First published in the UK 2006
by Quiller Press, an imprint of Quiller Publishing Ltd
The right of Robert Richardson to be identified as the author of this work
has been asserted in accordance with the Copyright, Design and Patent Act 1988.

Copyright © 2006 Robert Richardson

British Library Cataloguing-in-Publication Data
A catalogue record for this book
is available from the British Library

ISBN 1 904057 96 9
        978 1 904057 96 3

Designed by Jo Ekin
Set in AGaramond 12/14pt
Printed in the United Kingdom

Quiller Press
an imprint of Quiller Publishing Ltd
Wykey House, Wykey, Shrewsbury SY4 1JA, England
email: info@quillerbooks.com
Website: www.countrybooksdirect.com

NAPOLEON'S ULCER

and other medico-historical stories

Robert Richardson

Quiller Press

Contents

(continued overleaf)

Preface

Twenty-five years ago, in a letter to the *Journal of the Royal Society of Medicine*, I argued that so much worthless rubbish had been written about Napoleon's health that a case could be made for wiping the slate clean and starting again.

And that is precisely what I did. I cleared my mind and assembled only the records kept by doctors from the time of Napoleon's arrival on St Helena (I believe him to have been essentially healthy before he was exiled) to the time of his death and on to the post-mortem report. I allowed the diagnoses to emerge from the constellation of symptoms recorded by these doctors, rather than their being reached from symptoms selected to fit a preconceived idea or by their being based on erroneous or incomplete information. To this end, memoirs and reminiscences of non-medical writers – medically, notoriously unreliable or prejudiced – are ignored.

Moreover, I suspect the reason there is such confusion and controversy is because no one has previously assembled the day-to-day clinical records of the doctors who attended Napoleon on the island, together with Antommarchi's full post-mortem report, and used them to reach a diagnosis of his illnesses and cause of death. The problem, if such it is still considered to be, is clinico-pathological rather than historical.

The rest of the book consists of snippets from a broad sweep through history – mostly the history of medicine. It is a mixture of the completely new and a selection from my earlier writings – revised and brought up to date – that had appeared in obscure medical publications and seemed worthy of a larger audience. Although I have endeavoured to contact owners of copyright material, in some instances this has not been possible. I shall, however, be pleased to correct any omissions in future.

Robert Richardson 2006

Illustrations

NAPOLEON'S ULCER
I: Napoleon's medical history

When the sun had set on that glorious (for some) day at Austerlitz, the Emperor Napoleon exclaimed with prophetic insight: "One has only a certain time for war. I shall be good for another six years; after that I must stop myself". The implication of this was echoed 140 years later by Lord Moran (Charles Wilson – 1882–1977) who argued most persuasively in *The Anatomy of Courage* that courageousness in a man is not an inexhaustible quality. Four years after Austerlitz, in 1809, we can begin to sense, in his disregard for human life at the battles of Aspern-Essling and Wagram, that Napoleon really did believe his years were numbered. Could he have had good reason for this belief?

The diagnosis of disease in historical figures is beset with pitfalls, and especially is this so in the case of Napoleon: intrigue, politics, jealousy, hatred and much else besides conspired to cloud the pool both during his lifetime and afterwards. We therefore need to tread warily. In particular we need to be aware of the state of medicine at the time. To take but one instance, how much reliance are we prepared to put on the diagnosis of cancer of the stomach in Napoleon's father who died in 1785? Remember,

Napoleon Bonaparte. A cameo by Nicola Morelli (1800). O'Meara said that, allowing for the features having lost some of their sharpness, this bore a striking resemblance to the Napoleon he first saw in 1815. (*Napoleon in Exile.*)

Giovanni Morgagni's (1682–1771) *De Sedibus et Causis Morborum per Anatomen Indagatis* (the book that marked the birth of pathology by correlating clinical records with post-mortem findings) had only been published in 1761 and would not yet have begun to make its mark, and the microscopic study of diseased tissues still lay in the future. Medicine lagged a long way behind in the march of civilization.

Napoleon was 36 when he won at Austerlitz; in sixteen years' time he would be dead. There is nothing sinister about this in itself even though the cloud of symptoms that has gathered about him has intrigued and confused historians ever since; depending on one's selection they can be attributed to a quite alarming array of diseases: tuberculosis, gonorrhoea with urethral stricture as a consequence, bladder stones, gallstones, epilepsy, piles, peptic ulcer, Zollinger-Ellison syndrome (peptic ulcer associated with a tumour of the pancreas – Robert Zollinger, 1903–92; Edwin Ellison, 1918–70), stomach cancer, malaria, brucellosis (a diagnosis that can only be proved in the laboratory), schistosomiasis (no evidence of an initial gross haematuria or subsequent episodes of haematuria and, anyway, again the diagnosis can only be proved in the laboratory), amoebic hepatitis and abscess, pituitary deficiency, acromegaly (pituitary overactivity), hypogonadism, manic-depression, heart failure, partial or complete heart block, Klinefelter's syndrome (a chromosomal anomaly – Harry Klinefelter, 1912–90) and, the source of much discussion in the past fifty or so years, Fröhlich's syndrome or dystrophia adiposo-genitalis (Alfred Fröhlich, 1871–1953; *see* Chapter 3). All these and others have at one time or another been foisted upon him. Even today the diagnosis of a number of these conditions is obscure and far from easy – spot diagnosis is just not on. Portraits and contemporary descriptions tell us nothing more than that Napoleon was putting on

weight and we must be wary of romanticized portraits on the one hand and of propaganda and caricatures on the other.

Accounts of Napoleon's contacts with the medical profession are usually selective, the choice depending on space, the point one is trying to make, and the faith one has in the accuracy of the information. My contention is that, before St Helena, Napoleon was essentially a healthy man — certainly not sick to a degree that would alter the outcome of a battle or sway the fate of nations.

Napoleon campaigned for more than twenty years, admittedly not without respite and admittedly cushioned for much of the time against the worst of the rigours endured by his soldiers. Nevertheless physical fitness was at a premium and right until his military end he showed beyond doubt that he was a fit man. Even on St Helena, a variety of circumstances permitting, he rode on horseback, went for walks, gardened. and went for drives in a carriage.

Isolated instances do not prove a case, any more that one swallow makes a summer, but they may be pointers. A particularly illuminating passage occurs in a letter from Dominique Jean Larrey (1766–1842), Surgeon-in-Chief to the Imperial Guard, to his wife. It was written in Warsaw at the end of January, 1807, during the terrible winter campaign in the wastes of Poland that led up to the battle of Eylau. Larrey wrote: "His Majesty enjoys good health as always... The Pultusk campaign changed him a little and made him very tired, though several days' rest sufficed to restore his embonpoint. If I had food and lodging like his, I believe I would be as fit."

My second example is Napoleon's physical behaviour on June 17, 1815. Wellington, withdrawing from Quatre Bras to Mont St Jean in pouring rain, was pursued without any great show of enthusiasm despite the fact that the Emperor was directing the French in person and with irrepressible energy. It seems now like an omen of the outcome of the next day's battle.

And so we come to Napoleon's health. We are told he used to scratch pimples and scabs on his face until they bled, particularly in moments of stress as during the coup d'état of 18 Brumaire (November 9, 1799) – but most of us like a good pick from time to time. We are also told that he was

prone to open an old wound on the inner side of his left thigh just above the knee. This, most commentators say, was received at Toulon in 1793, but Barry O'Meara (1786–1836), the first of his doctors on St Helena, recorded in *Napoleon in Exile* (*see* Chapter 3) that Napoleon told him it had been a bayonet wound received in his first campaign in Italy (1796). It had been of sufficient severity for the surgeons to contemplate amputation and it left a deep scar. But wherever it was sustained, by reopening it Napoleon was probably consciously following the doctrine of the humours and creating an issue by means of which morbid material was removed from the body and the balance of the humours restored. This would be quite in keeping with the medical beliefs of the day.

The next recorded injury was in 1798 at the start of the Egyptian expedition when he was kicked in the right leg by his horse. The damage was more than superficial bruising as there appears to have been active bleeding into the deep tissues. Larrey, then Surgeon-in-Chief to the Army of the Orient, released the blood through a small incision, applied a dressing and did his best to make Bonaparte rest, but the general would have none of it – if anything he was more active than usual. With daily dressings the wound healed rapidly and satisfactorily.

Then, on April 22, 1809, he was wounded on the toe at the battle of Eckmühl – neither O'Meara nor Francesco Antommarchi (1770–1838; the last of his doctors on St Helena; *see* Chapter 3) enlighten us as to which toe. The next day, at the battle of Ratisbon (modern Regensberg), Napoleon was hit in an ankle by a stray shot, an event recorded by the artist, Claude Gautherot (1765–1825), who showed Alexandre Yvan (1765–1839), Napoleon's personal surgeon, dressing the right ankle. However, Antommarchi noted a scar just above the left ankle. Artistic licence probably got in the way of anatomical accuracy.

In his report of the post-mortem on Napoleon's body, which he had performed, Antommarchi recorded the presence of several scars. Apart from those already noted, there were two more on the left leg – one of which might have been from a wound at Marengo (1800) when, as O'Meara recorded, a cannon-shot took away a piece of his left boot and a little skin – one on the head and another on the inside of the left ring finger which had been inflicted by a wild boar while out hunting.

But wounds and attitudes to them and to surgeons are one thing – particularly at that period in history – sickness is quite another. As I said, I am prepared to accept very little of what has been written about Napoleon's health before Waterloo. The eyewitness accounts, even when utterly unbiased and objective, are notoriously difficult to interpret in terms of a modern diagnosis and the waters have since been muddied by half-forgotten reminiscences and an endless stream of commentaries. So, one tries to look for factual supporting evidence.

On the night before Borodino, in 1812, Napoleon was unwell. His aide-de-camp, Philippe de Ségur (1753–1830) tells us in his *Histoire de Napoléon et de la Grande Armée* (1825; vol. I, 356–7): "He was exhausted by the hardships of the previous days and nights, the cares and the expectations. The chill in the air seized him: an irritant fever, a dry cough, an excessive change in the vital functions consumed him! The remainder of the night he sought vainly to quench the burning thirst that devoured him. This new malady aggravated an old complaint: since the previous day he had been fighting against a painful attack of the grievous trouble, the ill-effects of which he had felt for a long time." (Ségur does not reveal the nature of this grievous trouble; a footnote simply states that it was 'dysuria'. However, in an undated 20th century edition dysuria has been incorporated into the text.) Nevertheless, at five o'clock in the morning, one of Michel Ney's (1769–1815) officers reported that the marshal had caught sight of the Russians again and was asking permission to attack. "This news appeared so to restore the Emperor's vitality that the fever abated."

The outcome of this episode inclines me to the belief that the 'fever' (I put it in quotes since the clinical thermometer had yet to be invented) was due to a flare-up of his bladder trouble ('gravel') and it is common knowledge that discomfort or pain can be forgotten in the heat of the moment. The symptomatic diagnosis of dysuria must be accepted without question since, on St Helena, Napoleon told Antommarchi that he had always had trouble with micturition which could sometimes be painful. And, as final supporting evidence, at the post-mortem Antommarchi found the bladder to contain a quantity of gravel mixed with a few small calculi. It is also more than likely that Napoleon suffered from straightforward difficulty in starting.

And so to 1815. A vast amount has been written about the reasons for Napoleon's defeat at Waterloo. In recent times much of it has concentrated on the man's physical health, ranging from the popular prolapsed piles, through foreknowledge that he would die of cancer of the stomach, to a tale of epilepsy. Napoleon's way of life may conceivably have predisposed to piles and he admitted to suffering from constipation; but the piles story only emerged years later when brother Jerome (1784–1860), on his deathbed, coyly proposed it as an excuse for the defeat – we are asked to believe that the secret was shared with Louis Marchand (1765–1851), Napoleon's valet, and his surgeon Larrey (*see* later).

Napoleon almost certainly worried about his stomach and may, understandably, have had a foreboding that he would die of stomach cancer since his father had died at the age of 39 from what was said to be that disease. Carlo Mario Buonoparte (1746–85) did have severe stomach pains before his death and the diagnosis was supported by the post-mortem, but, as we saw earlier, in 1785 pathology was scarcely a science and many other possible causes for his death were not yet recognized.

Napoleon. A miniature painted by J. Parent in 1815.

Moreover, cancer of the stomach is unusual before the age of forty. Yet, even if Napoleon was anxious on this score, it is highly improbable that the emotion assumed such devastating proportions at Waterloo when it must have been with him during his latter campaigns – *he* was 39 in 1808.

The diagnosis of epilepsy hangs by the most tenuous of threads. It is not a diagnosis that can always be made with ease today, but in Napoleon's case his outbursts of temper, usually after periods of prolonged physical or mental stress and

often thoroughly justified, have been confidently ascribed to epilepsy. The nadir was reached in a style typical of so much of the medical hash that has proliferated around the man. In 1920, Henry Orlando Marcy (1837–1924), the American who gave kangaroo tendon to hernia repair, and who was then 83, wrote in the *Boston Medical and Surgical Journal*: "The following two items which come to me from an accredited authority… are of more than usual significance.

"It is not generally known that Napoleon was an epileptic. He had been under an extraordinary continuous strain in preparation for his last campaign but was confident of the victory of the morrow. He left orders to be called at four in the morning of the battle of Waterloo. That night he was seized with an unusually severe epileptic attack and Baron Larrey allowed him to sleep until six. Who shall say that the destiny of Europe, which hung in the balance was not decided by those fateful two hours?" [The other item was an equally improbable tale of Napoleon's behaviour on receiving a letter from Edward Jenner (1749–1823 – of vaccination fame). He ordered Larrey to vaccinate the entire army!]

Marcy carried the secret of his accredited authority to the grave. Larrey, it should be noted, was not and never had been the Emperor's personal surgeon (*see* Chapter 12); at Waterloo he was Surgeon-in-Chief of the Grande Armée and had quite enough to do in that capacity without becoming involved with Imperial piles or epilepsy. The real cause of Napoleon's delay in launching the attack on Wellington's position was Antoine Drouot's (1774–1847) report that, until the ground had had a chance to dry out after the previous day's torrential rain, the artillery could not be manoeuvred. (Drouot was to the artillery what Joachim Murat (1771–1815) was to the cavalry.)

But as always in the Napoleonic saga there is yet another explanation: Walter Henry (1791–1860), in his *Trifles from my Port-folio or Recollections of Scenes and Small Adventures During Twenty-nine Years' Military Service*, said he had asked Henri Bertrand (1773–1844) why Napoleon did not act with heroism and lead the Guard (his reserve) into action; why he abandoned his men. Bertrand replied that "the Staff around Napoleon had seized the bridle of his horse, led him aside, and prevented him by force from heading the Guards when mounting the position."

And so I believe Napoleon set sail for St Helena with, apart from the possibility of some gravel in his bladder, a clean bill of health. What his state of mind might have been is another matter, particularly when he understood that his intention of living in deep retreat, under the name of a colonel who had been killed at his side, in England or America was not to be realized. He was to be treated as a prisoner of war.

2

NAPOLEON'S ULCER
II: The last days of Napoleon Bonaparte

The ex-Emperor Napoleon arrived off St Helena on board HMS *Northumberland* on October 15, 1815. Two days later, he and his staff landed at James Town, the capital. Both his intended medical attendant, M. Fourreau de Beauregard who had looked after him on Elba, and a young doctor, M. Maingaud, chosen to stand in until Beauregard could journey to the island, cried off when they learnt of the destination. So Barry O'Meara, ship's surgeon on HMS *Bellerophon*, was offered the job.

O'Meara had studied medicine in both Dublin and London and was a competent and experienced naval surgeon. He was fluent in Italian and French and had got on well with Napoleon on the voyage over from France to England. On St Helena virtually all their conversations were conducted in Italian and were written up, in English, by O'Meara at the end of the day. They were published in 1822 in his book *Napoleon in Exile; or a Voice from St. Helena*. So far as Napoleon's health was concerned, this record covered the years 1815 to 1818.

During his incarceration on St Helena, Napoleon was attended by four doctors: Barry O'Meara; John Stokoe, who was called in only for an

opinion; Francesco Antommarchi; and Archibald Arnott (1772–1855). Now, if you want a medical history, the obvious thing to do is to go to the doctor's original notes, but as far as I can make out, no one seems to have used the written records of these four doctors as a consecutive history and analysed them with a view to reaching a valid medical diagnosis. This is a pity as the two doctors who actually looked after Napoleon on St Helena from beginning to end – except for an unfortunate eighteen-month gap when he had no medical attendants at all – have left us excellent clinical and post-mortem descriptions of his medical problems. The reports of the other two provide confirmatory evidence (of a sort).

Napoleon was first lodged at the Briars, a pleasant estate of a few acres of highly cultivated land with excellent fruit and kitchen gardens and many delightful shady walks; it was the home of Mr Balcombe, the purveyor, and his wife, two young sons and two daughters both of whom were fluent in French. As O'Meara wrote: "Nothing was left undone by this worthy family that could contribute to lessen the inconveniencies of his situation." Napoleon and the twelve-year-old younger daughter, Betsy, struck up an easy friendship as she behaved quite naturally towards him and he responded in kind.

The interlude at the Briars was necessary while Longwood, Napoleon's future home, received much needed repairs and the building of an extension to accommodate some of his entourage. The house was far from being a desirable residence; it sat, bleak and exposed, on the summit of a mountain on the windward side of the island, nearly two thousand feet above sea level. The atmospheric temperature was twelve to thirteen Fahrenheit degrees colder than James Town on the coast. Water had to be brought from three miles away. The gum-woods, the only trees that would grow, were bent by the continuous humid blast of the prevailing southeast trade winds. The Longwood estate had a perimeter of some twelve miles and was usually enveloped in wet penetrating fog which, when it felt so inclined, would give way to the scorching heat of a tropical sun. The average annual rainfall in the three years, 1816–18, was 33·38 inches in contrast to London's 21·25 inches. It is small wonder that no inhabitant had ever made Longwood their permanent home. When Napoleon was installed there on December 9, it was generally supposed that a suitable

Longwood House, St Helena, where Napoleon was confined for nearly six years.
(*Napoleon in Exile.*)

winter home would be found for him when the new governor arrived.

The Governor at the time was Rear-Admiral Sir George Cockburn (1772–1853) who was fair but strict in his interpretation of the required security measures. He permitted Napoleon a degree of freedom in his movements and even gave several balls to which the French were invited, although Napoleon never attended. Sir George went on to become Admiral of the Fleet in 1851. But, as we shall see, things were to change when his replacement, Lieutenant-General Sir Hudson Lowe (1769–1844) arrived on April 14, 1816; from the start he got off on the wrong foot by sending a message to say he would visit Napoleon at nine the next morning. As Napoleon never received anyone at that hour, Lowe was greeted with the news that the emperor was indisposed and would see him at two the next day. Lowe and his abundant staff were thoroughly put out at this – it was pouring with rain!

O'Meara's first mention that something might be amiss appeared in the entry for July 26, 1816, when Napoleon complained of a slight pain in his right side and enquired about the causes of the liver disease that was prevalent on the island. At this date O'Meara also noted that Napoleon

often suffered from catarrh, colic, rheumatism and toothache. In those days 'catarrh' was a recognized symptom complex: it started as a common cold, then a tired feeling and a complaint of chilliness; the nostrils and upper lip became inflamed; hoarseness and a sore throat followed with pain and a sense of tightness in the chest and a dry cough. The patient was feverish. When muscular pains appeared patients lost their appetites and complained of feeling very thirsty. In other words, a barrage of non-specific complaints without a ready modern diagnosis.

On October 13, Napoleon complained of headache and a general uneasiness; he was a little feverish. O'Meara recorded that his gums were "spongy, pale, and bled on the slightest touch" – a pathognomonic sign of scurvy. For treatment he recommended a larger quantity than usual of vegetables and to take exercise (idleness was regarded as a cause of the disease). On the 26th Napoleon had tonsillitis and rigors. Then on November 1 his legs were swollen. But by the 7th he was almost better. (Swelling of the legs was reported by James Lind (1716–94) to occur in many cases of scurvy. His epoch making book *A Treatise of the Scurvy* was published in 1753.) Among the other possible symptoms of scurvy displayed by Napoleon were weakness and vague pains in the muscles and joints.

In March 1817 his legs were again swollen for a while. Then until the beginning of September he was generally in good spirits and good health – apart from episodes of toothache when the offending tooth was removed. However, with the arrival of September he complained of headaches and rheumatic pains.

By September 20 he was out of sorts and O'Meara again recorded spongy gums that bled at the slightest touch, and ankles and legs that were slightly swollen. He once more recommended antiscorbutic vegetables and insisted on the importance of exercise which Napoleon was most reluctant to take. His excuse – and it may be regarded as valid – was that while the restrictions imposed on him by the Governor remained in force "I will never stir out". His outside activities had been severely restricted by Lowe and he was no longer able to go for long horse rides; he had to be accompanied by a British officer and if he strayed off the track he was liable to be verbally abused by the sentries and could even have been shot at. Things remained much the same with a slight improvement until the

end of the month.

On October 1, 1817, O'Meara wrote: "Saw Napoleon in his bedroom at eight, a.m. He complained of a dull pain (*dolore sordo*) in the right hypochondriac region, immediately under the cartilages of the ribs, which he said he experienced yesterday morning for the first time. Sensation in the right shoulder, which he described as more of numbness than of pain.… Said he felt something in the right side which never was there before." O'Meara wondered whether it might be hepatitis "the prevailing disease of the island". Napoleon, true to his distrust of doctors and their remedies, refused treatment.

On October 3: "Examined the right side, and perceived that it felt firmer to the touch than the left. There was also a tumefaction evident to the sight, which when pressed hard, gave a little pain. Napoleon said, that this was observed about two months since. That he had thought nothing of it, and attributed it to obesity, but that now, from its being attended with pain, he imagined it might be connected with enlargement of the liver." However, the pain in the right upper quadrant of the abdomen, referred to the right shoulder, together with the two-month history of a visible and tender swelling in that quadrant point, not to hepatitis, but to inflammation of the gall-bladder – cholecystitis.

O'Meara recommended calomel, a mercury-containing compound, given as a purgative with other measures but, as he noted later, Napoleon took only those remedies he chose to.

When Lowe received O'Meara's written report he told him it was too detailed – in other words, it talked of hepatitis (but not of cholecystitis – *see* later) – and that he must write another that could be made public. This was the start of a serious falling-out between the two men with O'Meara insisting the patient be treated humanely and moved to a better climate and Lowe, intent on sending favourable reports back home (that is, ones that made no mention of any disease that could be attributed to the circumstances of his confinement) and attempting to keep the French in the dark over the true state of affairs.

On October 11 the pain in Napoleon's right side and shoulder increased. But when he discovered that O'Meara was reporting to the Governor and had to refer to him as 'General', Napoleon refused to

consult him about anything medical although they continued to talk about Napoleon's past and the present conditions on the island. Consequently, from that time on O'Meara gave only scrappy references to Napoleon's state of health, but he did note that he was never free of dull pain and that throughout January and February 1818 there seemed to be some improvement in his general condition.

Then on March 6, 1818, O'Meara stated that the progress of the disease (presumably in his mind he was referring to hepatitis) was advancing slowly. But on April 10 he was compelled to hand in his resignation because

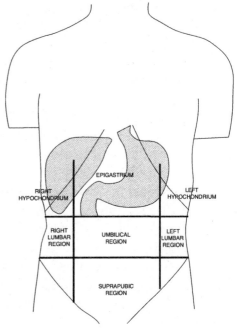

The regions of the abdomen

of his stubborn refusal to toe the political line in his reports and also because the Governor had been treating him atrociously with uncalled-for restrictions. Nevertheless, on June 11 he recorded that more troublesome teeth had been extracted and that, because his health had become much worse, Napoleon actually agreed to follow his advice regarding treatment. Even so, he had neglected the two most important things O'Meara had advised – exercise and diversions – he had not left his rooms for nearly six weeks.

On June 27 O'Meara noted that Napoleon was "much affected by a severe catarrhal affection, caused by the extreme humidity of his rooms." He discontinued some of the remedies his patient was taking and continued: "Napoleon's health required that I should prescribe for him a regimen, and prepare the medicines which it would be necessary for him to take in the absence of a surgeon, an absence likely to be of long duration, as I was perfectly sure he would accept of none recommended

by Sir Hudson Lowe."

So, in July 1818 at the end of months of political finagling, O'Meara was removed in disgrace from the island. Before he left, Napoleon presented him with a statuette of himself and a snuff box. (This was O'Meara's second snuff box; he had been given the first on New Year's Day, 1817.) Then, at their final meeting, Napoleon shook him by the hand, embraced him – a rare tribute to a member of the medical profession – and said they would never meet again. "Soyez heureux."

What diseases did Napoleon suffer from during O'Meara's stewardship? From O'Meara's accounts we can be confident that Napoleon had scurvy at the end of 1816 and again from the end of 1818 and could still have been suffering when O'Meara left the island. Being a naval surgeon, O'Meara would have been in no doubt when he saw a patient with scurvy. The presentation with spongy gums that bled at the slightest touch, swollen ankles, pains in the legs, lassitude and an aversion to exercise are all in agreement with Lind's description of 1753. Intriguingly, scurvy also carries with it a liability to peptic ulceration (*see* later).

Nevertheless, I can find no other report of scurvy on the island at that time. But to indicate that the disease was not unknown, a record from 1808 said that soldiers and others were brought to the hospital as far advanced in real scurvy as if they had just landed after a long voyage. Vegetables grown by the islanders were generally sold or bartered to the ships or troops. And though O'Meara may have listed the supplies allocated to the establishment at Longwood (consisting of forty-five people) between October, 1816, and June, 1817, there were constant complaints about their quality and quantity. Thus, as there can be no precise evidence of what antiscorbutic vegetables, citrus fruits and other vitamin C-containing foods actually entered the Imperial stomach, O'Meara's diagnosis of scurvy cannot really be challenged.

We can be confident also that Napoleon had hepatitis. The disease was seriously endemic on the island and O'Meara would be familiar with its manifestations – especially so as he had suffered from it himself in November, 1816. He had passed out at Napoleon's feet and had come round to find that Napoleon had lifted him into a chair, loosened his shirt

collar, dashed eau de Cologne over his face and was holding a bottle of vinegar under his nose. Napoleon's expression was one "of great concern and anxiety." When O'Meara left the room he heard him whisper to his valet, Louis Marchand, instructing him to follow in case he had another faint. (The cause of the collapse was more likely to have been the very profuse bleeding he had just undergone, rather than the hepatitis.)

All the symptoms necessary for a diagnosis of hepatitis are found in O'Meara's daily reports: the onset with fever to be followed by malaise, headache, nausea, loss of appetite, pain in the right upper quadrant of the abdomen and, in the acute phase, a moderately enlarged and tender liver; on occasion he had mentioned jaundice of the skin and sclera of the eyes. Precise dating of the onset in Napoleon's case is admittedly difficult, but if we accept that the cholecystitis began in October 1817 (though maybe two months earlier if we accept Napoleon's own timing), the July 26, 1816, episode could well have marked the beginning of the hepatitis and then, when the disease became chronic, the resulting fibrosis probably obstructed the neck of the gall-bladder.

Thus when O'Meara departed in July 1818, Napoleon was left without a doctor although he was offered, and declined, the services of James Verling, surgeon to the Royal Artillery. But, in January 1819, after a particularly unpleasant bout of ill-health, his household were so concerned that they persuaded Lowe to permit John Stokoe, surgeon on board HMS *Conqueror*, to examine Napoleon. He confirmed O'Meara's diagnosis of hepatitis.

On January 17, 1819, Stokoe wrote to Lowe reporting his visit that morning when he had found Napoleon to be extremely weak and suffering cruelly on his right side in the region of the liver and experiencing shooting pains in the shoulder. In the middle of the night he had had a violent headache followed by vertigo lasting about a quarter of an hour. When it passed, Napoleon took a hot bath which made him sweat abundantly and with great benefit. Stokoe believed that the presence of a doctor was indispensable in such a serious case.

The next day he wrote to Henri Bertrand, one-time Grand Marshal, saying that in spite of the symptoms of chronic hepatitis that had appeared some sixteen months previously and the disorders it was

responsible for, he did not believe that Napoleon was in imminent danger. The illness was, however, becoming every day more serious and would probably end Napoleon's life but, he repeated, he did not think there was any imminent danger. (Since the appearance of the symptoms, sixteen months previously, coincides with the probable onset of the cholecystitis, it would seem that neither he nor O'Meara made the distinction between cholecystitis and hepatitis; the significance of pain referred to the right shoulder was also not appreciated.)

Two more letters of the 19th and 20th to Lowe and one on the 21st to Bertrand reinforced what he had already said. For his pains, Stokoe was court-martialled and dismissed the service. Truth could not flourish in the prevailing political climate.

❧

Francesco Antommarchi, Napoleon's fellow Corsican, now enters the picture. He was to be one of the extra staff sent out by Madame Mère, Napoleon's mother (Letizia Ramolino-Bonaparte; 1750–1836) though the choice was actually made by Cardinal Joseph Fesch (1763–1839) her half-brother. It may seem a strange choice since Antommarchi was currently an anatomist and not a practising physician, but Fesch knew his man.

Antommarchi had been trained at Pisa and Florence and, in 1808, had received doctorates in medicine and philosophy from Pisa; in 1812 he obtained a diploma in surgery. In 1818 he was demonstrator in anatomy at the hospital of Sainte-Marie-Neuve of Florence, attached to the University of Pisa and as such was obliged to live there. But to do so he needed a permit; this was refused. Because he was a known Bonapartist he was harassed by the populace and subjected to police surveillance. In desperation he wrote to the Cardinal offering his services; Fesch replied on December 19, 1818, saying that he could have the job once he had completed the necessary formalities with the British officials in Rome. The insults and threats directed at him continued until he got his passport and was able to leave for Rome on January 7.

After he had been in the city about a month he received an answer to a letter he had written to O'Meara seeking information on Napoleon's

Francesco Antommarchi (1780–1838).

health. O'Meara responded with an excellent summary that was far more coherent than his day-to-day diary. He set out the history from September 1817 when the symptoms indicative of a disorder of hepatic function had begun. In passing, he mentioned the spongy, scorbutic appearance of the gums, the yellowness of the sclera and the evidence of indigestion. From October 1 there had been no let-up in the progress of the illness which he clearly identified as acute, progressing to chronic, hepatitis. He noted that the urine was pungent and strongly coloured (indicative of cystitis), that his bowel action had become irregular with abundant evacuation of bile-stained mucous stools and that he often vomited sour and viscid bile. O'Meara also drew attention to the pain in the right shoulder and recorded that Napoleon's pulse, which was usually 54-60 beats per minute, had increased to nearly 88. O'Meara wrote that on June 11, 1818, he had overcome Napoleon's resistance to internal medication and had persuaded him to take mercury pills and purgatives (unspecified) for his constipation. This treatment was continued on and off for a fortnight. It was started again on July 2 for a week but without effect. Towards the end of his letter, O'Meara mentioned that Napoleon was salivating a lot – the first mention of a symptom that can occur in patients with gastric ulcer.

O'Meara concluded by giving vent to his feelings about the conditions Napoleon had to endure: two years of inactivity, a murderous

climate, sordid and badly ventilated apartments, unheard of treatment by the Governor, isolation – everything that would upset his feelings. It was astonishing, he wrote, that the disease had not progressed more rapidly. He thoughtfully included copies of the letters written by John Stokoe.

Procrastination by other members of the party almost drove Antommarchi to abandon the project. In the end he did not arrive on the island until September 18, 1819. Napoleon had been without adequate medical cover for over a year.

Antommarchi was presented to his emperor on September 22; Napoleon was in bed in a small excessively gloomy room. After a long conversation, in Italian, he was instructed to return the following afternoon.

Like O'Meara, Antommarchi kept a daily record which was published in 1825 as *Les Derniers Moments de Napoléon*; his account of the first consultation reveals that he was indeed a thorough and competent physician. Napoleon was lying on a camp bed, this time in a well-lit room, and was quite chatty but hard of hearing (possibly a consequence of artillery fire). He said he had been habitually constipated and had had difficulty urinating since childhood. He had been off his food for several days. He complained of pain in the right hypochondrium that varied in intensity and had been present for a long time. He said he had had chronic hepatitis which had started two years previously. He also reported symptoms that O'Meara would have termed catarrh. He had not been out-of-doors for eighteen months.

On examination, Antommarchi recorded that Napoleon was ashen faced, with coated tongue and reddish-yellow conjunctivae; his entire body was excessively fat. He had a dry cough and violent and prolonged sneezing. The secretion of saliva was occasionally abundant. The pulse was small, regular and 60 beats per minute. The left lobe of the liver in the epigastrium was hardened and extremely tender to pressure. The gall-bladder was full, firm and palpable in the right hypochondrium; there was pain around the right breast and also in the right shoulder where it was extreme. His urine, though frequent, was normal.

Napoleon's non-specific symptoms came and went in many combinations and degrees of severity. They included weakness, anxiety,

depression, easy fatigability, insomnia, headache often severe, vague pains in the abdomen (later, Antommarchi occasionally recorded slight tenderness in the lower belly – a finding that could indicate cystitis), abundant sweating, cold legs and feet, skin dry and burning and so on. They were like background noise to the symptoms and signs of his developing illnesses. For symptomatic relief, he relied on hot baths (even as long as two or more hours) and mustard foot baths, but the relief was never complete. Since he rarely agreed to take purgative medicines, his constipation required frequent enemas. He took walks in the garden, sometimes with Antommarchi, and went for drives in a carriage.

Reading on through Antommarchi's diary, we find that on October 22, 1819, Napoleon had a very bad pain in the liver that extended into his right shoulder. Between November 12 and December 17 his health was sustained, but then relapsed with colic and insupportable pain in the liver. Antommarchi's daily reports then ceased until July 19, 1820, when he recorded that since the 7th Napoleon's health had been bad: the pain in the liver had returned with a vengeance and had extended into the shoulder; there was bilious vomiting and respiration had been difficult and painful. This episode had lasted until the 31st of the month.

By September 15 the liver pain had returned but more severely and there was a burning sensation in the right hypochondrium and in the epigastrium (the central part of the upper abdomen). By the 22nd he had recovered and, feeling the need of fresh air, had tried to mount a horse and then to get in a carriage but had failed. Feeling ill, he had come back in and gone to bed.

Moving on to October 5 Antommarchi recorded that the liver pain and the pain in the right shoulder had worsened, and that the right hypochondrium was uncomfortable and painful.

On October 13 a completely new pain appeared. It was in the spinal column and extended from the neck and shoulders into the middle of the back. On the 25th Antommarchi found Napoleon in a very depressed and unhappy state: "Is there anything more deplorable than my existence?" he asked. "It is not living, it is vegetating. I shall never get better." Two or three weeks later, on November 12, the pains over the liver and in the epigastrium were much worse, added to which severe pain in the thoracic

spine and left shoulder was again recorded. These reports of spinal pain are strongly indicative of perforation of a gastric ulcer which, as became evident at the post-mortem, was sealed off by adhesions to the liver.

There is an intriguing set of entries at the beginning of December when on the 5th and 6th Antommarchi said the emperor was getting better and better, but on the 7th Napoleon tells him that for three days he had had a sort of strangury (strangury can mean a severe pain in the urethra with intense urgency or the painful passing of just a few drops of urine). Antommarchi reckoned that the bladder had been seriously overdistended. Whatever the case, no further mention was made of the occurrence and this, taken with the casual references to urinary complaints, would seem to indicate that the cystitis was a chronic low-grade infection. At all events, as was proved at post-mortem, there had been no ascending infection to the kidneys.

⚭

Because the existence of peptic (gastric or duodenal) ulcer was not even suspected, Antommarchi could do no more than record what he observed. The presence of symptoms of both cholecystitis and gastric ulcer would have presented him with what, in those days, would have been an insoluble diagnostic problem. Gastric ulcer was described for the first time by Jean Cruveilhier (1791–1874) in his book *Anatomie Pathologique du Corps Humain*, published in Paris between 1830 and 1842. So, to give us an advantage over Antommarchi, this is some of what he had to say on the subject.

"Confused in practice sometimes with chronic gastritis and more commonly with cancer, simple chronic ulcer of the stomach does not appear to me to have attracted the attention of observers as a special disease." And again: "The principal symptoms are the following: loss of appetite or bizarre appetite, insurmountable distress, difficult digestion, nausea or heavy pains in the epigastrium, and sometimes epigastric pain extremely sharp during the process of digestion or indeed when there is no food in the stomach. The epigastric pain, or rather the xiphoid or substernal pain, is referred sometimes to a corresponding place on the

spine, and I have seen many patients complain more of a spinal point than of an epigastric point of tenderness." Interestingly, but not to be given significance in our argument, he commented that one of his patients (a twenty-nine-year-old man) was markedly obese.

❦

And so into 1821 when, on January 2, there was another instance of Napoleon's compassion towards his doctors. At 8.30 am Napoleon was still in bed when Antommarchi entered; as he felt the room needed airing he started to open the window but it slipped and cut the back of his right hand exposing three extensor tendons. Napoleon saw it happen and was most concerned, insisting that he went at once to find an English doctor. Antommarchi was off sick for three days.

Until January 27th Napoleon's health was improved, he had a good appetite and took walks in the garden and went out for carriage rides. But on that date his prostration was extreme and he complained of painful sensations in his stomach. By February 19 events were coming to a head. Napoleon found himself unable to eat meat, only milky and farinaceous foods. And on March 1 his digestion was extremely painful; nevertheless he went out for a carriage drive but by the evening he was feeling sick and vomited.

On two days (5th and 7th) in early March he asked for meat dishes but hardly touched them. From then on it was a matter of a light diet consisting of such items as soups, broths, fresh eggs, jellies, finger biscuits and a little claret well diluted with water. During one of his fairly frequent differences of opinion with Antommarchi over the value of internal medications, he commented: "What is written is written. The time of our death is written and nothing we can do can change that. I view death without emotion. I am not afraid to die."

By the end of the month, on the 26th, he was feverish and suffering episodes of meteorism and was in such a bad way that Antommarchi wanted to consult one of the English doctors. But Napoleon resisted saying that an English doctor could do no more than Antommarchi himself and, moreover, would be under the influence of Hudson Lowe.

However, he did eventually agree to let him have a word with Archibald Arnott, surgeon of the 20th Regiment, who simply advised raising blisters over the abdomen (a recommended contemporary measure), giving a purgative, and frequent sprinkling of the forehead with vinegar. Antommarchi does not record whether he acted on this advice, though when he returned he gave Napoleon a couple of enemas with a small result.

On April 1, Napoleon finally allowed Antommarchi to call in Arnott. But it was10.30 pm and Napoleon would not allow a light. So, in pitch darkness, Arnott took his pulse and palpated his abdomen.

By now, Napoleon had been in bed for a fortnight as a consequence of which the officer charged with reporting daily on his continued presence had been unable to do so. What really brought matters to a head was the enema affair. The windows in Napoleon's ground-floor bedroom were sufficiently close to the ground that passers-by could see what went on inside. So, when the time came for an enema, Charles Montholon (1783–1853) stood on one side while Antommarchi worked from the other; meanwhile Marchand stood at the window pretending to attend to the curtains. The officer on duty outside reported this to Lowe. Lowe was furious.

At first it seemed like checkmate. Napoleon would not allow a British officer into his bedroom and no one in the Imperial household was acceptable to Lowe. Furthermore, as in the case with O'Meara, Antommarchi would not refer to his emperor as General Bonaparte. The situation was resolved when both sides realized that Arnott would be an acceptable observer.

Like Napoleon's other doctors Arnott, too, kept a daily record which was published in1822 as *An Account of the Last Illness, Decease, and Post Mortem Appearances of Napoleon Bonaparte*. It agrees in essence with Antommarchi's diary over the same period, though there are different bits of information when one or other visited on their own. Arnott almost immediately walked into a political situation: on April 3, Antommarchi ran into a worried Sir Thomas Reade, the Deputy Adjutant General, who wanted to move Napoleon to better quarters. He was amazed that Antommarchi allowed him to stay in stuffy, unhealthy rooms when much

better apartments could be made available. Antommarchi reacted instinctively: "I understand! Killed in a hut, he must be seen to have expired in a palace. This combination is typically English!" Arnott was, however, in favour of the move and Napoleon listened to him for a while. But when he was asked for his opinion, he deferred to Antommarchi who replied that it would have serious consequences as the patient was too ill. Napoleon remained in his 'hut'.

Napoleon instinctively knew that his liver and stomach were responsible for his condition and on April 10 he asked Arnott to examine his liver. Arnott duly palpated the right hypochondrium and could feel nothing wrong. He told him "that I did not apprehend there was any disease of the liver; that perhaps there might be a little want of action in it."!! Napoleon knew he was pulling the wool over his eyes and Arnott knew which side his bread was buttered. The next day Napoleon suffered from alarming vomiting.

Over the next ten days what little food he took, he either brought back immediately or suffered from painful stomach ache. Arnott wrote: "After the vomiting, his stomach was much relieved, and he conceived himself better on the whole."

On the morning of the 27th, while Arnott was with him, Napoleon was seized with violent retching and vomiting. When Arnott looked in the basin he saw that the vomit resembled coffee-grounds and was very offensive. The vomiting continued till 3.30 pm. (The coffee-grounds appearance is due to blood that has been altered from bright red to brown by the action of the gastric acid.)

Napoleon continued to vomit during the night with the vomitus still looking like coffee-grounds but with the addition of small specks of blood. At 7 am he had some soup, a fresh egg and a finger biscuit dunked in a little claret. At 8 o'clock he talked to Antommarchi, giving him instructions about his post-mortem and saying that after his death Antommarchi was to go to Rome and tell Madame Mère and his family everything about his illness and death. In the small hours of the 30th he had had hiccups and had vomited but not so dark a colour as previously. Between 11 pm and midnight he had a rigor accompanied by great anxiety and dyspnoea. This was followed by another attack of hiccups.

In the morning (May Day) he was much worse, incoherent and in a terrible state. He was given an enema which "produced a copious evacuation". Arnott the next day recorded his pulse rate at 102 in the morning and 110 by evening. The end was near.

At 2 pm on May 3, Abbé Vignale administered the last rites. But an hour later Napoleon was rational and talked sensibly. At 6 pm Arnott wanted to give 10 grains (about 0·6 gram) of calomel. Antommarchi vehemently opposed this, but the dose was nevertheless given. Five-and-a-half hours later it produced a series of five copious fetid tarry stools. (A tarry stool results from blood having passed through the digestive tract.)

Napoleon's condition steadily deteriorated to the accompaniment of severe and continuous hiccups. His last morning (May 5) began at 5 am with the vomiting of coffee-grounds. During the day he was delirious, inarticulate and in severe abdominal pain.

The Emperor Napoleon (*pace* Hudson Lowe) died at 5.49 pm on May 5, 1821. The cause of death was haemorrhage from a gastric ulcer.

3

NAPOLEON'S ULCER
III: The post-mortem

And so we come to Napoleon's post-mortem which, we might hope, would reveal all. Alas, no. The lasting achievement of the official British report was to provide a rich storehouse for speculators to plunder. It read:

"Longwood Saint Helena May 6th 1821

"Report of appearances on dissection of the body of Napoleon Bonaparte.

"On a superficial view the body appeared very fat which state was confirmed by the first incision down its centre where the fat was upwards of one inch thick over the sternum, and one inch and a half over the abdomen. On cutting through the cartilages of the ribs and exposing the cavity of the thorax a trifling adhesion of the left pleura was found to the pleura costalis – about three ounces of reddish fluid was contained in the left cavity and nearly eight ounces in the right. [One fluid ounce is the equivalent of 2·84 ml.]

"The lungs were quite sound.

"The pericardium was natural and contained about an ounce of fluid.

"The heart was of the natural size but thickly covered with fat. The

auricles and ventricles exhibited nothing extraordinary except that the muscular parts appeared rather paler than natural.

"Upon opening the abdomen, the omentum was found remarkably fat and on exposing the stomach that viscus was found the seat of extensive disease. Strong adhesions connected the whole superior surface particularly about the pyloric extremity to the concave surface of the left lobe of the liver, and on separating these an ulcer which penetrated the coats of the stomach was discovered one inch from the pylorus, sufficient to allow the passage of the little finger. The internal surface of the stomach to nearly its whole extent, was a mass of cancerous disease or schirrous portions advancing to cancer. This was particularly noticed near the pylorus – the cardiac extremity for a small space near the termination of the oesophagus was the only part appearing in a healthy state. The stomach was found nearly filled with a large quantity of fluid resembling coffee grounds.

"The convex surface of the left lobe of the liver adhered to the diaphragm. With the exception of the adhesions occasioned by the disease in the stomach no unhealthy appearance presented.

"The remainder of the abdominal viscera were in a healthy state.

"A slight peculiarity in the formation of the left kidney was observed."

The report runs to 330 words and was signed by Thomas Shortt, Physician and PMO; Archibald Arnott, Surgeon 20th Regiment; Charles Mitchell, Surgeon HMS *Vigo*; Francis Burton, Surgeon 66th Regiment; and Matthew Livingstone, Surgeon Honourable East India Company. Not one of the five had taken part in the dissection, they were simply among the seventeen or so observers, as was Walter Henry, Assistant Surgeon 66th Foot, who wrote the document but was too junior to be a signatory. On instructions from the Governor, Sir Hudson Lowe, the report was heavily biased towards British political interests: Napoleon had to be seen to have died from nothing that could cast aspersions on the way the British had cared for him; cancer of the stomach was an ideal diagnosis. Any suggestion that he might have died from a liver complaint had to be suppressed as hepatitis was endemic on the island and mention of liver disease had already been responsible for diplomatic headaches.

The official post-mortem report on Napoleon Bonaparte signed by five British doctors.

That the report was deliberately intended to mislead was a point not lost on Francesco Antommarchi, who performed the autopsy, or Thomas Shortt, the senior medical officer. Shortt simply expressed to the Governor his concern that there was no mention of enlargement of the liver and was sent away with a flea in his ear. He took the matter no further; he had seen what had happened to John Stokoe. Any value the five signatories might have hoped for was totally lost through political interference; it did, however, establish the belief that Napoleon had died from cancer of the stomach.

Henry, however, seized an opportunity he saw for ingratiating himself with the establishment. In 1823 he wrote a letter, based on notes he had made at the time, to Hudson Lowe (*Hudson Lowe Papers*, British Museum. Add. Mss., Vol. 20. 214, folios 200–1). The relevant passage reads:

"The whole surface of the body was deeply covered with fat. Over the sternum where, generally, the bone is very superficial, the fat was upwards of an inch deep, and an inch and a half, or perhaps two inches, on the Abdomen. The skin was noticed to be particularly white and delicate as were the hands and arms. Indeed the whole body was slender and effeminate. There was scarcely any hair on the body and that of the head was thin, fine and silky. The pubis much resembled the <u>Mons</u> <u>Veneris</u> in women. The muscles of the chest were small, the shoulders were narrow and the hips wide." Henry concluded his observations: "The Urinary Bladder was small and contained a few gritty particles. The Penis and Testicles were very small, and the whole Genital system seemed to exhibit a physical cause for the absence of sexual desire and the chastity which had been stated to have characterized the Deceased."

Henry was evidently intending to heap further ignominy on the fallen emperor by making him out to have had an effeminate body and, generally, not to have been much of a man. But what an extraordinary contradiction for him to say that the whole body was slender and effeminate when he had just drawn attention to the whole surface of the body being deeply covered in fat. Henry was just trying too hard. Yet he had not laboured in vain as we shall discover later.

In Antommarchi's eyes the official report was such a travesty that he

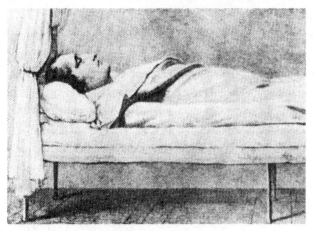

Napoleon on his deathbed.

refused to sign it. With his reputation, such as it was, at stake, he wrote his own version and published it in his two-volume work, *Les Derniers Moments de Napoléon* (1825). A paperback edition of the book, published in 1975, omits the post-mortem report on the grounds that, although meticulous, it was dry, without interest and said nothing that was not already evident; the footnote gave the cause of death as the perforation of a pre-pyloric ulcer which might possibly have been cancerous but was not proved to be so as Antommarchi seemed to believe. Oh, dear! there is far more to it than that.

Once Lowe had been assured that the body really was Napoleon's, there was almost a crisis as Madame François Elisabeth (Fanny) Bertrand had not yet received a parcel of limestone for taking the death mask. Fortunately, Dr Burton knew of a deposit of gypsum on the island and a ship's boat was put to sea. When it returned several hours later, Antommarchi heated the fragments to produce a plaster and took the impression. He then shaved Napoleon's head so that members of the family could be given locks of his hair.

Before starting the dissection Antommarchi recorded his impressions: The emperor was considerably thinner than at their first meeting. His eyes were closed and he appeared to be deeply asleep, not to be dead. A sardonic smile hovered about his mouth. Antommarchi noted the scars of Napoleon's wounds and also the mark of the cautery that had been applied to his left arm as treatment.

"The body had been lying for twenty-and-a-half hours. I proceeded

with the autopsy." What follows here is a translation of Antommarchi's complete report:

"I opened first the thorax. Here I observed something remarkable: The costal cartilages were in large part ossified. The left pleural cavity contained around a glassful of yellowish fluid.

"A thin layer of coagulable lymph covered part of the costal and corresponding pulmonary surfaces of the pleural membrane of this side. The left lung was slightly compressed by the fluid, stuck by numerous

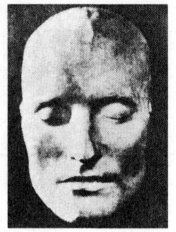

Napoleon's death mask.

adhesions to the posterior and lateral aspects of the chest and pericardium; I dissected it with care, I found the superior lobe to be studded with tubercles and several small tuberculous cavities.

"The right pleural cavity contained about two glassfuls of yellowish fluid. The right lung was slightly compressed by the fluid; but was of normal consistency. The two lungs were generally crackly and of normal colour. The mucous membrane of the trachea and bronchi was quite red and coated with much thick and viscid mucus.

"Several bronchial and mediastinal [lymph] nodes were a little enlarged, nearly degenerated and suppurating. The pericardium was normal and contained about an ounce of yellowish fluid. The heart, slightly bigger than the subject's fist, was, although healthy, fatty at the base and along its sulci. Both the ventricles and the atria were normal, but pale and entirely empty of blood. The orifices of the heart showed nothing abnormal. The great arteries and veins were empty and in general normal.

"The abdomen revealed the following:

"Distension of the peritoneal cavity due to a large quantity of gas.

"An unremarkable, clear and diffuse exudate covered the entire extent of the contiguous internal surfaces of the peritoneum.

"The greater omentum was normal.

"The spleen and the liver, which was hardened, were enlarged and swollen with blood; the substance of the liver, of a reddish-brown colour,

showed no other notable change to its structure. The gall-bladder was filled and distended with extremely thick and clotted bile. The liver, which was affected by chronic hepatitis, was closely adherent along the whole extent of its convex surface to the diaphragm; the adhesions were strong, organized and of long standing. The concave surface of the left lobe was closely and strongly adherent to the corresponding area of the stomach, above all along the lesser curvature of that organ, in like manner to the lesser omentum. At all points of contact the lobe was perceptibly thick, swollen and hard.

"The stomach appeared at first sight to be in a mostly healthy state; no trace of irritation or inflammation. But on examining the organ with care, I discovered on the anterior surface, towards the lesser curvature and three fingers' breadth from the pylorus, a slight scirrhus-like congestion, of very small extent and well circumscribed. The stomach was penetrated through and through in the centre of this small induration. The adhesions at this part of the left lobe of the liver had obstructed the opening.

"The volume of the stomach was smaller than is the usual state. On opening this viscus along the greater curvature, I discovered that it was partially filled with a considerable quantity of matter of poor consistency mixed with much very thick mucus that was of a colour resembling coffee-grounds; it gave off an acrid stench. When this had been removed, the mucous membrane of the stomach was found to be in a normal state between the lesser sac and the greater sac of the peritoneum, along the greater curvature. Nearly all the rest of the internal surface of this organ was taken up by a cancerous ulcer which had its centre superiorly and extended along the lesser curvature while its irregular margins, finger-like and tongue-shaped, stretched over the inner surface from the cardiac orifice to within an inch or more of the pylorus. The opening, which was round and slanted, penetrated obliquely into the inner surface of the stomach, and was scarcely four or five lines [a line is one-twelfth of an inch] in diameter on the inside and two-and-a-half lines at the most on the outside; its circular margin there was extremely narrow, irregular and blackish, and formed only by the peritoneal covering of the stomach. This penetration had an ulcerated, greyish, smooth lining; it would have allowed the cavity of the stomach to communicate with the abdominal cavity had the

adhesions to the liver not prevented it. The right extremity of the stomach, to within an inch of the pylorus, was encircled by a swelling or rather a circular scirrhous hardening, several lines wide. The pyloric orifice was entirely normal. The margins of the ulcer presented some remarkable swollen fungosities the base of which was hard, thick and scirrhous and likewise extended over all the surface covered by this cruel condition.

"The lesser omentum was contracted, swollen and extremely hard and degenerated. The lymph nodes of this peritoneal fold – those that are found along the curvatures of the stomach – and also those adjoining the crura of the diaphragm, were somewhat enlarged, hardened and several were even suppurating.

"The digestive tract was distended by a large quantity of gas. On the peritoneal surface and on the peritoneal reflections, I noticed some small, scattered, very pale red spots and plaques of varying sizes. The membranous lining of the tract appeared normal. The large intestine was filled with a blackish, extremely viscid matter.

"The right kidney was normal; the left was displaced backwards onto the lumbar vertebral column; it was longer and narrower than the right, it appeared normal. The urinary bladder, empty and very contracted, contained a quantity of gravel mixed with a few small calculi. Numerous red plaques were scattered over the mucous membrane; the walls of this organ were in an abnormal state.

"I wished to examine the brain. The state of this organ in a man such as the Emperor was of the very greatest interest; but I was officiously stopped; I had to give up.

"I concluded this sad undertaking. I removed the heart, the stomach, and put them in a silver vase filled with esprit-de-vin. I then put the separated parts together and closed them with a suture, I washed the body, and handed over to the valet…"

This report has the distinct feel of having been written by a man who knew what he was doing but, in making an analysis, we once again have to be alert to the state of medical knowledge at the time. Antommarchi used two words that have since caused trouble: cancerous and schirrous (which today implies cancerous hardening). To Antommarchi, what he saw *was* cancer, it could not have been anything else; difficult though it may be for

us to appreciate today, there was just no other diagnosis available to him. As we saw in the last chapter, the existence of gastric ulcer was not even suspected until the early 1830s when it was described by Jean Cruveilhier. He noted: "Almost always single, simple ulcer is situated most commonly either on the lesser curvature or upon the posterior wall of the stomach.... Simple ulcer of the stomach does not present other than a gross resemblance to cancerous ulcer with which however it has always been confused. The base of it does not show any of the characteristics of either a hard cancer or a soft cancer, one does not find the circumscribed hypertrophy which practically always accompanies cancer and which has been taken so often for a cancerous degeneration itself."

Had Antommarchi realized that what he was looking at was not cancer, he could have found a place in medical history as the first person to describe a gastric ulcer. Not only are the essentials of an accurate clinical history to be found in his reports, but he was also correct pathologically as regards its site and margins. The great majority of gastric ulcers start on the lesser curvature and extend along it from just below the cardiac orifice to a point about an inch or more before the pylorus – precisely as he described. As the ulcer spreads it encroaches onto the anterior and posterior walls of the stomach to become saddle-shaped or irregular – again as he described the appearance of the right extremity of the stomach to within an inch of the entirely normal pylorus. His description of the appearance of the ulcer also agrees with that of one that has perforated and been sealed off by strong adhesions of the lesser curvature to the liver. Then there are the lymph nodes lying along the lymphatics that drain the stomach: these he described as somewhat enlarged, hardened and some even suppurating – a clear indication of chronic inflammation, not of cancer. Moreover, scirrhous cancers, such as he thought he was describing, are infrequently associated with ulceration.

Antommarchi's descriptions of the state of the liver and gall-bladder confirm the clinical diagnoses of hepatitis and cholecystitis and the contents of the large intestine confirm, if confirmation were needed, that the dying man had been bleeding into his digestive tract. The condition of the urinary bladder provided evidence that Napoleon had indeed suffered from cystitis. The normality of the kidneys indicates that there had been no ascending spread of infection.

Of interest, in view of the fact that Napoleon is said to have had tuberculosis, is the finding that the upper lobe of the left lung was studded with tubercles – indicating infection in the distant past, and almost certainly asymptomatic, that had been successfully overcome – and several small tuberculous cavities suggesting re-activation, possibly the result of his poor health and the general conditions of his captivity on the island. But whatever the case, neither O'Meara nor Antommarchi recorded any symptomatic evidence of re-activity; as such, the findings in the left upper lobe may be regarded as incidental and of no clinical significance.

Antommarchi's other observations may safely be attributed to the state of Napoleon's health in the preceding weeks and to the body having lain for twenty-one hours.

The post-mortem thus confirmed the clinical diagnoses of haemorrhage from a gastric ulcer (the cause of death), cholecystitis, chronic hepatitis and a low-grade chronic cystitis.

❧

Antommarchi returned to Europe a poor man with few friends and many enemies. After a brief stay in England he travelled to Paris and Rome where he gave a grief-stricken Madame Mère an account of her son's treatment on St Helena. With Europe no place for a Bonapartist he emigrated to California, practising as an ophthalmologist, before moving to Santiago, Cuba, where he died of yellow fever on April 3, 1838. A sad and lonely end for a good doctor who simply was on the wrong side at the wrong time and has, for many historians, stayed there.

❧

Now that would be the end of the story of Napoleon's ulcer were it not for one or two loose strands that need to be tidied up. The most important of these is the widespread belief that he was poisoned.

The suggestion of poisoning took off almost as soon as his body was cold. But from the start it was no more than a conspiracy theory – sheer speculation. The chief suspect is that dodgy character, Charles Montholon

(1783–1853), a close member of the household, acting either independently or as an agent of the Bourbons, who is supposed to have poisoned Napoleon's wine with arsenic.

A theory that Napoleon was assassinated is closely associated with the poisoning theory and would seem to have had its origins in conversations recorded by Antommarchi. (Where he used the word assassination in the French, I have retained it for the English translation.) One such took place on February 20, 1821:

Antommarchi had just finished examining the emperor, finding him irritable, tired and thoroughly worn out.

"Will it be soon, then," Napoleon asked, alluding to his death.

"No, Sire, your illness is settling down."

"As always, Doctor! When will you tire of telling me I'll recover?"

"When your health is restored."

"In that case you'll be promising me for a very long time."

"No, it will be sooner than Your Majesty might think. Moreover, your health would benefit from taking the waters at a spa."

"Do you really believe they [the English] would acknowledge that? And if they did a refusal to allow it would bring them into the open. It would be like admitting to my assassination. Poor *capocorsino*! You do not understand them."

"But surely Sire, when your health demands it, when your doctor advises it, it would be inhuman to forbid it."

"Precisely!"

Napoleon was referring to the perverse refusal of Sir Hudson Lowe and the British Government to entertain any idea of a move to a healthier location where he might expect more humane treatment, as urged by both O'Meara and Antommarchi. This he made explicit in what amounted to a monologue on April 19 the same year:

After talking for a while Napoleon directed his remarks to Arnott (who does not record them in his own book) with Bertrand acting as translator.

"It was your government that chose this frightful rock, where the lives of Europeans are destroyed in less than three years, to end mine by assassination.... For a home on this inhospitable island you have given me

the least habitable spot where the murderous tropical climate makes itself most felt.... You have been assassinating me for a long time, piecemeal, with malice aforethought and with the infamous Hudson as the chosen executioner of your government."

Accidental poisoning through the medications Napoleon was prescribed is another possibility, but that assumes he was given the appropriate medicines in sufficiently large doses. Arsenic is again the drug that has been most hotly pursued, particularly as it was the active principal of Fowler's solution (a 1 per cent solution of potassium arsenite). Introduced in1786, Fowler's solution in small doses was a popular tonic, but arsenic had numerous other indications including obstinate skin diseases, ague, syphilis – you name it and arsenic was probably used. Indeed, a highly regarded neurological textbook of 1940 recommends arsenic for disseminated (multiple) sclerosis and syphilis and it may even be prescribed for a form of leukaemia today.

A trawl through O'Meara's, Antommarchi's and Arnott's books to discover precisely what medications Napoleon had been prescribed (and taken) and in what doses unfortunately gets us nowhere at all. Mostly the drugs were not specified or if they were they were not potentially poisonous or were prescribed in acceptable doses at acceptable intervals. Furthermore, as O'Meara said, Napoleon would take only those medications he chose to take.

There still remains the possibility of environmental sources such as his hair pomade (surface contamination) and the wallpaper (inhalation and surface contamination) at Longwood. The wallpaper in his room has been shown to contain Scheele's green (Carl Wilhelm Scheele, 1742–86), a mixture of solutions of copper sulphate and sodium arsenite. When exposed to heat and dampness, as would have been the case during Napoleon's long hot soaks in his bath, the paper could have exuded arsenical vapour. The green flock paper on the walls of the drawing room could also have given off arsenical vapour in the damp climate of St Helena. In total, sufficient to be absorbed and to kill him?

The arsenic theory received 'scientific' support in a paper by a Swedish dentist, Sten Forshufvud and others, published in 1961 (*Nature*, **192**, 103–05). The medical history was massaged unmercifully to fit a

diagnosis of arsenical poisoning and this provided the motive for applying an activation analysis technique to the study of a sample of hair "probably taken immediately after his death" – in the title of the paper – or "probably on the day after his death" – in the text. The provenance of the hair as given in the paper was non-existent, simply that it had been made available by M. le Commandant Henri Lachouque, the great French expert on Napoleon's life. Where had he got it from?

The analysis gave a value for the level of arsenic of 10·38 parts per million (ppm) compared "with the normal mean arsenic content of about 0·8 parts per million." Any further studies on the distribution of the arsenic along the hair were not possible as no more samples were available. So far so good it might seem, even though there had been no procedure to remove any surface contamination before analysis.

In July, 2005, a paper appeared in the *Lancet* (**366**, 332–5) by Timothy Cox and others, entitled "King George III and porphyria: an elemental hypothesis and investigation". No mention of Napoleon whatsoever. The authors' starting point was their belief that exposure to heavy metals might play a part in the manifestations of the attacks of acute porphyria, the almost certain cause of the king's illness. The provenance of the sample of hair was well authenticated and the analytical technique impeccable. Before analysis the hair was treated to remove any surface contamination.

The results revealed the unexpectedly high concentration of arsenic of 17 ppm compared with values in control hairs (taken from adult men and women volunteers) of 0·05–0·25 ppm. In their inspection of the Royal Archives the authors discovered that the source of the arsenic had been the disturbingly large doses of tartar emetic (potassium antimony tartrate) given to the king during his illnesses. If antimony seems a strange source for the arsenic, we have to remember that the two are often found together in nature and that such medicines as tartar emetic were, in those days, contaminated by up to five per cent arsenic. The authors calculated that the amount of tartar emetic given to the king would have been well able to produce chronic arsenical poisoning, particularly in view of the slowness of excretion of the metal.

George III, 17 ppm. Napoleon, 10·38 ppm. On this evidence, if

anybody really had been trying to poison Napoleon, they made a pretty rotten job of it.

Regrettably, however, so far as answering the question of whether Napoleon died from arsenical poisoning, these results tell us nothing except that a hair contained arsenic – the controls are inadequate. What is needed are hairs from people who have died from chronic arsenical poisoning and also from those who have died from acute arsenical poisoning. They would provide true, but obviously impractical, controls.

∽✠∾

As we said earlier, young Walter Henry had not laboured in vain. The physical signs described in his letter to Hudson Lowe were seized upon by a Scottish physician, Leonard Guthrie (1858–1918) as sufficient to justify a diagnosis of hypopituitarism. His paper in the *Lancet* (1913, ii, 823–6) was entitled "Did Napoleon Bonaparte suffer from hypopituitarism (dystrophia adiposo-genitalis) at the close of his life?" Regrettably, his inclusion of the words dystrophia adiposo-genitalis has led to trouble ever since.

The problem arose because Alfred Fröhlich (1871–1953) had, in 1901, described the case of R.D. a fourteen-year-old boy who had presented with physical and sexual infantilism and fatness, particularly on the abdomen and in the region of the genitals, which had developed simultaneously with local symptoms and signs indicative of a tumour of the pituitary (*Wiener Klinische Rundschau*, 15, 883–6; 906–08). The English translation of the title of Fröhlich's paper reads "A case of tumour of the hypophysis cerebri [the pituitary] without acromegaly." The great importance of Fröhlich's paper, and the reason the syndrome was named after him, was that previously *only* acromegaly (hyp*er*pituitarism) with local cerebral symptoms had justified the diagnosis of pituitary disease, and R.D. showed evidence of hyp*o*pituitarism. Subsequently, the role of the pituitary in the production of the obesity part of the syndrome was doubted and it is now regarded as being due to the pathological lesion interfering with the function of the neighbouring hypothalamus.

[R.D. was operated on and a probably benign adenoma removed from the pituitary. In 1908 he was generally improved, had had some

"Vive l'Empereur!"

growth of body hair and also erections. He was, however, still of infantile appearance and showed no decrease in his bodily fat. This status was unchanged when he was last seen in 1913.]

Fröhlich's syndrome therefore *only* describes children with physical and sexual infantilism, local cerebral symptoms and the described distribution of obesity caused by the presence of a tumour in the region of the pituitary. It does *not* and cannot apply to any other type of juvenile obesity – to saddle these children with a diagnosis of pituitary deficiency would be a gross diagnostic error. So whatever diseases Napoleon may have suffered from, Fröhlich's syndrome cannot possibly be among their number. However, this has not stopped the diagnosis being applied on and off for generations and being dug up again whenever it suits an argument.

Nowhere in his paper did Guthrie use the term 'Fröhlich's syndrome' but as the expression 'dystrophia adiposo-genitalis' had been coined in

1906 by Max Bartels and had become a synonym for Fröhlich's syndrome, it is no wonder that before long Guthrie was held to have said that Napoleon had suffered from Fröhlich's syndrome.

What Guthrie was suggesting was hypopituitarism in his later years. He based his argument first on Henry's description, and second on his reading of Napoleon's mental and physical decline from about 1809. He wrote: "It is pitiful to trace the mental decadence of this intellectual giant in the sordid details of his closing years." And of his lassitude on St Helena: "Fatigue and prostration readily induced by exertion were, in fact, signs of the insidious onset of hypopituitarism."

The problem with the diagnosis of hypopituitarism bears a resemblance to the one we encountered with poisoning. Some of the features that would be needed for the diagnosis can be found in the medical history but they would have to be exaggerated and manipulated to fit the theory. Since Guthrie's day, understanding of the physiology and pathology of the pituitary has greatly expanded and from today's clinical point of view the diagnosis will not stand up to critical evaluation.

Guthrie also suggested that at an earlier period in his life Napoleon had suffered from dyspituitarism, though whether hypersecretion or hyposecretion he could not decide. He seemed to favour hypersecretion on the strength of Napoleon's urinary and sexual histories. His arguments are invalid today.

❦

"I should have died at Waterloo", Napoleon remarked after he arrived on St Helena. Even if he had, he would still have held on for four years longer than he prophesied in the golden moment of Austerlitz. But, more to the point, he would have deprived generations of biographers, historians and other assorted theorists of much innocent pleasure.

4

ASPECTS OF
MENOPAUSAL LIFE

D uring the Napoleonic wars the French army surgeon, Pierre
François Percy (1754–1825), remarked in disgust at the
prevailing attitude to casualties: "A man ceases to be a man when
he can no longer fight." Likewise, in the popular mind down the ages a
woman ceased to be a woman when she could no longer menstruate.
Rudolf Virchow (1821–1902), at the end of the 19th century, expressed
this feeling in more biological terms: "Woman", he is reputed to have said,
"is a pair of ovaries with a human being attached; whereas a man is a
human being furnished with a pair of testes."

In contrast to a man who slides without abrupt change from one
stage of his life to the next, a woman's progress is charted by a number of
distinct physiological events – the menarche, defloration, pregnancy,
labour, lactation, the menopause – all of which leave their mark. Except
for the last, these events have been subject to ceremonial, taboo and
superstition and abundantly celebrated in myth, folklore and legend. But
about the cessation of menstruation there is silence; the pages of the book
are missing because they were never written.

One reason for this omission may be that the climacteric has only

comparatively recently had a serious impact on the social scene. At the beginning of the 20th century a woman could expect to live to about 48 years; now, her life expectancy approaches 80 years (in the free world). As the expectation of life increased and it became the rule rather than the exception for a woman to live beyond the climacteric, so the changes associated with this period of life intruded more into the social consciousness.

(Here it would be as well to define our two main terms. The menopause, or change of life, refers to the cessation of the menses; it is an event that can, in retrospect, be precisely dated. The climacteric is the period – usually lasting

Time destroying beauty. A painting by Pompeo Girolamo Batoni (1708-87). (*National Gallery, London.*)

between one and five years – during which ovarian function fails and finally ceases. The Greeks believed that at certain ages, which they referred to as climacteric periods, the body underwent definite changes. There were five of these periods and the ages at which they occurred were generally multiples of seven. The word did not enter the English language until 1601. The menopause marks neither the beginning nor the end of the climacteric; it is simply one of the major events of this period and precedes the end of ovulation by months or maybe years.)

However, the fact that life expectancy was only 48 at the start of the last century – 35–40 a hundred years earlier, 25–30 in medieval Europe, and 20–25 in Greece and Rome – does not imply that the menopause was unknown. The figures indicate the expectancy at birth and since infant,

child and maternal mortality rates were distressingly high in the past, a fair number of women lived well beyond the expected years (at birth) for their time. So again we must ask why an event of such significance to the individual woman passed almost without notice sociologically, anthropologically and medically. And the only answer thrown back from the silent past is that the menopause was a negative event of no importance in the life of the community.

So, when a woman's usefulness was seen to be ended, she ceased to be a woman. Indeed in one of the exceedingly few studies in this area, Margaret Mead (1901–78), the American anthropologist, found that pre-pubertal girls and post-menopausal women were, in many societies, treated very much as men. The only reference she made in her book *Male and Female* to the social role of women after the menopause emphasized this point: "Where reproductivity has been regarded as somewhat impure and ceremonially disqualifying – as in Bali – the post-menopausal woman and the virgin girl work together at ceremonies from which women of child-bearing age are debarred." She continued:

"Where modesty of speech and action is enjoined on women, such behaviour may no longer be asked from the older woman, who may use obscene language as freely as or more freely than any man." Nevertheless the post-menopausal woman must have been something of a conundrum to primitive people living close to nature, as the human is the only female animal to live to any significant extent beyond her reproductive years.

⚜

Underlying the many superstitions and taboos surrounding menstruation is the belief that the menstrual flow is a means of ridding the body of poisonous material; as a consequence menstruating women are unclean. But there is more to it than this. Primitive man has a deeply ingrained fear of menstrual blood, amounting at times to terror. Sir James Frazer (1854–1941), in *The Golden Bough*, recorded examples that illustrate the universality of this dread. The sight, for instance, of a menstruating woman of the American Déné tribe was believed to be dangerous and she was compelled to hide herself beneath a special skin

bonnet with fringes falling over her face and breast. The women of a tribe in South Australia left camp during their monthly periods and the boys were told that if they saw menstrual blood they would become prematurely grey-headed and lose their strength.

The influence of menstruating women on crops and staple industries could be particularly disastrous. In New Guinea it might cause the tobacco plants to be diseased; in Sumatra, the rice crop to fail; in one of the Torres Straits islands, the fish to die; and in North America it might spoil a hunter's expedition. In the Lebanon, shadows of these women cause flowers to wither and trees to die. The cattle of certain tribes in South Africa perish if a menstruating woman drinks their milk or if a drop of her blood falls across their path. For a menstruating Baganda woman to touch something of her husband's is to make him ill, and should the object be his weapons he will be killed in his next battle.

Among Europeans the list of misfortunes, according to Pliny the Elder (23–79), is swelled by the sophistication of civilization. To blighted crops, miscarrying mares and dying cattle are added blunted razors, rusted iron and tarnished brass, dimmed mirrors, soured beer, wine, and milk, and much else besides. And let the sailor beware, for the presence aboard of a menstruating woman is bound to conjure up a storm.

But these superstitions and taboos are not the prerogative solely of primitive peoples and of our own forefathers. In the remoter parts of the British countryside today you may still meet with the farmer's wife who will assure you that milk handled by a menstruating woman cannot be churned to butter or that hams will not take salt at her hands.

These and the many other taboos of a similar nature attached to puberty and events of the childbearing years of a woman's life contrast strikingly with the dearth of beliefs and practices associated with the cessation of menstruation.

ож

About the only aspect of the menopause that has aroused any interest is the age at which it occurs – and, linked to this, the oldest age at which a woman has given birth. One suspects, nevertheless, that the motivating

factor is a search for the unusual or the sensational which in the end finds gold only among travellers' or old wives' tales. From Classical Greece to the 21st century women have reached the menopause at between 45 and 50 with a spread of perhaps five years at each end. Cessation of the periods before or, more especially, their continuance after these years should make us highly suspicious of a pathological or iatrogenic cause.

Hippocrates (460–377 BC) suggested that the menopause occurred at 42, but this may have simply been because the number was a convenient multiple of seven. Aristotle (384–322 BC) wrote in his *Politics*, "for the most part 50 marks the limit of women's reproductive capacity." Soranus of Ephesus, who lived in the 2nd century AD, was prepared to commit himself to a lower as well as an upper limit; menstruation, he said, usually comes to an end not earlier than 40 and not later than 50. Aetius of Amida (6th century AD) extended the range slightly. Periods ceased "not before the 35th year, and not after the 50th, though in rare instances menstruation continues until the 60th year." In the opinion of Avicenna (980–1037), the influential Arabian physician, "there are women whose menstruation lapses quickly to end in their 35th or 40th year; but there are others in whom it lasts until they reach 50."

The 11th-century Salernitan manuscript attributed to Trotula varied the age according to the woman's bodily constitution. Menstruation lasts "until the 50th year if the woman is thin; until the 55th or 60th if she is moist; and until the 35th if she is fat." (Moist is not a concept that we would understand today as it is part of the doctrine of the humours. According to this, old age is due to the body drying out. Thus it is only to be expected that a manifestation of ageing – the menopause – should appear later in a woman whose constitution was 'moist'.)

John of Gaddesden (*c.*1280–1361) in *Rosa Anglica, Practica Medicina*, wrote that the menses "cease naturally at 50, though sometimes they stop earlier, at 35, 40, or 45, according to the various natures of women" which, although he was referring to the humoral theory, is as neat a way as any of saying that the age at the menopause depends on the individual.

In more modern times attempts have been made to discover the factors that influence age at the menopause. Many have been considered – heredity, constitution, social status, climate, race, sex life and

childbearing among them – but it is well-nigh impossible to control all except the one being studied. Speculation remains the order of the day. Nevertheless heredity would appear to have a genuine influence and social status, insofar as it relates to malnutrition, overwork and poor general health, may play a part. For instance, in 1935 some investigators found possible evidence that the menopause occurred earlier (by about two months) in the lower than in the upper classes. They also concluded that a warm climate seemed to postpone the menopause, though this does not agree with the view of Charles François Menville (1805–?) who, in 1840, wrote that in Asia a woman was no longer young at 30 and in Java was unable to conceive at that age. In Persia the menopause was reported to occur at 27.

One occurrence in a woman's life might perhaps reasonably be expected to indicate the time of her menopause, and that is the age at which her menses began. Unfortunately for those who like things in tidy packets, there is little or no correlation between the two events.

In the search for the oldest menopause in the medical literature (to give it an air – spurious maybe – of authority) the palm must go to the patient of G.H. Maasius. This woman first menstruated at 20; her first child was born when she was 47, and the last of her eight children when she was 60. Her periods thereupon ceased, only to reappear at 75; they continued until she was 98 when they stopped again, this time for a mere six years as they returned at the advanced age of 104. That was in 1812, the year Maasius saw her; her subsequent history is unknown.

A pity though it may be to spoil a good tale, Maasius undoubtedly had the wool pulled over his eyes, most likely by two or three generations having run together in the patient's mind – not necessarily with intent to deceive. Travellers' tales of aged women with very young children often have a similar explanation: the true relationship is perhaps that of grandmother and granddaughter, but because of a language barrier the wrong impression is given. However, on the evidence available, this would not apply to the best known instance of an apparently post-menopausal woman giving birth. In Genesis we read:

"And God said unto Abraham… I will bless her, and give thee a son also of her:… Then Abraham fell upon his face, and laughed, and said in

his heart, Shall a child be born unto him that is an hundred years old? and shall Sarah, that is ninety years old, bear?" (Ch. 17, v. 15–17).

These ages indicate only that Abraham and Sarah were no longer youthful. Abraham had been "seventy and five years old" at the beginning of the journey south into Egypt and at that time Sarah was extremely beautiful (Ch. 12). But when God announced the forthcoming birth of Isaac, Sarah had ceased to menstruate: "Now Abraham and Sarah were old and well stricken in age; and it ceased to be with Sarah after the manner of women" (Ch. 18, v. 11). Nevertheless she was still sufficiently attractive to be taken by Abimelech, king of Gerar (Ch. 20) – possibly an instance of the sexual beauty of the mature woman (a consideration that we shall return to later).

So without going into the question of whether Sarah had really passed her menopause but was still ovulating, or whether there was some other cause for the amenorrhoea (malnutrition, change of climate perhaps), there is one explanation that could fit the facts. Barren women not infrequently conceive after they and their husbands have adopted a child. Sarah was barren and ten years after their return from Egypt she said to Abraham, "Behold now, the Lord hath restrained me from bearing: I pray thee, go in unto my maid; it may be that I may obtain children by her... And he went in unto Hagar, and she conceived" (Ch. 16, v. 2 and 4). And when the child, Ishmael, was born he was brought up in the house of Abraham and Sarah.

The oldest, reliably documented mother appears still to be Mrs Ruth Alice Kistler of the USA. (Unfortunately, the waters have become muddied since the arrival of fertility treatments and in vitro fertilization, both of which should, in the present context, be regarded as cheating!) At all events, Mrs Kistler was born on June 11, 1899, and gave birth to a daughter on October 18, 1956, at the age of 57 years, 129 days. The British record is some two or three years less.

⚬✺⚬

Until modern science began to unravel the hormonal complexities of menstruation there could be no valid medical attitudes to the menopause,

only to the menopausal woman – and these were conspicuous by their almost complete absence.

The scientific trail began in 1672 when the Dutchman, Reignier de Graaf (1641–73), published his description of the structures in the ovary which have since become known as Graafian follicles. Yet another one-hundred-and-fifty years had to pass before Karl Ernst von Baer (1792–1876), an Estonian by birth, showed that these follicles were not the ova but merely their containers. Towards the end of the 18th century the ovaries were thought in some way to be connected with menstruation as their absence or destruction was always associated with amenorrhoea, but von Baer's discovery in 1827 opened the way and twelve years later Augustin Nicolas Gendrin (1796–1890) put forward the theory that menstruation depended on periodic ovulation. Various misconceptions, such for instance that ovulation and menstruation occurred simultaneously, however, persisted until the beginning of the 20th century. The next important step was the isolation by Edgar Allen (1892–1943) and Edward Adelbert Doisy (1893–1986) of St Louis in 1923 of a hormone from the follicular fluid which was capable of inducing oestrus in oophorectomized animals. This ovarian hormone (oestrone) was crystallized from the urine of pregnant women by Doisy and his colleagues in 1930.

The ovarian role – its failure – in the menopause was investigated by French physicians from the early 1890s onwards (though ignored by the Germans for another two decades). For a while at the turn of the century dysfunction of the thyroid and, to a lesser extent, of the adrenal was thought to be the major cause of the climacteric symptoms. Then in 1915, Gregorio Maranon (1887–1960), a Spaniard, stated that all the endocrine glands were involved at this critical period. Although the ovary is the gland primarily affected, its functions are so integrated with those of the others (especially the anterior pituitary) that its failure upsets the balance of the whole endocrine system.

So it is against this background of centuries of physiological ignorance that we take a look at centuries of neglect of the menopausal woman. Among the ancients, Soranus was one of the few to adopt a positive approach. In the 2nd century AD he wrote:

"But in women who are about to menstruate no longer, their time for menstruation having passed, one must take care that the stoppage of the menses does not occur suddenly. For in regard to alteration, even if the body be changed for the better, all abruptness disturbs it through discomfort; for that which is unaccustomed is not tolerated, but is like some unfamiliar malaise. The methods we employ at the approach of the first menstruation [general hygiene, avoidance of tension and inflammation, and measures to tone up the body] must now be marshalled forth during the time when menstruation is about to cease; for that which is able to evoke the as yet absent excretion is even more able to preserve for some time menstruation which is still present. In addition, vaginal suppositories capable of softening and injections which have the same effect should be employed, with all the remedies capable of rendering hard bodies soft."

A little further on he continues, "And the fact that they do not menstruate any more does not affect the health of women past their prime, nay on the contrary, the drawing off of blood makes the majority more delicate." This view of menstruation as harmful is in disagreement with Galen's opinion that the menses were simply a natural blood-letting necessitated by overfeeding with its resultant plethora. Indeed Galen (130–c.200) remarked, "a woman who takes a little exercise must needs be abundant in many menstrual periods in order that in this respect she may be in good health." And Galen's doctrines, distorted by time and inaccurate translations, were the authority for the next 1500 years with the result that phlebotomy was freely resorted to for treating the ills of post-menopausal women, just as it was for treating most other ills. The negative attitude to the menopause is well demonstrated here since Galen's contributions to gynaecology were weak and mostly second-hand, whereas Soranus's work and teachings formed the basis of future practice – except so far as the menopause was concerned.

At the beginning of the 18th century Johann Christoph von Ettner (1654–?), otherwise known as the 'Faithful Eckarth', gave a poetic, but thoroughly demoralizing, description of the physical changes at the menopause:

"Just as in young women, so long as their blooming takes its orderly

course, all is in full flower and motion, so with those women who have lost their bloom, all spirit and briskness decline. The colour which excites love changes to a faded paleness; the once tense muscles and flesh-covered fibres become slack, and wrinkles take the place of the former smoothness and beauty; indeed the whole form is altered so that when one compares the present figure with the earlier beauty, it is difficult to find any likeness. The eyes which used to dart hither and thither, like those of falcons, become dull and glazed. The lovely cheeks fall in; the beautiful round breasts hang down like bags; the ruby lips become plum colour, brown and dull; the well-grown spine curves and bends and with it the erect neck; the beautiful white, ivory-like skin becomes yellowish; the flesh disappears from those pretty hands and feet. In fine, all that a lover once held beautiful, is now repulsive to him and arouses in him a disgust and horror of uncomeliness." One suspects that the Faithful Eckarth must have had an unfortunate experience at some time in his life!

A hundred years later Pierre Roussel (1742–1802) gave evidence that the Galenic view of menstruation still flourished, though he wrapped it up in a highly decorated parcel. Menstruation, Roussel maintained, was not an inherent function of women but one that had been acquired through heredity or custom. Menstruation did not take place during woman's primeval existence or among savage tribes (his anthropological knowledge was sorely deficient); it was a healthful crisis that had been artificially acquired by civilized woman. Once accustomed to the luxuries of civilization and excesses in dietary, her system became overcharged with blood and to save her health from danger the menstrual flow took place.

Théophile Charles Emmanuel Edouard Auber (1804–73) believed he could go one better than this and in 1859 proposed the view that menstruation was caused by enforced continence. He, too, had some pretty peculiar anthropological ideas as he said that in the savage state a woman could always gratify her sexual impulses without restraint, and when these impulses had been satisfied by reproduction or had ceased by reason of age there was no need for menstruation. But when civilization appeared, woman had to restrain her sexual instincts. As a result, "there arose irritation of the uterus, and haemorrhagic crisis followed. Hereditary beliefs which had given rise to the idea that these haemorrhages were

natural in women, would then favour the return of these phenomena in succeeding generations."

Such male fantasies could hardly be expected to further the cause of the menopausal woman, but reason was asserting itself on our side of the Channel where Edward John Tilt (1815–93) in 1851 had written "that habits which have lasted more than thirty years cannot be set aside without frequently entailing very serious ill health." Tilt divided women into those endowed with a strong constitution and those with a weak. The latter need make no change in their style of living at the menopause (as this already embodied the precautions he advised), but those with a strong constitution suffered more from the change of life and would do well to take a light diet; tight lacing, late revelries such as routs and balls, and horse-riding should be avoided, though walking and bathing were encouraged. In an attempt to preserve the woman's health by taking over from Nature, who was abdicating her responsibilities, he also bled his patients and gave them purgatives and sudorifics – the ancient doctrine of the humours took an unconscionable time a-dying.

Tilt was not unaware of the mental hazards of the menopause: "The full conviction that age has stamped them with its irrevocable seal may indeed ease [send] a momentary gloom over the imagination, but in a well-trained mind it must soon be dispelled, if not by the consciousness of a useful career, at least by the knowledge that this epoch proclaims an immunity from the perils of child-bearing and the tedious annoyances of a monthly restraint; that it may even promise them a length of life and strength of constitution superior in general to that of the opposite sex similarly advanced in years."

In a subsequent book published in 1857, Tilt quoted two authors who recognized the disturbances that might accompany the menopause: G. Bedford who stated that "in addition to structural and malignant disorders so frequent at this period, there are many forms of eccentric nervous disturbance, various forms of temporary or permanent paralysis, and that the varieties of simple nervous irritation, without involving any peculiar lesion, are beyond calculation." And Jacques-Louis Moreau de la Sarthe (1771–1826) who said that "the change of life is characterized by headaches, syncope, leipothymia [fainting], general or partial spasmodic

affections, hypochondriasis, the varied symptoms of hysteria, and by many forms of insanity."

Nevertheless, Tilt bemoaned the fact that to many others the change of life was a period of no importance, and in another of his quotes we meet for the first time reference to an attitude that, regrettably, is with us still: "Thus, Sir C.M. Clarke, commenting on the diseases of the epoch, states that 'It is not unusual with women to refer all their extraordinary sensations to the "c. of life", and to consider that, when they have thus accounted for their diseases, they have at the same time cured them; and in this, most medical men, judging at least from their practice, seem to be of the same opinion.'"

As the 19th century progressed, so more and more attention centred on the ovary, and in its last decade treatment with the gland in one form or another came into medical practice. This was largely due to the enthusiasm of Charles Edouard Brown-Séquard (1817–94) in Paris who followed up his rejuvenation experiments, using testicular extracts, with work on the ovary. At first, according to Charles Vinay, he tried giving two sheep's ovaries a day sandwiched between slices of unleavened bread and when this failed he prepared extracts of ovaries taken from animals (cows, mares, sheep) in the full blush of sexual activity. As with the testicular extracts, these ovarian extracts were given by subcutaneous injection. Speaking at a meeting in London in 1893, Brown-Séquard commented: "Of the ovaric liquid I will only say that it acts with less power than the orchitic liquid. However, sixty old women in Paris have derived benefit from its action, according to an American lady physician, Mrs Brown."

The work of the great French surgeon, Théodore Tuffier (1857–1929), on ovarian grafting has on occasion been misinterpreted. He did not graft ovaries to relieve menopausal women of their symptoms. Between 1906 and 1921 he performed 230 operations in which he grafted or transposed the ovaries; however, 210 of these were autografts and only 20 homografts. In all patients the ovaries were grafted or transposed for valid surgical reasons; homografts were employed when the patient's own ovaries were unusable for one reason or another. In none of the 20 homografted patients did menstruation return and menopausal symptoms were never suppressed.

Ovarian extracts were given with greater or, usually, lesser degrees of success in the management of the menopause until the arrival of the natural oestrogens and, later, of the synthetic oestrogens such as stilboestrol. Nevertheless, the remark of E. Von Graff is scarcely less true today than when it was written some seventy-five years ago: "The various disturbances connected with the 'critical age' in female life known to laity and physicians alike are often not seriously considered by the latter, and have become a kind of 'stepchild' in medicine which frequently happens with fields that border between pathology and physiology."

✺

Opinions are in conflict about a woman's sexual emotions at the menopause. Gregorio Maranon speaks for one side and Isabel Hutton (*d.*1960),writing in 1936, for the other.

Maranon sees a tendency for women to enjoy avidly those pleasures which – they imagine – are about to end. But beyond this, he believes that at the climacteric there is an increase in libido in many women of irreproachable sexual integrity. It shows itself in "a thirst for risqué conversation or questionable jests, sometimes of an extremely erotic character. [Echoes here of Margaret Mead's findings.] Yet such conversation or jokes they would have refused to give ear to formerly." An aspect of the amorous feelings that he finds intriguing is "the frequency with which the individual who arouses them is of a younger age than the menopausal woman." He regards this as "an instinctive tendency to seek in another's youth the warmth which her own waning power requires." But in Isabel Hutton's view: "Popular novels often give the impression that women are unduly amorous at this time and inclined to break loose from all decorum. We are familiar with the kind of literature in which women, at what is called 'the dangerous age,' fall in love with young men and make themselves ridiculous with their overtures. These novels lead us to suppose that women are pursuing a last love affair before reaching the age which is supposed to be the end of their sex-life.

"In all the writer's experience, not a single case of this kind, directly attributable to the climacteric has ever been met with. An amorous, flighty

woman will continue so throughout the 'change of life' and afterwards, but she does not suddenly develop these characteristics between forty and fifty years of age."

Sex apart, the climacteric is a fertile time for domestic crises. Isabel Hutton sees a previously trusting wife gradually become jealous and suspicious of her husband. The wife craves for more affection and when it is not forthcoming she begins to imagine that he no longer loves her. She becomes apprehensive of losing him. Then the fear that he is interested in someone else grows into a certainty and his most innocent actions seem to her to point towards this. She starts nagging and in the end may drive him to giving her genuine cause for complaint.

Margaret Mead saw, in 1950s' America, rather different possibilities for crisis. With the last child having left home the woman imagines her purpose in life fulfilled; although she is still too young to be retired, she feels she should be. This is reinforced by the emotional fears that surround the menopause – that she will lose desire and cease to be desirable, that she will no longer be attractive, and that she may become emotionally unstable. The husband, too, may have problems of his own at this time; he is quite likely to have reached the final plateau in his job, and now simply works to stay still, not for promotion. The family crises may well be further intensified by difficulties with elderly parents which increase their consciousness of growing old. It is in critical circumstances such as these that the woman may have a last baby or she may take up voluntary work or return to her old job. But work in itself may lead to fresh crisis as the husband contrasts her new enthusiasm and prospects with his own treadmill existence. And what is the solution?

"To the extent that both are able to re-plan their lives together," Margaret Mead offers, "they make of the crisis a step forward rather than a step back. It is probable that society will recognize this period as a period in which professional counselling is needed as much as in adolescence. For each married couple alone in a home of their own is exposed to pressures and difficulties unknown in differently organized societies."

Although many women must have been of menopausal years when they walked through the pages of fiction none, until quite recent times, was permitted to influence the story by virtue solely of her physiology. Unless, of course, we accept Phaedra as belonging to their number: then we have a tale of a woman whose behaviour was utterly at the mercy of her hormones – or as one French author called it, "Le drame de l'age critique."

In Greek mythology Phaedra was the wife of Theseus – but we had better start nearer the beginning. When Theseus returned from slaying the Minotaur (with the help of Ariadne, daughter of the King of Crete, whom he subsequently abandoned on Naxos) his next expedition was to the country of the Amazons where he abducted Antiope (or, according to another version, her sister, Hippolyte). Antiope (or Hippolyte) bore him a son, but instead of marrying her he married Phaedra (sister of Ariadne) for whom he had evidently been nursing a passion for some time. After a visit to Sparta he introduced Helen to his household, but the influence of this on future happenings is open to conjecture. At all events, when Theseus came home from yet another expedition he found himself in the middle of an almighty domestic crisis. Helen's brothers, the Dioscuri, had arrived to take her back to Sparta; but worse than that, Phaedra had fallen hopelessly in love with her stepson, Hippolytus (the son of Hippolyte – or Antiope). The young man, as he now was, could not return her advances since he had taken a vow of chastity and this completely unbalanced Phaedra. She accused Hippolytus to Theseus of having made an attempt on her virtue and thereupon committed suicide. Theseus, credulous, distraught and furious, prayed to Poseidon to kill the youth and that same afternoon a sea-monster panicked the horses during Hippolytus's drive along the seashore and he was dragged to his death beneath the chariot.

This legend provided the theme for *Hippolytus*, Euripedes's (480–406 BC) tragedy, and for Racine's (1639–99) *Phèdre* (1677).

Not surprisingly, in view of their scientific interest during the latter part of the 19th century, it was the French who incorporated the emotional aspects of the menopause into the literature of the period. In his comedy, *La Crise* (1882), Octave Feuillet (1821–90) showed remarkable insight and perceptiveness. Julia, the heroine and a previously well-balanced personality, reflects:

"What name can be given to this moral affliction, to this discontent with myself and with those about me that I have felt for some months. My husband is, doubtless, the best of men. But nothing that he says or does pleases me. His watch charms irritate me above all else. Yet these charms and I have lived together in peace for 10 years. Then suddenly, one fine day, we hate each other. My husband has the insufferable habit of jingling them while he is talking – making an unbearable clinking. At the very instant that I write these lines he is in his room, winding his watch and making a noise with those charms."

Her husband, M. De Marsan, a magistrate, visits his doctor. "It is not", he says, "a question of extravagant symptoms that would attract the attention of outsiders, but of shades, each day more marked, which do not escape an intimate like myself. For 10 years I have said I possessed a treasure in my wife. Then suddenly this sweet Julia takes on the air of a martyr – obedient, but irritated. This woman of the world, this refined woman now speaks a language full of sharp, bitter words, harsh and peevish maxims. I find in her conversation – previously so mild – a banal melancholy, a sharp poetic flavour, with a socialistic tendency which fills me with uneasiness… At the same time that the wife changed, the mother changed too. Her husband is now a tyrant, the children a heavy burden. She scarcely speaks to them. They are left to themselves. Here, then, doctor, is what has happened to me. Here is the crown of thorns which Julia has put upon my innocent head, without the least provocation on my part. What is the explanation?"

The doctor replies: "Perhaps I have it – your wife's age." He then continues, "It is a normal disease that may attack the best of women as they reach the threshold of maturity. Such is the attraction of the evil fruit which Eve held for the first time in her hands. Thus the most honoured woman may sense a desire not to be resigned to death without having tasted it."

Thus, belatedly, both literature and medicine acknowledged that a woman's emotions are disturbed at the menopause – "though her years were waning, her climacteric teased her like her teens" wrote Byron (1788–1824) in *Don Juan* (canto 8, st. 47) – but fortunately the sensual extremes of a Phaedra are few and far between. And what of the physical

body? The Faithful Eckarth gave no encouragement and even those who compare this stage of life with the golden maturity of autumn cannot ignore the imminence of winter.

Maranon believed in the sexual beauty of some women such, for instance, as Madame Julie Bernard Récamier (1777–1849) whose influence over men began in earnest when she was 36. He quoted the Spanish philosopher and humanist, José Ortega y Gasset (1883–1956) who, in 1919 when he was 36 wrote: "What woman is the most beautiful? I believe that every sensitive spirit prefers in woman the ripeness of autumn, when in her gracious features are mingled the echoes of the girl and the uneasy anticipations of infirmity. In this moment the woman is her whole self. She brings us the essence of her past springtime even while diffusing the rigor of snows to come." This sexual attraction of overlapping seasons is no doubt the reason why white wigs were the fashion in the 18th century.

And in this same mood we shall conclude, more optimistically, with the words of Jules Michelet (1798–1874). In *L'Amour* (1858) he said, "The autumn of life is an epoch full of the mystery of all that is unperturbed. It is similar to a wide plateau on a mountain-top, swept by a fresh breeze, beneath a fair and cloudless sky, when the earth is contemplated with equal serenity by night and by day. It is the stage of recollection and most sincere happiness." And again, when he was 60, "If the face is faded, does that say that the flesh is less firm? In these cases not rarely is the body twenty-five while the face is forty. There are wrinkles around the eyes and on the cheeks, it is true. But usually, the knees and elbows previously angular, now show pretty dimples." Compensations can be found for many human afflictions if we know where to look!

5

ASPECTS OF HAIR

Man has made the most of what hair remains to him by pressing it into the full and uninhibited service of his psychological needs. Posing mainly as a phallic symbol, the hairs of his head have been prominent in mythology, folklore, superstition and the art of adornment ever since Adam and Eve – in an Arabian version of the story – lost their full covering of long flowing hair when they ate of the forbidden fruit.

Depending on one's attitude, hair is symbolic of either sexual or spiritual energy – though in the end both amount to the same thing in the sense that either will explain the involved mythological and superstitious associations; and some explanation is certainly needed. The symbolism of hair is far from straightforward.

"From the most primitive times," C. Berg wrote in 1936, "man has given much time to various forms of interference with his Hair. The primary advantage of this behaviour is, perhaps, that it keeps his hair out of his eyes and from interfering with his activities." He followed this marvellously logical statement with another: "Perhaps the true explanation of why Hair should be signalled out as a phallic substitute par

excellence may be in its physical relationship to sexual maturity."

But, alas, as Berg himself well knew, the subject cannot be left in such delightful simplicity. The unconscious has been at work and has turned our hair into an invaluable way of expressing our emotions, drives and lost conflicts. Thus it features in taboos, mourning behaviour, sexual complexes and tales of strength or beauty with remarkable similarities in different times and in different places. And, finally, its symbolism is entangled in the motives for scalping.

⚭

To the primitive mind certain persons, conditions or things are endowed with the mystical property of taboo. They are a source of danger and as such must be fenced about by ritual to protect the individual or the community. Although the distinction is not made in the primitive mind, the tabooed person or object may be either sacred or unclean – or both, under different circumstances.

The head is, for many peoples, an especially sacred part of the body as it is believed to be the home of a powerful spirit. This creates many difficulties, not least of which is how to cut the hair without incurring the spirit's retribution should it be hurt or insulted. Then, having overcome this hurdle, there is the problem of disposal: the sympathetic union between man and every part of his body continues even when the physical link is broken. Therefore a man may be harmed or killed if his cut hair (or nail parings or whatever) is damaged or falls into the hands of someone who wishes him ill.

The simple answer is not to cut the hair at all, and this is the solution reached by the priests of the Hos tribe of West Africa and, in the Dark Ages, by the kings of the Franks; to have their locks shorn was to renounce their right to the throne. These two instances demonstrate the fact that the more sacred, regal or divine the person, the stronger the taboo.

An extension of the taboo is the belief in an association between hair and the elements. At sea the Romans, for instance, would cut their hair (or their nails) only during a storm – when, in fact, the damage was done and things could not be made worse. (An alternative explanation is that

they cut their hair to appease the gods and bring calm.) In the Scottish Highlands no girl whose brother was abroad in a boat would comb her hair at night. And the Maoris used to cast spells to avert the thunder and lightning which they believed were caused by cutting the hair; they first consecrated the knife, and afterwards both the person who had had his hair cut and he who had cut it were tabooed for a period.

If we were to delve into the depths of the unconscious we would probably find that the act of cutting the hair (a phallic symbol) was a symbolic representation of a socially unacceptable desire – castration. In consequence, when cutting the hair we are faced with an unclean taboo because we are denying the reality of the desire. The situation was sufficiently serious for the Namosi chiefs in Fiji to eat a human sacrifice after they had had their hair cut.

Fortunately, though, it is not difficult to get round the problem of an unclean taboo: we simply turn it into a sacred one by giving it ceremonial status. It then represents a socially acceptable fulfilment of the repressed desire. For instance, in some parts of New Zealand the most sacred day of the year was chosen for ceremonial hair cutting of the assembled population. Perhaps the parallel most easily grasped is that with killing: murder is individual, unclean and socially unacceptable whereas war is communal, sacred and socially acceptable.

Variations on the sympathetic magical properties of hair are found from one end of the world to the other. It is popular knowledge that if you wish to do your enemy harm, one technique is to obtain a lock of his hair and weave spells over it. Beliefs of this nature are particularly prevalent in the South Seas, Australasia and Africa. So powerful is the magic that the Nandis of East Africa put it to a use that makes Dartmoor look like an open prison. They shave the heads of their captives and hold the hair as a pledge of good behaviour. When a ransom has been paid, both prisoners and hair are returned together.

One must also beware of animals. In Germany, headaches were sometimes attributed to birds building their nests with the cut hair, and the inhabitants of the Carpathians had to take great care to keep the clippings from mice – if they used the hair for nesting madness might strike.

So, to save the shorn hair from falling into the wrong hands an array of precautions is available. It may be buried in temples or other sacred places or under the threshold of your house. The hair of the Vestal Virgins, newly cut when they took up their temple duties, was hung on an ancient lotus tree. A sad little commentary, however, comes from Thailand. When the top-knot of a Siamese child has been cut, the short hairs are put in a plantain leaf and floated away down-river taking with them all that is harmful or bad in the child's character. The long hairs are kept until the time of the first pilgrimage to the holy Footprint of Buddha at Prabat. Here the priests make brooms of the hair to sweep the Footprint; but so much hair is offered that as soon as the little pilgrim turns for home much of the hair is burnt. However, in many places – and the more isolated parts of Europe are not exempt – hair is burnt to protect its owner from witchcraft.

Other peoples, who believe in the resurrection of the body, go to great pains to preserve their hairs and their nail parings. The Incas of Peru were among these, keeping shed or cut hairs stuffed in cracks in the walls; if an Indian saw that some had fallen out he would return them to avoid the chaos that would ensue when all the resurrected bodies were searching for their own bits and pieces. Turks and Armenians have similar beliefs and in Drumconrath in Ireland the women used to push their hairs into the thatch of their cottage roofs – they had taken literally the two passages in the Bible: "The very hairs of your head are all numbered" (St Matthew, Ch. 10, v. 30) and "But there shall not an hair of your head perish" (St Luke, Ch. 21, v. 18).

⚛︎

The Old Testament contains many references to shaving the head at times of general or private grief. For instance, when Judah was invaded by the Persians "in that day did the Lord God of Hosts call to weeping and to mourning, and to baldness, and to girding with sackcloth" (Isaiah, Ch. 22, v. 12). On hearing of the calamities that had befallen his family at home "Job arose, and rent his mantle, and shaved his head" (Job, Ch. 1, v. 20). And when Ezra learnt of the people of Israel consorting with

undesirable strangers, "I rent my garment and my mantle, and plucked off the hair of my head and of my beard" (Ezra, Ch. 9, v. 3).

When Ajax and Menelaus brought the slain Patroclus back to the Greek camp, Achilles, his cousin, strewed the corpse with his own hair. On the death of Hephaestion (*d.*324 BC), his bright shadow and intimate friend, Alexander the Great (356–323 BC) not only cut off his own hair but also ordered the tails and mains of the horses and mules throughout his army to be shorn. And when Adonis died, the little cupids are reputed to have cut their own locks.

The reason why, at times of grief, the unconscious picks on the hair both in reality through the hands and metaphorically can be explained in terms of the Oedipus situation: as punishment for his unconscious death wish towards his father, the son symbolically castrates himself.

❧

Psychoanalysts tell us that one of the two most important repressions is the castration complex (the other is incestuous craving). This postulate holds up for women as well as men – the male has an organic phallus, but this does not prevent the majority of those who are so inclined taking out their repressions indirectly on their hair. The female has, through her hair, a symbolic phallus and instead of organ castration her repressed fear is of loss of love. Characteristic of civilization is a subduing of the purely physical to the intellectual and, pursuing the psychoanalytical line of attack, it may well be that short hair styles represent this subjection in the guise of symbolic partial castration. By the same token long hair styles would represent a less civilized but less repressed (more permissive) state of affairs.

Hair, in general, symbolizes energy, whether this be spiritual or sexual. When long or golden it represents the sun's rays and (besides getting one involved in the vast complex of sun symbolism) is characteristic of the solar heroes of mythology. Brown or black hair reinforces the symbolic energy and an auburn or coppery shade implies a demoniacal element.

Folklore abounds with tales in which a man's soul or strength is

connected with his hair, either in toto or with a strand. Moreover prisoners under torture often lost their will to resist and confessed if their hair was cut off or, indeed, if this was only threatened. In Europe, the evil powers of witches and wizards was thought to reside in their hair and so, in France, people suspected of sorcery were shaved, perhaps over the entire body, before being brought to trial. Similar beliefs existed in places as far apart as India and Mexico.

In the psychoanalytical context, where strength is equivalent to sexual potency and hair is a phallic symbol, the significance of cutting a strong man's hair becomes readily apparent.

Hair has been a source for adding to the adornment of the person, both male and female, since the beginning of recorded history; and because its phallic significance is so highly symbolized it is quite acceptable as an object of beauty. In Biblical times long hair on a man was highly regarded: "But in all Israel there was none to be so much praised as Absalom for his beauty: from the sole of his foot even to the crown of his head there was no blemish in him. And when he polled his head, (for it was at every year's end that he polled it: because the hair was heavy on him, therefore he polled it:) he weighed the hair of his head at two hundred shekels after the king's weight" (II Samuel, Ch. 14, v. 25, 26) – the weight has been variously estimated but was probably about 850 grams. Yet his hair was his undoing when it caught in the boughs of a great oak while he was riding a mule: hanging there he was slain by Joab and his men.

David's words of lamentation over his son are well known, but many centuries later they were adapted by a London barber who displayed a sign showing the unhappy Absalom hanging in the oak tree. Underneath was written:

"O! Absalom, my son, my son, If thou had'st worn a periwig thou would'st not been undone."

Josephus, the 1st-century AD Jewish historian, tells us that on ceremonial occasions King Solomon was preceded by forty pages (some say it was his bodyguard), all of noble family and all with their hair sparkling in the sun from being liberally sprinkled with gold dust. The Romans followed suit but also used powdered lapis lazuli.

Joab slaying Absolom caught by his hair in an oak tree.

Some five hundred years after Solomon when Greece was on the threshold of her glory, the Spartans wore their hair long and before going into battle would carefully comb and dress their heads. Before Thermopylae (480 BC), spies reported to the Persian commander, Xerxes (c.519–465 BC), that Leonidas (d.480 BC) and his troops were doing just this. Xerxes was incensed by what he regarded an insult; however, he misjudged the Spartans as their behaviour was part of their religious observance and equivalent to a funeral rite – which, in this case, proved all too necessary. (Leonidas, who was killed in the battle, was credited by Plutarch (c.46–120) with a heart covered in hair. This, as with other instances in the literature, was almost certainly a fibrinous pericarditis.)

One of the worst calamities that could befall many peoples was to have their heads shaved. It was considered a great dishonour and was used as a form of punishment; for instance by the Lombards and the Saxons for petty theft. Yet it is women who suffer the ultimate in disgrace: since Classical times adulteresses have had their heads shaved and usually were

not allowed to grow it again for a year. Isaiah (Ch. 3, v. 24) includes among the many punishments for pride in a woman, "instead of well set hair [she shall have] baldness". In recent times the punishment was meted out to the collaboratrices in France and was encountered among the atrocities committed in Northern Ireland. As Lucius Apuleius (*c.*123–*c.*170) wrote: "Even Venus herself, were she destitute of hair, though surrounded by the Graces and Loves, would have no charms to please her own husband – Vulcan."

The last request of Ancient Britons condemned to be beheaded was that no slave should touch and no blood should stain their hair. The Goths regarded cut hair as an indication of slavery and it had been this same reason that had earlier persuaded Julius Caesar (*c.*102–44 BC) to crop the heads of the prisoners he took in Gaul. To the Anglo-Saxons and the Danes hair was an object of great beauty.

However, in the New Testament when Paul was defining the rules for divine worship he frowned on long hair for men. "Doth not even nature itself teach you, that, if a man have long hair, it is a shame unto him? But," he continued, "if a woman have long hair, it is a glory to her" (I Corinthians, Ch. 11, v. 14, 15). Previously, in verse 5, he had laid down that a woman should not pray or prophesy with her head uncovered. Then, in verse 10, he explained why – not because of men in the congregation lusting after her but: "For this cause ought the woman to have power on her head [a covering to indicate that she was under the power of her husband] because of the angels."

This was, in fact, a very serious belief since angels are of dubious moral character. Their reputation for misbehaviour began way back at the beginning: "And it came to pass, when men began to multiply on the face of the earth, and daughters were born unto them, that the sons of God saw the daughters of men that they were fair; and they took them wives of all which they chose." (Genesis, Ch. 6, v. 1, 2). Verse 4 indicates the very close parallel that existed in those early days with the gods and heroes of other mythologies: "There were giants in the earth in those days; and also after that, when the sons of God came in unto the daughters of men, and they bare children to them, the same became mighty men which were of old, men of renown." The one survived, flourished, and is remembered;

the other faded, was superseded, and peeps through only in places – as, for instance, we shall see with the hero Samson.

⚹

Although best known among the Indian tribes of North America, scalping is – or was – a considerably more widespread habit. It was – or is – practised by the Indians of South America; some tribes of the Gran Chaco used the scalps as drinking vessels in the belief that the victim's spiritual force was imparted to the drink. Herodotus (*c*.484–424 BC) reported the custom among the Scythians and Strabo (*c*.63 BC–AD 24) among the Karnians. It also occurred among the Samoyeds and Ostiaks of Siberia (the Ostiaks believed that by scalping the enemy they could prevent his ghost from walking). And as late as the 9th century AD it was practised by the French and Germans.

Scalping, said Carl Jung (1875–1961), is closely connected with the ancient rites of flaying and their magical significance. In general, flaying signifies the transformation from a worse state to a better, and hence renewal and rebirth (*cf.* a snake shedding its skin). It finds its parallel in the association of the shaven head with spiritual transformation or initiation – many priests, as those of Isis, were shaved bald and the tonsure is still worn.

Nevertheless, while flaying seems reasonable in a ceremonial sacrificial context, the idea of Indians wishing to ensure the spiritual transformation of their foes to a better state is rather hard to accept. More likely, scalps were taken originally for their magical value – to capture the strength of the dead man. They also had the convenience value of counting how many men the warrior had slain and were thus a measure of his courage and war-like qualities.

⚹

The powerful symbolism of hair ensures it a place in many myths and fairy tales throughout the world – though how one interprets that symbolism is a matter of personal choice. It is also not really surprising

that the themes from widely separated places should often resemble one another quite closely and that the same theme should appear in different stories within a mythology.

In Greek legend, Amphitryon was unable to conquer the Taphians so long as their king, Pterelaos, retained a golden hair that grew on his head. But Pterelaos had a daughter who, conceiving a wild passion for Amphitryon, plucked out the hair. Alas for her, the victor viewed her deed with contempt and had her put to death. (While Amphitryon was on this expedition avenging the slaughter of his wife's brothers, Zeus appeared to Alcmene in her husband's likeness. The result of the visit was Heracles.)

Similarly, Nisus, King of Megara, had a purple (or maybe golden) hair growing in the middle of his head. It so happened that when the Cretan, Minos, was besieging the port of Megara, Scylla, the king's daughter lost her head over him and killed her father by cutting off this special hair. Minos was horrified and either drowned the wretched girl or simply turned his back on her and set sail. Somehow or other Scylla turned herself into a fish and swam in pursuit until her father's soul, in the guise of a sea eagle, pounced on her and she became a bird.

The Celts have a legend (containing many of the qualities peculiar to legends) in which Fionn is loved by the two daughters of a smith, Miluchradh and Aine. Aine says she will never marry a man with grey hair, so her sister persuades the gods to cast a spell over a lake that whoever bathes in its waters shall become grey. Along comes Fionn chasing a doe; but he jumps into the lake to recover the ring of a woman sitting on the shore. When he emerges the woman has gone and Miluchradh gets a grey-haired husband.

Water appears again in the numerous legends of creatures who sit by rivers or lakes combing their hair and usually having an unfortunate effect on passing men. The best known is the beautiful Lorelei who lives on her rock in the Rhine and lures sailors to disaster. The river and lake sprites of Macedonia have horrible snake-like bodies and vile temperaments; they sit on the banks combing their hair and destroy those whom they inveigle into dancing with them. If they see a man in the water, they loosen their hair and use it to entangle and drown him. The water nymphs of Russia, the Rusalka, who love men and entice them into their clutches, emerge

The cave of the storm nymphs. A painting by Sir Edward J. Poynter. Water, hair and beautiful women have become closely entwined in the mythological beliefs of many peoples. This picture, painted in 1903, is the embodiment of those legends in which beauty lures man to disaster. These three nymphs do not bear all the physical characteristics of the legendary Sirens, though the one sitting high on the rock is playing their attribute – a lyre, usually, as here, fashioned from a shell.

from the river at dawn in the shape of naked women and comb their long black hair. If they are frightened they throw themselves into the water so quickly that they often leave their combs on the bank. The variations on this theme are many; sometimes the nymphs are clothed and sometimes they have green hair.

The Vily or fairies of the Slavs are beautiful women, eternally young and dressed in white. Their long hair is fair or golden and their life is believed to depend upon it. If a Vily looses a single hair, she will die. The Slovenians maintain, however, that a Vily will only show herself in this, her true form, to the person who succeeds in cutting off her hair.

The Indians of the Great Plains of North America regarded his hair as a man's life and strength. When a boy was initiated into manhood a

lock was cut from the crown and dedicated to Thunder, the god of strength. When the hair had grown again a special lock was parted in a circle and braided by itself. War honours were worn on this plait, which was also the lock taken when these Indians were scalped.

The Greeks and Romans had similar customs when boys reached puberty: Theseus, for example, travelled to Delphi for the ceremony and dedicated his locks to Apollo. In attenuated form the custom extended well into the Christian era when the first cutting of a child's hair was done by someone held in special esteem by the family. If this could not be done in person, the first-cut lock was sent, as a token of regard, to the individual who became a spiritual godfather.

Hair can be found entwined in the myths and beliefs surrounding both the beginning and the end of life. In Mexico, the first man, Piltzintecutli, was given for wife a woman made from a hair of the goddess, Xochiquetzal. And, at the end, Thanatos (Death) – a son of Nyx (Night) – would come forth and clip a lock of hair from the dying Greek to hasten his last breath. For much the same reason the Turks would shave their heads, leaving only a single lock on the top by which they hoped Azrael, the angel of death, would seize them when bearing them to their last abode. And, to ensure that the journey of the dead to the next world will be unhindered, the Samoyed women allow their hair to fall unbound during a burial.

Yet undoubtedly the best-known and possibly the greatest hero of mythology whose strength was symbolically bound up with his hair was Samson. The link between his long hair and the sun is strengthened by the probability that his name is a derivative of the Hebrew word for sun, *shamash*. He is thus a hero on a par with those of ancient Greece and could well be identified with Heracles. According to H.S. Barahal, writing in 1940, the myth of Samson and Delilah serves as a beautiful example of the male's eternal and ever-present craving for incest (represented by Delilah) accompanied by a fear of the consequences (castration, loss of strength and death).

On the straightforward clinical level the most likely explanation is that Samson suffered from a pituitary tumour and was an acromegalic – the great strength which failed and then returned in the last moments before death; the blindness caused by pressure on the optic chiasma, rather

than physical gouging out of his eyes; and the jawbone of an ass which in reality applied to the size of his own. The long hair was a ritual among his people: "That he told her [Delilah] all his heart, and said unto her, There hath not come a razor upon mine head; for I have been a Nazarite unto God from my mother's womb: if I be shaven, then my strength will go from me, and I shall become weak, and be like any other man" (Judges, Ch. 16, v. 17). And verse 19:

"And she made him sleep upon her knees; and she called for a man, and she caused him to shave off the seven locks of his head; and she began to afflict him, and his strength went from him."

But besides his hair being symbolic of physical strength, it was symbolic also of spiritual power: "And he wist not that the Lord was departed from him" (v. 20 – when he awoke after his head had been shaved). It seems that the chronicler had been handed down a mass of disjointed facts about a remote hero and he had to make the best of them, given the knowledge and beliefs of his time.

One other 'myth' needs to be mentioned: Beauty and the Beast. Seemingly against the odds, this has nothing to do with hair – the fact that the Beast is hairy is irrelevant. This 18th-century story by Jeanne-Marie Leprince de Beaumont (1711–80) is the old Oedipus theme of the son killing the father to marry the mother, rearing its head again; the difference in this case is that the son replaces the father not by killing but by metamorphosis.

⚛

Usually when an event is as celebrated in the popular mind as hair turning white 'overnight', one can uncover some foundation in fact. But alas for the romantics, the only foundations are either deceptive (not necessarily deliberate) or illusory. In the former case an already white- or grey-haired person is for some reason deprived of their colouring cosmetics, and in the latter there is a rapid fall of darker hairs leaving only the white behind – in alopecia areata the white hairs in the diseased patches are well-known to be frequently spared, though admittedly the role of emotion in the causation of alopecia areata is seriously challenged.

What is known about the behaviour of hair supports this cynical attitude towards sudden whitening. Hair grows in cycles. Active growth of a scalp hair lasts for between two and four years (elsewhere on the body, this period may be anything between a few weeks and several years). When a hair stops growing it enters a resting phase, the duration of which is extremely variable, but usually between one and three months. The follicle then becomes active again and a new hair starts to grow; but before its tip reaches the surface the old hair (referred to as a club hair because of the shape of its root) falls out. Sometimes, however, the old and the new hairs may be seen side by side.

At any one time, about eighty-five per cent of the hairs on the scalp are growing and the other fifteen per cent resting. But unlike rodents and other animals which shed their hairs all at once (moulting), human beings shed theirs quite haphazardly. The daily loss is about seventy hairs.

A full, healthy head of hair contains roughly a hundred thousand individual hairs. They grow at a rate of about 0·37mm (0·014in) a day which, give or take a little, is some six inches a year. The colour is determined by the amount of melanin that enters the outer part of the hair in the depths of its follicle during the growing phase – dark hair contains more of the pigment than does fair, and in red hair the pigment is spread more diffusely than the granular distribution found with the other colours. The theory that sudden greying is due to a sudden increase in air bubbles in the shaft has been pricked.

Hair is dead. The only live part is the bulb at the bottom of the follicle where growth takes place. The significance of this is that the colour of the hair we see above the surface of the scalp is already determined and will stay that colour whether it remains attached or is cut off; the only way its colour may be changed is by outside physical influences such as dyes, bleaches, exposure to the sun and so forth.

Yet so strong is tradition, that despite inadequate documentation and patently romantic associations, the belief in sudden whitening persists. The customary causes are fright, grief or some sort of mental stress – for instance, sentence of death, torture, shipwreck, climbing accidents. In cases where absolution was possible (such as torture and the death sentence) the happening frequently led to a pardon.

"For deadly fear can time outgo, And blanch at once the hair." Thus Sir Walter Scott (1771–1832) in *Marmion*.

And Byron (1788–1824) in *The Prisoner of Chillon*: "My hair is gray, but not with years; Nor grew it white In a single night, As men's have grown from sudden fears."

St Irenaeus (120–202), a disciple of St Polycarp (*c*.69–*c*.155), who was in turn a disciple of St John, wrote that his master had often heard the beloved disciple say that the hair of Our Lord had already turned white when He began His mission. Although, if true, this would only be an instance of *premature* whitening, it does provide a powerful force in the white hair tradition.

From among the many characters who were supposedly so afflicted we will select just a few as examples. The hair of Giovanni Battista Guarini (1537–1612), the 16th-century Veronese poet, turned white after he had discovered the loss of an irreplaceable old Greek manuscript. Within two weeks of the death of Mumtaz Mahal (1593–1630), his favourite wife who had borne him fourteen children, Shah Jahan's (1592–1666) hair is said to have turned white. He built the Taj Mahal in her memory.

Sir Thomas More (1478–1535), having already upset Henry VIII (1491–1547) by his opposition to the marriage with Anne Boleyn (1507–36), was imprisoned in the Tower in 1534 for high treason – he refused to take the oath of Supremacy. On the night before his execution the next year, when he was 57, his hair and his beard became white.

In her youth, Mary, Queen of Scots (1542–87), had genuine, beautiful, pale auburn hair, but during her long, last imprisonment she is reported to have become grey in the space of a few days. At all events when her executioner eventually completed his task he bent to pick up the head for display. In his hand he held an auburn wig, while rolling away from his feet was the head with its close-cropped grizzled pate. Mary was 45.

Marie Antoinette (1755–93) was another tragic queen with auburn hair that turned white overnight. Some reports say that this happened during the night before her execution in 1793, which is quite probable as she was denied her dyes and cosmetics in prison. However, two earlier traumatic occasions have also been proposed: on the return from the flight

to Varennes in 1791, and on the execution of her husband, Louis XVI (1754–93), early in 1793. She was 38 at the time of her death.

For almost a year General Charles Gordon (1833–85) defended Khartoum against the Mahdi. In 1883 his hair and whiskers were touched with grey. In 1885 the hair on his severed head was snowy white. He was 52.

One other instance, though not of a well-known historical character was related by a Dr Parry and appears in many reviews. A 24-year-old Sepoy in the Bengal army was taken prisoner in 1858. While he was being questioned his jet black hair turned grey in the space of half an hour. Despite the cachet of authenticity this case has acquired, it sadly lacks supporting evidence which would exclude deception and the detail of the time serves only to increase suspicion.

So, if the medical evidence to support sudden whitening of the hair is tenuous to the point of non-existence, why is the belief in its possibility so strong? The symbolic interpretations are on the thin side, too. Barahal offered the suggestion that premature greying of the hair was due to an unconscious tendency to simulate a dead father and to take his place when dealing with the mother.

Most people choose to ignore the truth of Theocritus's (*c.*310–*c.*250 BC) remark that "white hairs are a sign of age, not of wisdom" and to agree more with Metellus in *Julius Caesar*: "His silver hairs Will purchase us a good opinion And buy men's voices to commend our deeds." White hair is generally regarded as a mark of distinction, as synonymous with age, wisdom and reverence. Maybe the belief in its sudden appearance represents the plea of the unconscious for mercy; wisdom has been acquired and the lesson learnt.

⚬✹⚬

Man has for long regarded baldness as an affliction and in consequence has devoted a great deal of time, effort and money to the search for the magic formula that will restore the lost growth. A popular belief in the past was that for every disease a cure could be found in nature – and nature was kind enough to leave clues around; for instance, plants

with heart-shaped leaves provide a cure for heart disease. So hairy plants were sought, boiled, concocted and rubbed into bald pates.

This idea was resurrected by the makers of quack medicines early in the 19th century, but with a difference. They reasoned (as, in fact, had the medical profession some hundreds of years previously) that because bears had thick fur there must be some special hair-producing power in their subcutaneous fat. A pomatum made from this fat became extremely popular until someone wondered where all the bears were coming from – the market collapsed when it transpired that sheep, bullock and pig fat had been used for quite a while.

During this period the remedy in oriental countries to prevent the hair falling out was an ointment consisting of the bruised fresh bulbs of *Asphodelus bulbosus*, or of garlic, mixed with gunpowder!

However, instead of trying to fight the inevitable, man has had, since the days of Ancient Egypt, the alternative of covering it up. Indeed there have been few eras in history when wigs did not play an important part in adorning the social scene, whether their wearers were bald or simply shaven. In Rome, wigs of flaxen hair from Germany were highly favoured and inspired Martial (41–104) to write: "The golden hair that Galla wears Is hers: who would have thought it? She swears t'is hers, and true she swears, For I know where she bought it."

Sometimes, particularly among women, baldness was not a natural event but the result of some of the more pernicious preparations used to dye or bleach the hair. In one of his elegies Ovid (43–17 BC) wrote to his mistress:

"Did I not tell you to leave off dying your hair. Your own hand has been the cause of the loss you deplore; you poured poison on your own head. Now Germany will send you a slave's hair; a vanquished nation will supply your ornament."

Phoebus, who could not afford a wig and instead painted the locks on his bald head, has been immortalized in another of Martial's often cruel epigrams: "Phoebus belies with oil his absent hairs, And o'er his scalp a painted peruke wears; Thou need'st no barber to dress thy pate, Phoebus; a sponge would better do the feat."

Perhaps the last word should go to William Montagna who, in 1959,

wrote "it is unfortunate that baldness has been approached with an eye toward 'regrowing' or 'restoring' hair, and this with a tendency towards commercialism. Locked within the metamorphosing hair follicles in the balding scalp are all the secrets of growth and differentiation. Searching for these secrets should transcend the eagerness to 'regrow' hair on a bald scalp, an achievement which is of no great consequence. When we know these answers, we shall have the key, not to hair growth alone, but to all growth, which is, after all, the basis of all biological phenomena."

Nevertheless when we recall the symbolic significance of hair, it is scarcely surprising that baldness has remained throughout the centuries something to be prevented or, when the inevitable is accepted, perhaps to be hidden.

6

ASPECTS OF AGEING

"Whom the gods love, die young" – to which one is tempted to add "and if the gods don't love you, no one else will". Old age and the prospect of old age are so surrounded – submerged almost – by emotional attitudes of a largely unpleasant nature that it is practically impossible to view the matter objectively.

These attitudes are the product of social mores, tradition, false beliefs, prejudice, ignorance and of cultural immaturity and insufficiency. In addition we all have a strong desire to reject things that are unpleasant. Then, colouring the whole, is a feeling of aggression – aggression born of a personal, deep-rooted fear and directed at old age and death, not at the aged person. (But this is rather an academic point as it is the old people who have to bear the brunt of our attitudes.) Generally speaking, these attitudes have been with humanity since the beginning of recorded history, the only difference now being that we think less picturesquely.

During the reign of Cronus, in ancient Greek mythology, Accursed Old Age was numbered among Night's dread children. Later, when the Olympians held sway, old age was one of the afflictions let loose by Pandora. We can only be thankful that Hope decided not to fly away too

– without hope, mankind's approach to old age would have been vastly different.

However, the myth that so admirably sums up the attitudes to old age that have endured throughout the centuries – and are therefore part of our heritage – is the story of Eos and Tithonus. Eos (the Greek counterpart of the Roman Aurora, the Dawn), daughter of Hyperion and Theia and wife of Astraeus, rejoiced in the affliction common to many mythological characters: she could not resist a pretty young man. Orion and Cephalus were followed in her affections by Tithonus, half-brother to Priam, king of Troy. She carried him off to the land of the Aithiopians where she bore his son, the dark-skinned Memnos. So intense was her passion that she begged Zeus to grant Tithonus immortality. Zeus obliged. But the passing years took their toll – Eos had omitted to ask that Tithonus should be given perpetual youth to accompany his immortality. When she could no longer bear the sight of him, she shut him away in a room from where only the faint crying of his voice could be heard. But eventually she took pity and ended his misery by turning him into a cicada.

The important components of this story are hope, confusion and rejection: hope that life can be prolonged, so that the delights of youth may be enjoyed for ever; confusion about the true objective; and rejection of old age when it comes, as inevitably it must. The only lesson mankind learned from the unfortunate Eos was to be sure to ask for perpetual youth, not just immortality. Thus medieval alchemists spent their lives in search of the philosophers' stone which, besides transmuting base metals into gold, would give them the youth to enjoy the fruits of their success.

Nevertheless, someone appreciated that immortality, however framed, could be a harsh burden. In the legends of the Wandering Jew and the Flying Dutchman, both men are in the prime of life but condemned to wander the earth or sail the Seven Seas until they find redemption – the one in the second coming of Our Lord, the other in the love of a woman. This outlook is in keeping with Democritus's (*c.*460–357 BC) view that, although most people want a long life, few know how to enjoy it.

Over the past decades we have made a great issue of attending to the material and psychological – as opposed to the therapeutic – needs of old people. And, in terms of our society, we have made progress. Yet are we really doing more than easing our guilty consciences? To a young and middle-aged society, and particularly one that is rootless, unproductive old people are a nuisance; but the nuisance is getting bigger and beginning to have a say in the matter. Nevertheless, we still choose to care for our aged in special homes of one sort or another where, in reality, we simply isolate them – Tithonus was shut away where his feeble cry for help could go unheeded.

Our approach to old age, from whatever angle, is hampered by our lack of knowledge. The handicap is particularly noticeable in therapeutics where we scarcely make an attempt to apply such knowledge as we do possess. At least from the time of Hippocrates (460–377 BC), man has appreciated that an ageing body is a changing body; and, to contend with this, various essentially similar hygienic regimens have been proposed at intervals throughout history. With amazing prescience, Arnold of Villanova, in the 13th century, even said that care should be taken over the doses of medicines as the elderly were more susceptible to some drugs than were the young. Obviously, this advice could not be acted upon scientifically until clinical pharmacology became an established discipline, yet even so it is still too often ignored.

⟡

Research into ageing is mainly directed to discovering its nature. As Alex Comfort (1920–2000) wrote: "Our object in studying the biology of ageing is to find out why it occurs, and whether and how it can be controlled. This is not a new ambition." How true! Thus today we still seek the philosophers' stone as eagerly and as diligently as ever. Present research is in the direct line of descent from the alchemical laboratory, the main difference being that work is now carried out at molecular and sub-molecular levels.

The pursuit of this dream is an acceptable escape from reality, more particularly as we can be tolerably certain that no one concerned with

current research will have to face the monumental consequences of success. The philosophers' stone is well hidden, and Jew and Dutchman will have to roam the world alone for many a long year to come.

Nevertheless, though individuals have from time to time pleaded earnestly for a humane and sensitive approach to the care of the aged, it has, unfortunately, always been prejudiced and irrational society that has taken the action. Social attitudes are formed and hardened over many centuries, and reform consequently finds itself faced by some pretty formidable barriers. In the remote – and not so remote – past the attitudes towards old age were closely linked with those towards death. Old age was merely the clearly recognizable threshold of death. As few people lived long enough to become old it is not surprising that our ancestors were really more concerned with death, and it is only in the past hundred and more years that old age has become a major problem in its own right.

At this point we should be perfectly clear about the distinction between life expectancy and life span. Life expectancy is the average number of years that a person at a specified age may expect to live. As, historically, the specified age is usually taken as birth, one is inclined to get a distorted picture of the age structure of an ancient population. Infant and child mortality rates were distressingly high in the past and improvements in life expectancy figures largely reflect the declining mortality rates at younger ages. Thus the expectation of life (at birth) in Greece and Rome was 20–25 years; in medieval Europe, 25–30 years; in Europe at the start of the 18th century, about 33 years; at the beginning of the19th century, 35–40 years; and by the start of the 20th century most Western populations had a life expectancy approaching 50 years. During the last century the figure steadily climbed, as medical and public health measures made their influence felt, until it now stands at about 75 years for a man and 79 years for a woman (though with uncomfortably wide variations depending on a number of factors such as social class and geographical location).

In all these times people exceeded the life expectancy in fair numbers

and some lived to a great age, but none can have exceeded the life span, since this is the maximum number of years beyond which it is impossible to live. The life span for human beings is generally believed to be about 115 years.

Stories of people living beyond the span of 115 or so years can be discounted for one reason or another, most usually because reliable evidence of the date of birth is lacking. The crucial point is whether the 115 (or thereabouts) is an absolute figure or not. Some maintain that it is, and that nothing can be done to prolong a life beyond that span. Others believe that it is too low an estimate and that one day it will be possible to provide the right conditions for prolonging it to, say, 200.

✧

The attitudes to age that we find throughout history are complex, confused, often contradictory and vary from era to era, culture to culture and people to people. Every shade of emotion from deepest respect to final rejection is encountered. Some primitive peoples venerated their old folk, others mercilessly killed them.

As a generalization, it seems that agrarian communities on the threshold of civilization, such as the ancient Scandinavians, Polynesians and some African tribes, were those most likely to indulge in slaughter. They adopted this course for three reasons: fear that the mere presence of the old would, in some magical way, harm the harvest; sympathy for their unhappy plight; and because the old were an unproductive burden on the community. It is, in fact, quite a humbling experience to contemplate how close this attitude – and the response – is to that of modern Western Society.

With cultural development the attitudes tended to change. For example, among the North American Indians the old occupied a privileged position and the elders of the tribe were looked to for guidance and for interpretation of the laws which had been passed down by word of mouth. They were the cornerstones of a changeless society. In Middle Eastern societies, even today, old age is the climax of this life and great age is regarded as a divine blessing and the reward of virtue.

When a society becomes affluent it is inclined to dissociate itself from the aged; admittedly it makes provision for their basic care but this, as we saw earlier, is mostly institutional (along with society's other 'misfits'), and concern for the individual as a human person is lacking.

The crux of the situation, in whatever era or whatever country, is the value of the individual to his society. In a static, moderately cultured society the experience and wisdom of age are appreciated and respected; but in a mobile, productive and progressive society the emphasis is on vitality and youth, and age is forced into the background.

The fundamental problems of whether old age is physiological or pathological – a natural phase or a disease – and whether it is inevitable or can be temporarily averted have come no nearer to solution over the years. In fact, the more we learn and the more we strip disease away, the more insoluble do they appear. When the diseases that are often *associated* with age were considered to be part and parcel of the ageing process, matters were considerably simplified.

Both Greeks and Romans considered old age to be an incurable and progressive disease which they explained to their own satisfaction in terms of the doctrine of the humours. Hippocrates (460–377 BC) recognized that some diseases occurred only in old age and others more or less frequently than earlier in life. Moreover, and quite as we would expect from an acceptance of the humoral theory, he realized that some diseases ran a different clinical course in old people.

Galen (130–*c*.200) believed that old age was neither a disease nor a state of complete health. He was really forced to adopt this attitude because he maintained that Nature did nothing in vain (originally an Aristotelian concept). Therefore old age could not be a disease since it was not contrary to Nature. Nevertheless, the aged body was susceptible to disease because its humours were unbalanced and all its physiological functions reduced and weakened.

The elderly had always enjoyed respect in Eastern countries and so it is not surprising that special homes for their care first appeared in China

and India. From there they spread through the Arab countries and the Byzantine Empire into Western Europe. A home was established in 6th-century Rome and the medieval monasteries made special provision for the aged poor. Thus by the end of the Middle Ages age and poverty had become associated in men's minds to the detriment of the great majority of the elderly. People dreaded the mental, physical and social disabilities of age and vented their fear in mockery and hate of the old person.

Yet the most powerful driving force along the way was the belief that old age was a disease, the implication being that it could be cured – a departure from the teachings of Galen. As a result, signs of a changing attitude within the medical profession began to appear. John Smith (1630–79), in *The Pourtract of Old Age*, urged his colleagues not to ignore the old "as though they were altogether uncapable [*sic*] of having any good done unto them." And Sir John Floyer (1649–1734) exhorted them to apply their skills with more than ordinary diligence to all the ways by which they could preserve the health of old men. He firmly believed that prophylaxis and the treatment of disease in the elderly should be on a strictly individual basis, since each constitution and each type of cacochymia (disorder of the body humours) demanded different management. There were no general rules applicable to all people.

The 18th century was notable in the present context mainly for its pessimistic attitude towards ageing. This was due to the progressing destruction of the doctrine of the humours and the absence, so far, of any sound edifice to put in its place.

Yet even though the accumulation of data was slow, the medical world at last became receptive to the problems of old age and the man who set the ball rolling was Jean Martin Charcot (1825–93), better known as a neurologist than as a geriatrician. His important contribution to the medical attitude on age was to show that old age was not the decayed end point of adult life, but a new (albeit the last) stage of human life with its own physiology.

After this it was inevitable that the study of old age and its diseases would get caught up in the 19th/20th century move towards specialization. But a specialty needs a name to give it a sense of purpose and 'geriatrics' was coined by Ignatz Leo Nascher (1863–1944) in 1909. The

name neatly conveyed the parallel with the already established specialty of paediatrics, and indicated its concern with the study, treatment, and prevention of disease in the aged person.

∞✵∞

Throughout history the search for long life has been virtually inseparable from the quest for rejuvenation and, as we have already seen, the two goals are often hopelessly confused.

The attitudes towards old age conveyed in the idea of rejuvenation are the most appealing, the most romantic and the most escapist of all. They are also potentially the most morally destructive: Faust sold his soul to the Devil to regain his lost youth. But according to the proponents of prolongevity this moral viewpoint – that to tamper with fate or the process of ageing must lead to some form of retributive disaster – is pious nonsense and has served merely to hold back modern scientific research. Rejuvenation is a typical eat-your-cake-and-have-it situation, since it holds out the promise of youth enriched with the knowledge of maturity. As such it has appealed to a gullible public from the very beginning until the present day and will doubtless continue to do so long into the future.

The rejuvenation theme has appeared in most cultures in history in one guise or another. A popular, and at first completely innocent, form of prolonging life was that practised by King David (I Kings, 1:1–4): Abishag the Shunammite gave him the warmth of her body. One of the most successful exponents of Shunammitism, as the method came to be known, was the Roman, Hermippus. The inscription on his tomb was given by Hufeland:

"Dedicated to Aesculapius and Health by L. Clodius Hermippus who lived 115 years and five days due to the breath of young girls. Even after his death the physicians marvel not a little. Thus must you, his successors, lead your life." Regrettably not everyone is so well placed for following this advice: Hermippus was a master in a school for young ladies.

Roger Bacon (1214–92) recognized the benefit to the old of associating with youth – a fact that few would deny today. "There is a breath that emanates from people and animals. Those who are healthy and

strong, especially if they are young, refresh and rejuvenate old people by their very presence, and with their breath, their healthy pleasant exhalation in particular."

A high point in the rejuvenation story was the period when the alchemists were in full cry after the philosophers' stone. Their earnest desire to transmute base metals into gold had, as we know, the double objective of wealth and eternal youth – gold was wealth, but it also, in their eyes, preserved innate heat because of its astrological association with the sun. Besides the stone, two other rejuvenation themes enjoyed wide credence, the fountain of youth and what can only be called the 'chopping-up' theme. Both originated in Greek mythology.

The fountain theme probably sprang from a universal belief in the healing powers of certain springs and streams, though Zeus is credited with the transformation of one of the nymphs into a fountain whose waters possessed the power of rejuvenation. In the Middle Ages, India was a strong contender for the site of the legendary fountain. In the *Livres de Merveilles*, a 15th-century French manuscript, John Mandeville describes his voyage to India and how he found there a fountain, set deep in the jungle. The waters of this fountain perfumed the air and whoever drank of them, while fasting, was both healed of his sickness and made young again. (John Mandeville was probably Jean d'Outremeuse of Liège and his book was full of fantastic inventions.)

The influence exerted by the legend in the practical affairs of the time is seen in the fact that in 1512 Juan Ponce de Léon (*c.*1460–1521) mounted an expedition specifically to discover the fountain of youth. He discovered Florida instead, the irony of which should not be lost on us today.

An example of the 'chopping-up' theme is seen in the seventh parable of the *Splendor Solis* of about 1582. In this it is recorded how a sage, in his search for rejuvenation, was told to "allow himself to be cut in pieces and decocted to a perfect decoction, and then his limbs would re-unite and again be renewed in plenty of strength." We are left to wonder whether the sage submitted himself to this treatment.

Another high point in the interest in rejuvenation coincided, not unsurprisingly, with the great scientific and medical advances of the late 19th and 20th centuries. Charles Edouard Brown-Séquard (1817–94), a respected

The seventh parable of the *Splendor Solis*. *(British Museum, London.)*

French physiologist, began it all when in 1889, at the age of 72, he announced that for some time he had been injecting himself subcutaneously with extracts of fresh guinea-pig and canine testicles and had felt rejuvenated both physically and mentally as a result. Popular enthusiasm was unleashed and an eager public found many practitioners only too willing to pander to its desires.

Elie Metchnikoff (1845–1916), another respected physiologist, searched for a single specific serum that would stimulate the ageing cells. While looking, he advocated drinking sour milk to kill off the putrefactive bacteria which were responsible for autointoxication (and hence ageing and death). Alexander A. Bogomolets (1881–1946), another Russian, concluded that ageing began in the reticuloendothelial system and prepared a special antiserum that was supposed to enhance resistance to disease.

These were simple methods compared with the efforts of the surgeons, particularly Eugen Steinach (1861–1944), a Viennese, and Serge Avramovitch Voronoff (1866–1951), of Paris, popularly known as the 'monkey gland man'. Steinach and his associate, Robert Lichtenstern, transplanted human testicles (removed at operation for valid reasons) into prepared sites in the abdominal musculature of the recipient. Steinach also

ligated the vas deferens in the firm belief that blocking the exit of seminal fluid would allow the hormone-producing interstitial cells of the testis to develop and multiply; it was intended as a treatment for impotence. Voronoff dispensed with complex theory and experiment and straight-forwardly transplanted the testicles of anthropoid apes. When impoverished young men offered their own testicles for a fee controversy, already simmering, began to seethe.

The post-war years witnessed the popularity of Paul Niehans (1882–1971), a Zürich urologist, who had many well-known patients and based his rejuvenating technique on the injection of fresh tissues and living cells, and of the Romanian, Anna Aslan (?1896–1988), with the intramuscular injections of 2 per cent novocaine (vitamin H_3).

⚭

Society changes its attitudes when it is good and ready, not before, and there is little we can do to speed the process. So deeply rooted in superstitious fear – with the superimposed religious and mythological beliefs – are the attitudes to ageing in Western society that, for the moment, we must accept the Eos-Tithonus situation. Whether the process of ageing is natural or pathological makes no difference, the fact remains that the physiology of old people is no longer the same as it was in their maturity. This was appreciated on and off while the humoral theory held sway and was acted upon to the best of contemporary ability through the medium of the various hygiene regimens. Thus the object of treatment of disease in old age is – as Ignatz Nascher observed nearly a hundred years ago – to restore the diseased organ or tissue to a state normal in senescence, not to a state normal in maturity.

7

ASPECTS OF BLOOD

Blood is life. In the confused and misty beginning of things, man was puzzled by bloodless death – there seemed to be no reason, no explanation. So, to ease his discomfort in the face of the unknown, he conjured up a host of malevolent demons. But when he was confronted with death from a terrible wound, he could actually see life ebbing away. Blood and life were as one. Ever since this realization came to him – and who are we to say he was wrong? – blood has occupied a central place in myths, folklore and religious beliefs all over the world; it has contributed to the imagery of language and has given the medical profession much to think about.

When man in his primitive state had grasped the connection between blood and life, he exploited the discovery with enthusiasm to meet his spiritual needs and later, as his experience widened, to serve his medical theories. For a long while religious and medical thinking on blood proceeded in close company: "Hence it is said that the divine spirit is in

the blood, and the divine spirit is itself the blood... as is taught by God himself" wrote Michael Servetus (1509–53) in *Christianismi Restitutio,* the treatise in which he described how blood was turned to a bright colour in the lungs before being sent to the heart – and was also responsible for his death at the stake for heresy.

This popular view of the nature of blood was supported by Servetus's more famous contemporary, the physician and priest, François Rabelais (*c*.1495–1553) who, in *Pantagruel,* wrote "Life consisteth in blood; blood is the seat of the soul; therefore the chiefest work of the microcosm is to be making blood continually."

Indeed, the power possessed by blood in the primitive mind has been diluted remarkably little over the centuries. The crude savagery of blood sacrifice may no longer be with us, but only because the outward expression of the underlying beliefs has been attenuated by the influences of civilization. Some of these beliefs, if stated bluntly in modern language, may seem rather far fetched particularly when we try to sort out their contradictions; yet despite ourselves they still keep their hold over us.

It all began when man equated blood with God. The steps in his reasoning were probably quite simple: he had deduced that blood was life, but life was also something he associated with the Being he grew to know as God. Thus blood was seen as the means by which man could communicate with God – and beyond this was the possibility of a direct union between man and God through the flow of blood.

The obvious paradox here was explained by H.C. Trumbull in *The Blood Covenant* (1887): "Blood is not death, but life. The shedding of blood, Godward, is not the taking of life, but the giving of life. The outflowing of blood towards God is an act of gratitude or of affection, a proof of loving confidence, a means of inter-union. This seems to have been the universal primitive conception of the race. And an evidence of man's trust in the accomplished fact of his inter-union with God, or with the gods, by blood, has been the also universal practice of man's inter-communion with God, or with the gods, by his sharing, in food-partakings, of the body of the sacrificial offering, whose blood is the means of Divine human inter-union."

This belief in union through blood was given expression in different

ways by different peoples. But as time passed, the original purpose was adapted to the particular needs of the community and the role of blood in religious ritual became ever more complex and involved. Generally speaking, the more barbaric a people, the more bloody was their form of worship and so we find a gradation from what to us are the cruel excesses of human sacrifice to the exquisite act of union in symbolic form. Yet the common origin remains and, as James Frazer (1854–1941) wrote in *The Golden Bough*, the true character of ideas such as rebirth and the remission of sins through the shedding of blood was often disguised "under a decent veil of allegorical or philosophical interpretation, which probably sufficed to impose upon the rapt and enthusiastic worshippers, reconciling even the more cultivated of them to things which otherwise must have filled them with horror and disgust."

Yet there is a reason why the rites should have persisted when the sacrifice itself had long been abandoned. The horror and disgust were an integral part of the effect of the ceremony on the mind – they drew the participants together. Everyone in the community would benefit from the sacrifice, therefore everyone had to take part so that there could be no recriminations afterwards. The 'communion' is expressed very clearly in the Christian religion: "And as they were eating, Jesus took bread, and blessed it, and brake it, and gave it to the disciples, and said, Take, eat; this is my body. And he took the cup, and gave thanks, and gave it to them, saying Drink ye all of it; For this is my blood of the new testament, which is shed for many for the remission of sins" (St Matthew, Ch. 26, v. 26–28). Here the disguised thing "which otherwise must have filled them with horror and disgust" was human sacrifice and cannibalism. Those whose subconscious cannot reconcile itself to this view are probably among the number who regard Holy Communion as symbolizing the triumph of life over death.

The Jewish law as set out in a number of places in Leviticus and Deuteronomy is in distinct contrast: blood shall not be drunk. When a man caught "any beast or fowl that may be eaten; he shall even pour out the blood thereof, and cover it with dust. For it is the life of all flesh; the blood of it is for the life thereof: therefore I said unto the children of Israel, Ye shall eat the blood of no manner of flesh: for the life of all flesh is the

blood thereof: whosoever eateth it shall be cut off" (Leviticus, Ch. 17, v. 13–14. *See also* Deuteronomy, Ch. 12, v. 16,23–25).

Similarly, when a sacrifice was made, whether as a peace, sin or trespass offering, the priest sprinkled some of the animal's blood before the Lord, some on the horns of the altar, and poured away the remainder – the precise details varied with the nature of the sacrifice (Leviticus, Ch. 3–7). Never was it offered as a libation.

An example of communion with a god by means of blood being smeared on the body rather than being taken internally is provided by the Moru tribe of Central Africa. The ceremony, which took place annually, seems to have been for the remission of sins as the people arrived in sadness and left in happiness. After the preliminaries, a lamb was sacrificed by a priest who sprinkled the blood four times over the assembly before applying it individually. He then prayed that everyone would show kindness. This ceremony was practised on a smaller, family scale at times of crisis, illness or bereavement to avert any further trouble.

The most common variations of the blood ritual in early times were, however, those directly concerned with the annual growth and decay of vegetation and the vital importance of a successful harvest. Myths were created to explain the cycle of birth, death and rebirth and a variety of gods and goddesses were worshipped with the inevitable sacrifices. In these ceremonies the blood was shed to ensure the fertility of the earth.

⚮

What are myths to us were often religions to ancient peoples. The stories may seem harmless enough flights of imagination to explain the behaviour of nature, but the gods they contain could whip their worshippers into a frenzy of blood lust.

In mythology, the natural seasons were viewed in terms of human experience and were dependent upon the fluctuating powers of the gods and goddesses (originally simple plant spirits). So the vegetation gods were born, married, reproduced and died, to be reborn the next spring. They were life in conflict with death; but, by imitating the effect they wished to achieve, the worshippers believed they could help their gods – the

principle of homoeopathic or imitative magic (like produces like) has been practised since very early times. Religions based on this belief were widespread in the so-called fertile crescent of the eastern Mediterranean from Egypt (where the god was Osiris), through Babylon (Tammuz), Syria (Adonis – adopted later by the Greeks), to Phrygia in Asia Minor (Attis – imported by the Romans in 204 BC with the Phrygian Mother of the Gods). These four gods can all be identified with one another; indeed Tammuz and Adonis were identical in all save name.

As with so many myths, there are numerous variations about a central theme: but the essence of them all is that the corn god is killed and descends into the underworld where his goddess-love follows and strikes a bargain with the resident deity that allows the corn god to spend part of the year on earth provided he returns to Hades for the remainder. His worshippers annually mourn his death and rejoice at his rebirth – compressing the two occasions into a single, if protracted, ceremony and festival, usually in the spring.

The only one of these gods whose myth does not feature blood as a main ingredient is Osiris. In his worship, water played a dominant role, which is not really surprising when we remember that Egypt owed its fertility to the flood waters of the Nile. Nevertheless, there is evidence that in the long-ago the Egyptians did sacrifice a human being who represented Osiris; his dismembered body was then buried to quicken the seed in the earth.

Adonis, the beloved of Astarte (or Aphrodite) was worshipped particularly at Byblus in Syria. He had been killed by a boar (the jealous Ares in disguise) on Mount Lebanon and from the fallen drops of his blood there sprang the scarlet 'poppy' anemone. Every year, too, the river Nahr Ibrahim (known in ancient times as the Adonis) sweeps down from the mountains stained with his blood. In their mind's eye, the inhabitants of Byblus really saw the reddish-brown swirl of mud spreading out to discolour the bright blue Mediterranean waters as the crimson life-blood of their god.

In her haste to reach her lover's side, Aphrodite (Astarte) was caught by the thorns of a white rose bush. As she tore herself free, her blood touched the white flowers and dyed them red for ever. (It seems likely that she had been held up somewhere previously as the anemone blooms in spring and the damask rose in summer.)

The rites of Adonis were harmless, though as with Osiris there is a possibility that in much earlier days human beings representing the corn spirit were sacrificed on the fields at harvest time. Their blood was believed to fatten the next year's ears of corn. In the worship of Attis, however, considerable emphasis was given to the bloodier aspects of the rites.

Attis was a good-looking young shepherd beloved by Cybele (the Phrygian Mother of the Gods) – or he may have been her son. At all events, he, too, was killed by a boar – or more likely he emasculated himself under a pine tree and bled to death. Whichever it was, violets sprang from the ground where his blood fell.

Both the Phrygian and the Roman festivals took place at the end of March and both seem to have followed the same pattern. On the third day, known as the Day of Blood, the high priest drew blood from his arms in imitation of the self-inflicted death of Attis and offered it to the god – this may have been a substitute for a human sacrifice of earlier times. While this was happening the lesser priests were working themselves into a frenzy to the sound of cymbals, drums, flutes and horns, until at the height of their ecstasy they slashed their bodies and bled freely over the altar and over a special sacred tree – a pine, felled on the first day of the festival, wreathed in violets and decorated with an effigy of Attis. This Day of Blood was in mourning for the god and may have been designed to recall him to life, giving him strength for his resurrection (and thereby for the resurrection of nature). The following day was a carnival for those still capable.

The worship of Attis also included other mystic ceremonies about which we know little, though they probably included a sacramental meal and baptism with blood for the initiate. The young man stood in a pit while a bull was slaughtered on the grating above. As the blood showered down the man bathed every part of his body, washing away his sins to emerge reborn to eternal life.

Although the Greeks adopted the milder rites of Adonis in preference to the bloody festivals of Attis, they were not above inventing a savage ritual of their own, though admittedly it originated some eight hundred years BC among the more barbaric and drunken of the tribes in Thrace. Like Osiris, with whom he has been identified in a number of his aspects, Dionysus (known as Bacchus to the Romans) began his existence as a

The young Bacchus. Painting by Carlo Dolci (1616-1686). (*Fine Arts Museum, Craiova.*)

personification of the changing seasons. And, like the gods of vegetation, he died a violent death. In some accounts he was simply chopped to pieces (as was Osiris): in others he was immediately resurrected – but common to many of the stories is the belief that from his blood grew the pomegranate.

The cult of Dionysus spread like a bush fire through Greece, and on the way acquired for him the attributes and powers of a number of other gods (again as happened to Osiris in Egypt). However, a fairly consistent feature of the rites was for the worshippers to tear live bulls and calves to pieces with their teeth – in some of the myths, Dionysus had been in the guise of a bull when torn apart by the Titans. Other myths had him take the form of a goat and so sometimes a goat was eaten. On the islands of Chios and Tenedos in the Aegean a human being was killed, though later a goat was substituted.

In all these rites the worshippers believed they were killing the god and then eating his flesh and drinking his blood: by means of this sacrament they were entering into a mystic community with the god – in other words, transubstantiation. But as time passed, the people lost touch with the origins of the ritual and came to regard the goat as an enemy of Dionysus (because it had trampled on the vine) and therefore as an object to be offered sacrificially to the god. Thus we reach the ridiculous situation of a god being his own enemy and himself being sacrificed to himself – but that's mythology for you!

During Odysseus's long journey home from Troy he was sent by Circe to seek advice from the dead seer, Teiresias. He sailed to the River Oceanus and, at the entrance to their land, summoned the spirits of the departed by pouring the blood of a sacrificed ram and a black ewe into a trench. Quickened for a while by their drink of sacrificial blood, the pale shades, who included Odysseus's dead comrades and his mother, talked with the hero and showed him the miseries of their dismal home (Hades). Teiresias also appeared and delivered himself of some well-chosen warnings about the future which, true to mythological form, Odysseus ignored and in consequence lost all his remaining companions.

The practice of obtaining temporary inspiration through drinking blood was common throughout the world. For instance, a lamb was sacrificed once a month at the temple of Apollo Diradiotes at Argos; its blood was sucked by a chaste woman who, thus inspired by the god, was able to divine the future. At Aegira on the Gulf of Corinth, the priestess of Earth found her inspiration for prophesy by drinking the blood of a bull. In Southern India a priest of the Kuruvikkarans was inspired by the goddess Kali when he sucked the blood gushing from the cut throat of a goat. And in the Northern Celebes a priest forecast the outcome of the rice crop each year after drinking blood from a sacrificed pig.

Among the other Greek stories that feature blood is one connected with Perseus and Medusa. When Perseus had beheaded the Gorgon he was astonished to see Pegasus, the winged horse, spring from her blood. Then, as Perseus flew on Pegasus's back to Ethiopia, pursued in vain by the other two Gorgons, drops of blood leaked from the head through his pouch and where they fell gave rise to a breed of poisonous serpents.

In one version of their myth, the Sirens – winged demons of death – were born of the blood that fell to earth from the broken horn of Achelous. This river god had changed himself into a wild bull after being vanquished by Hercules.

Finally from Greece comes the story of Hyacinthus, a Spartan prince (though in origin an earth deity). Being a Spartan and well-favoured, it was inevitable that he should be loved by a god – in fact, by three: Apollo,

Zephyrus (the West Wind) and Boreas (the North Wind). The two gods of the winds were jealous and one day when Apollo was throwing the discus they blew it off course so that it hit Hyacinth on the head and killed him. The flower that grew from his blood was (need it be said?) the hyacinth.

✢

The dwellers in the fertile crescent were not alone in their belief in the power of blood to stimulate crop production. The Gonds of India would kidnap Brahman boys and sprinkle their blood over the ploughed fields or the ripening corn. The Finnish-Ugrian tribes living along the banks of the Volga sacrificed animals, such as cows and sheep, to the Earth Mother; they allowed the blood to run into the soil and carefully buried the bones to ensure a good crop of corn and grass.

But blood had many other ritual uses and blood sacrifices were commonplace. When the tribes of the Celebes built a house they sacrificed a goat, a pig or a buffalo and smeared its blood over the woodwork. If the building was a temple, the animal was a dog or a fowl which was killed on the roof and its blood allowed to run down the slope – one tribe, the Tonapoo, considered it stronger magic to use a human sacrifice. In all cases the underlying reason was the propitiation of the tree spirits who might still be living in the timbers.

The flow of blood has been used for rain making in countries from Africa to Australia where life depends on rainfall. In Central Australia the Dieri, for instance, believe that the spirits of their remote ancestors (the Mura-muras) can give them the power to make rain. Two magicians who have been inspired by the Mura-muras are cut about the forearms by an old and venerable man. Then, in a specially constructed hut, they fling the blood over the men of the tribe sitting huddled on the floor. While doing this they also throw handfuls of feathers into the air which float down and stick to the blood-stained bodies of the tribesmen. The blood represents the rain and the feathers the clouds. This part of the ceremony is followed by another, not concerned with blood, that takes place outside and can be seen by the Mura-muras.

When rain was needed in Java, two men would thrash each other's

backs till the blood flowed; and, in a part of Ethiopia, village would engage village in a bloody, murderous battle every January to bring the rain. Once, in the middle of the 19th century, the emperor forbade the ritual – the subsequent rainfall was inadequate, and the emperor was compelled to allow the battle to continue in subsequent years but in modified form.

Blood sacrifices frequently took place to transfer the qualities believed to be inherent in blood to someone in need – by reason of sickness or death, for instance. When an animal was sacrificed for a sick Yoruba (West African) tribesman, the blood was smeared on his forehead and spattered over the walls of his hut. The idea was to transfer the animal's life force to the sick man. Some Finnish-Ugrian peoples cut the throat of a hen when one of their number died and with the first drops of blood painted the eyebrows of the dead saying, "Save with this blood thine own blood from death." Others simply sacrificed the hen, saying "Soul for soul and body for body."

The belief that the characteristics of the donor would be transferred to the recipient surfaced in England in the 1660s when Christopher Wren (1632–1723), Robert Boyle (1627–91) and Richard Lower (1631–91) were experimenting with blood transfusion. Most of their work was carried out between animals but on occasion they did transfuse animal blood into a human being. The popular donors were sheep or lambs, but the choice of animal aroused considerable speculation with people wondering what the effect would be if the blood of a lion was used; regrettably no one seems to have attempted this courageous experiment. In France, Jean Baptiste Denis (?–1704) had some initial success transfusing patients with lamb's blood – none developed lamb-like qualities!

Another popular belief was that by drinking another man's blood the soul power would pass with it; this was held by, amongst many others, some of the Finnish-Ugrian tribes who also believed that the soul wandered about within the body. As an extension of this practice, blood was drunk to obtain specific qualities of the dead man desired by the slayer. The Tolalaki (head hunters of the Central Celebes) and the Italones of the Philippines, for example, drank the blood of their slain foes to acquire their courage.

During the Middle Ages, the treatment of wounds by the weapon salve method enjoyed a considerable vogue. The wound itself was left alone or covered with a piece of dry linen while the weapon that had caused it was solemnly dressed every two or three days with the salve (of various compositions, but often containing powdered mummy, earthworms and the like). For preference, treatment should start before the blood had dried on the weapon. Although the weapon salve has since been regarded with derision and typical of the mentality of the age, it had the merit of leaving the wound to heal undisturbed. Moreover, its antecedents extend far back in the realm of sympathetic magic. According to this there is a sympathetic connection between a man and the weapon that has wounded him, which in turn probably derives from the idea that the blood on the weapon continues to 'feel' with the blood in the body. This is why some people, such as the Papuans, destroy their dirty bandages: if these fell into the wrong hands they might be used to cause them injury by sympathetic magic. (This is analogous to the immense trouble some peoples will take to destroy their nail parings or hair cuttings, for example.)

The taboo on blood is also found in West Africa where any blood spilt on the ground is carefully covered and trampled into the soil or, if it falls on something wooden the affected area is cut out and destroyed. The nobility of the Betsileo on Madagascar employed a class of men specifically to lick up their spilt blood and swallow their nail parings. But, in the past, should the blood of a Maori chief fall on any object, that object whatever it was, became sacred to the chief and automatically his property.

There has always been a marked reluctance to shed royal blood, and in particular to shed it on the ground. In consequence, when a royal life had to be taken devious means were adopted to prevent the contamination of 'divine' blood with earth. In 17th-century Siam a king was put to death by being placed in an iron cauldron and pounded with wooden pestles. Kublai Khan (1216–94) executed his rebel uncle, Nayan, by having him wrapped in a carpet and tossed to and fro.

The Bantu believe that blood is sacred and that if removed it cannot be regenerated and the unfortunate subject loses his strength or becomes blind or impotent. This has important implications for the practice of

modern medicine in Africa because the Bantu imagines that the white man wants to take blood in order to dominate him.

Two other examples help to illustrate the wide-ranging nature of the general beliefs about blood. In Norse mythology the Valkyrie are supposed to ride, raining blood from the sky, before a battle; and, in gentler vein, when Siegfried had slain Fafner, he put some of the dragon's blood to his lips, whereupon he could understand the songs of the forest birds.

〜❧〜

Superstitious belief in the vampire – the unquiet spirit in human form that rises from the grave at night to suck the blood from its sleeping victims – is as old as history itself. Although its origin is generally thought to be Slavic it can in fact be found in many cultural traditions; in India, for instance, the theme can be traced back to the Atharva Veda, one of the earliest of Sanskrit documents.

Although vampires are often depicted as male, it seems that originally they were associated with the destructive aspect of the feminine (the negative side of the Great Mother, whose positive or creative side was concerned with the crops). Hecate, who began life as a moon goddess and finished as a divinity of the underworld, was probably the vampire of Greek mythology since she was not averse to sucking blood from young boys. She haunted crossroads, cemeteries and the scenes of crimes and was often worshipped where three roads met. On the eve of a full moon offerings would be left before her image, which had three heads or faces to correspond with her power in the heavens, on earth and in the underworld.

〜❧〜

The strikingly close resemblances between the practices and beliefs in the New and the Old Worlds might seem uncanny, unless we remember that virtually the same conditions were operating in both. Blood was there to flow and be equated with life, and life depended on the success of the maize harvest.

At the great Aztec festival to the Maize Goddess, Chicomecohuatl,

which took place in September just before harvest time, a girl of twelve or thirteen was chosen to be the personification of the goddess. She was bedecked with maize cobs and wore a green feather upright in her hair to represent an ear of maize. After the preliminary rituals and ceremonials, this girl was borne on a palanquin to the temple and into a sacred chamber strewn with the first fruits of the harvest. Here she stood while the entire population in order of precedence passed before her with saucers full of the dried blood drawn from their ears during the previous week of penance and fasting. As each one's turn arrived, he or she squatted down and scraped their blood onto the ground. This done, they all returned home to feast and drink. On the next day they re-assembled to watch the grim finale as the priests threw the girl onto a heap of corn and slashed off her head. The blood was caught in a large bowl and then sprinkled over a wooden image of the goddess, over the harvest offerings and over the walls of the chamber. After this, the headless body was flayed and a priest donned the skin together with the girl's clothes and adornments before dancing at the head of the concluding procession.

Thus by offering their own blood, the people paid homage to the goddess and gave thanks for her kindness to them. But throughout the other aspects of the ritual we can clearly see the parallel with the Adonis/Attis ceremonies of death and resurrection. The goddess had to die (the spilling of her blood on the harvest was to ensure its success), but she also had to be re-born (the man wearing her skin) for the cycle to continue. A young girl was specially chosen so that the divine powers would be perpetuated with youthful vigour.

Among the North American Indians, the Pawnees also sacrificed a young girl who personified the Maize Goddess. Her blood was sprinkled over the seed corn to inspire a plentiful crop.

Blood was very potent magic for the American Indian and bloody self-castigation was commonplace in rituals designed to influence the course of natural or human affairs. Many of the tribes believed that by drawing blood they could produce or enhance certain desirable qualities, such as strength, stamina, courage and skill. For instance, the Creeks and the Oyana among others would scratch their legs to help them endure long marches; some tribes would scratch their arms to give them strength

with bow or paddle; others would scratch themselves about the mouth and eyes to improve their accuracy with the bow or blowpipe.

The use among the Indians of bleeding as a panacea for sickness has about it a strong flavour of the doctrine of the humours, as we shall see in the next chapter where we discuss this ancient Greek theory. The Indians' idea was to let out the bad blood which had caused the illness, though the place of bleeding was more closely related to the site of illness than was usual with blood-letting in the Old World. For example, the afflicted limb was scratched to relieve rheumatism, and headache was treated by letting blood from the temple. Moral failings, too, could be dealt with by bleeding which was thus a popular form of punishment for children among the Creeks, the Abipones and the Aztecs.

When blood escapes from the body, its magic power is released; this belief is put to practical use by tribes in northern South America who smear blood from castigation rites over their sick or weakly brethren. During funeral ceremonies, the Bororo women of Brazil allow this blood to fall on the basket containing the remains to give them life. And in Patagonia the blood is painted as a protective on a person's body to ward off evil spirits.

At first the castigatory scratching was done with the nails and the amount of blood thus drawn was considered quite sufficient. But as time went by and the idea of sacrifice to a god became a prominent feature, instruments such as thorns, teeth and knives were used and the practice became more and more barbarous as the tribesmen vied with one another in an orgy of self-mutilation (as happened, for instance, during the worship of Attis).

❦

So strong is the association between blood and life that the existence of myths about the Creation in which blood plays a part is only to be expected.

The pre-Maori people of the Chatham Islands, for instance, have a myth that man originated from a clot of blood placed by two deities in a hollow tree. But other inhabitants of Oceania believe instead that he was

born by the bursting of blood blisters or boils on the body of one of the deities. The problem of where the materials originally came from is neatly illustrated by a story of the Creation from New Britain: a 'being' drew two human figures on the ground. He then cut himself with a knife, sprinkled the drawings with blood, and covered them with leaves. In due time these figures came to life.

The idea of a god using his own blood is also found in Central American mythology where Quetzalcoatl created man by kneading the flour of a magic bone taken from the underworld with blood drawn from his penis. And in India an 11th-century collection of tales by the poet Somadeva records how Shiva created the world from a drop of blood that fell into the primeval water. An egg formed from this drop and out of it stepped Perusha, the Supreme Soul; while from the two halves of the egg itself there emerged heaven and earth.

According to Siberian mythology Buga, the Heaven god, made the first two human beings out of materials gathered from the four quarters of the earth: from the north, earth; from the south, fire; from the east, iron; and from the west, water. Out of the earth, he created flesh; out of the fire, warmth; out of iron, the heart; and out of water, blood.

Other peoples view the Creation in completely the reverse manner – not man from the earth, but the earth from man: out of the microcosmos, the macrocosmos. The Kalmucks, for instance, believed that the solar system was formed from the body of Manzashiri. His body became the earth; his eyes, the sun and moon; his teeth, the planets; his blood, the seas; his blood vessels, the trees; his bones, iron; his hair, grass; and the warmth of his body, fire. A similar belief is found in Teutonic mythology where the earth and sea were created from the flesh and blood of – variously – dwarfs, men or gods. The Chinese are less romantic, for they have a story in which the blood of Pan-ku becomes the rivers and his vermin, man.

❦

The bond of blood relationship is extremely strong, though it has been corroded by civilization. Now, other links (typified in the old school tie and by loyalties to the crown, the regiment, the team and so forth) can

be equally, if not more, important. Primitive man, however, accepts only the blood tie and resents any so-called civilizing influence that will weaken or replace it.

Where a blood relationship does not exist, two men can become blood brothers (as any schoolboy knows) in various ways, such as sucking each other's blood or binding their cut wrists together. In *Götterdämmerung*, the bewitched Siegfried and Gunther the Gibichung cut their arms with their swords and allowed the blood to mingle with wine in a drinking horn. Each placed two fingers on the horn and then, swearing an oath of blood brotherhood, drank. In a Scandinavian rite, men swore blood brotherhood by letting their blood flow together into a footprint – this is connected with the belief that souls come from Mother Earth. The bond of blood brotherhood is sacred and endures for life.

Blood vengeance is a more complicated subject and should not be confused with the modern idea of capital punishment by means of which a murderer get his just deserts. The concept of blood revenge demands that the dead man's kin shall lay his ghost. The law of Israel concerning murder, set out in Numbers, Chapter 35, supports blood revenge, though it distinguishes between accidental and deliberate homicide, granting the accidental killer a city of refuge where he is safe from the revenger of blood unless he strays outside. The killer becomes a free man again on "the death of the high priest, which was annointed with the holy oil."

Blood revenge was restricted to the murderer himself: "The fathers shall not be put to death for the children, neither shall the children be put to death for his own sin" (Deuteronomy, Ch. 24, v. 16). And, to prevent the situation degenerating into an endless family feud, the revenger of blood was deemed not to be guilty of blood (Numbers, Ch. 35, v. 27).

◌⚭◌

Many seemingly strange happenings or appearances in nature have a perfectly logical explanation when the cold eyes of reason and science are turned upon them but to the simple, superstitious or over-stimulated mind they are magical or imbued with symbolic meaning. When Alexander the Great (356–323 BC) was building his causeway across the

sea at the siege of Tyre, a soldier, eating his evening meal, cut into his bread and was horror-struck to see blood oozing out. Alexander, himself in fear, sent for his physician-astrologer, Aristander, who with his usual common sense read the omen as favourable: since the blood came from inside the bread, it could only mean that blood would flow from inside the city. And so it happened after six long months of siege. The two most likely explanations are either that some small animal had been caught in the poorly baked bread or that the bread was contaminated with *Chromobacterium prodigiosum*, which produces a red pigment.

A similar phenomenon with, probably, a similar cause is the Bleeding Host frequently recorded in the Middle Ages. This was thought at the time to be caused by unbelievers stabbing the sacramental bread or, if one was not prepared to accept such a comparatively materialistic explanation, to be a real miracle with Christ's blood appearing in the Host.

Christ's blood also appears in the legend of the discovery of the True Cross in Jerusalem by the Empress Helena (*c.*248–328 – mother of Constantine the Great) at the beginning of the 4th century AD. Blossoming from the blood at the foot of the Cross she found the royal herb, basil.

The blood of St Januarius, martyred in AD 305, is kept in the cathedral at Naples and is believed to this day to liquefy. On special occasions the dark red solid in its silver and glass container is brought out and solemnly up-ended and righted until the 'blood' becomes fluid. Whatever the substance is, it cannot be blood; yet, even in this sceptical age the ceremony survives – and reliquaries containing the saint's 'blood' can still be found in antique shops.

An early form of psychological lie detector was the Ordeal of the Bier, of Germanic origin and dating from the time of the fall of the Roman Empire. For the test to be positive, the body of a murdered man

St Helena. The Invention of the True Cross. 13th-century manuscript. (*Bodleian Library, Oxford.*)

had to bleed at the touch of his murderer. Simple belief in its value was usually sufficient to make the guilty person give himself away by his reactions, and largely for this reason the ordeal (or cruentation) survived into the 16th century.

The story of the River Nile being turned to blood by Moses and Aaron and told in Exodus (Ch. 7, v. 17–25) is probably an example of an overgrowth of red organisms or plants in favourable environmental conditions. Verse 21 encourages this belief: "And the fish that was in the river died; and the river stank, and the Egyptians could not drink of the water of the river; and there was blood throughout all the land of Egypt" – sufficiently extensive overgrowth can have this effect by lowering the oxygen content of the water. This same explanation also accounts for other tales of seas turning to blood, though in the case of the Nile there is another possibility. Admittedly schistosomiasis would not account for the natural phenomena but the story could be allegorical, and certainly the disease with its bloody water has been a plague in Egypt for centuries.

Folk beliefs involving blood are practically universal where the natural soil is red or reddy-brown. In the myth of Adonis we have already seen how the rain washing the red soil down from the mountains of Lebanon was regarded as the god's life-blood – and so, in the sense of its being the fertile top soil, it was. The Albanian peasant until relatively recently saw the stain of slaughter in streams running red with earth, and the labourer in the New Forest used to consider the marl he dug was red with the blood of his old enemy, the Dane. In contrast to the beliefs and the actuality of blood as fertilizer was the West Sussex view that ground on which human blood had been shed would always remain barren. From farther away comes the story that the soil, the trees and the flowers are for ever reddened at the place where Buddha offered his own body to feed the starved tigress's cubs. And, in the red of the cliffs of Cook's Straits, the Maori sees the stains made by Kupe when he cut his forehead with pieces of obsidian while mourning the death of his daughter.

The folklore and beliefs about blood have enriched our language and probably nowhere can this be better appreciated than in Shakespeare's (1564–1616) plays where examples abound. In addition to numerous references to blood as blood, we come across the word used in many different senses, most of which are familiar still.

Life. 'Farewell, my blood." (King Richard II. *King Richard* II, I, 3.)

Royalty. "And they will almost Give us a prince of blood, a son of Priam." (Calchas. *Troilus and Cressida*, III, 3.)

Lineage. "He is the next of blood, And heir-apparent to the English crown." (Beaufort. *II King Henry VI*, I, 1.) "I am no less in blood than thou art, Edmund." (Edgar. *King Lear*, V, 3.)

Ownership by right of descent. "That blood which ow'd the breadth of all this isle." (Pembroke. *King John*, IV, 2.)

Relationship. "The obligation of our blood forbids A gory emulation 'twixt us twain." (Hector. *Troilus and Cressida*, IV, 5.)

Brotherhood. "We'll mingle our bloods together in the earth, from whence we had our being and our birth." (Helicanus. *Pericles, Prince of Tyre*, I, 2.)

Men of spirit. "Rome, thou hast lost the breed of noble bloods." (Cassius. *Julius Caesar*, I, 2.)

Youthful spirit. "How giddily 'a turns all the hot bloods between fourteen and five-and thirty?" (Borachio. *Much Ado About Nothing*, III, 3.)

Courage and cowardice. "Stiffen the sinews, summon up the blood." (King Henry V. *King Henry V*, III, 1.) "To prove whose blood is reddest, his or mine." (Prince of Morocco. *The Merchant of Venice*, II, 1.) Red blood was traditionally considered a sign of courage; in contrast, cowards "have livers white as milk," (Bassanio. *The Merchant of Venice*, III, 2). This is confirmed by Falstaff who said, "The second property of your excellent sherris is, the warming of the blood; which, before cold and settled, left the liver white and pale, which is the badge of pusillanimity and cowardice." (*II King Henry IV*, IV, 3.)

Cruel. "Proud, subtle, bloody, treacherous." (Duchess of York of King Richard III. *King Richard III*, IV, 4.)

Condition. To be in blood is a term of the chase and implies that the beast is in good condition. It was used by Talbot in a human context: "If we be English deer, be, then, in blood." (*I King Henry VI*, IV, 2.)

Temper. "Blood ill-tempered." (Cassius. *Julius Caesar*, IV, 3.) "With too much blood and too little brain, these two may run mad." (Thersites. *Troilus and Cressida*, V, 1.)

Passion – hot and cold. "Madam, you have bereft me of all words, Only my blood speaks to you in my veins." (Bassanio. *The Merchant of Venice*, III, 2.) "O, my lord, wisdom and blood combating in so tender a body, we have ten proofs to one that blood hath the victory." (Leonato. *Much Ado About Nothing*, II, 3.) "Lust is but a bloody fire, Kindled with unchaste desire." (Sir Hugh Evans. *The Merry Wives of Windsor*, V, 5.) "I thank God and my cold blood." (Beatrice. *Much Ado About Nothing*, 1,1.)

Free from passion. "We should not, when the blood was cool, have threaten'd Our prisoners with the sword." (Lucius. *Cymbeline*, V, 5.) "Who cannot condemn rashness in cold blood." (Alcibiades. *Timon of Athens*, III, 5.)

Murderous. "Some bloody passion shakes your very frame." (Desdemona. *Othello*, V, 2.)

Temperament. "Our bloods No more obey the heavens than our courtiers Still seem as does the king." (First Gentleman. *Cymbeline*, 1,1.)

Emotions. The notion that blood was thickened by the emotions is referred to by Polixenes: "And with his varying childness cures in me Thoughts that would thick my blood."(*The Winter's Tale*, I, 2.) "Or if that surly spirit, melancholy, Had bak'd thy blood, and made it heavy-thick." (King John. *King John*, III, 3.) "When the blood is made dull with the act of sport." (Iago. *Othello*, II, 1.)

8

THE NATURE OF BLOOD

From what we know of the power of blood in religion, mythology and folklore it can surely come as no surprise to discover that blood was the essential fabric in the theory that dominated medicine for the best part of two-and-a-half thousand years – and still lingers with us today in spirit, if not in admitted fact.

The doctrine of the humours was the outcome of a strange amalgamation of seemingly incompatible theories extending back into the astrological recesses of Babylon, Chaldea and Egypt. We need join the story only at the point where Pythagoras (580–489 BC) and his school at Crotona produced the doctrine of the four elements: earth, fire, air, water. Everything was reckoned to consist of different mixtures of these four, whose qualities were manifested, respectively, as cold, heat, dryness, moisture. These manifestations were termed contraries – heat and cold were active contraries, while dryness and moisture were passive ones.

Developing separately and a little later in time – though inspired by the natural philosophical theory of the four elements – was the idea that the body contained four humours which were found in the blood. Attention was probably drawn to blood because of its vital importance

and also because it behaved most intriguingly when shed: at first there was a surface layer like a bright red jelly (this was blood the humour); then, as coagulation proceeded, the serum was extruded as a transparent yellow fluid (yellow bile), leaving a dark red jelly consisting of the red corpuscles enmeshed in fibrin (black bile); and from this jelly a pale greeny-white upper layer separated out, consisting mainly of white cells and platelets – the buffy coat, known in the past variously as crusta sanguinis, crusta inflammatoria, crusta phlogistica (this was the humour, phlegm). Each humour was formed and stored in a different part of the body: the blood in the heart; the yellow bile in the liver; the black bile in the spleen; and the phlegm in the brain. Admittedly, the eye of faith must have been required as the buffy coat really only appears as such after centrifugation.

Quite how these four humours became linked to disease is rather obscure, though Anaxagoras (500–428 BC) is credited with being the first to suggest an association. Nevertheless, if you believe the body to be composed of four elements and to contain four humours, it seems reasonable to postulate that when things go wrong there is an imbalance between the component parts. And in fact the ancients were nearer to the truth – as we understand it – than they could possibly have imagined. Apart from the more esoteric changes that take place in the blood during disease, one extremely common alteration (in pregnancy, trauma, haemorrhage, infections and many other conditions) is leucocytosis which shows itself in the increased thickness of the buffy coat – and it was excess of phlegm that was blamed for so many diseases.

The humoral system of pathology matured over a number of years as indicated by the absence of any mention of black bile in the 'genuine' works of Hippocrates (460–377 BC), though it appears in the complete compilations from his school. In the early days the balance between the humours was evidently not appreciated since, in *On the Nature of Man*, Hippocrates wrote: "According to some doctors, man is nothing but blood in the humoral sense, to others, only bile, and to yet others only phlegm. They pretend, in fact, that there is a unique substance (chosen and named arbitrarily by each one of them) and that this unique substance changes its appearance and properties under the influence of heat and of cold, becoming thus pleasant, bitter, black, white and everything else. For my part, I think this is not so."

When, as soon happened, the natural philosophical and the pathological theories came together the resultant doctrine was to serve medicine until displaced by the modern scientific approach. Besides the four humours and the four elements, there were also the four associated temperaments. In very simplified form the end result of the amalgamation was as follows:

Blood: air: hot and humid: sanguine.

Black bile: earth: cold and dry: melancholic.

Yellow bile: fire: hot and dry: choleric.

Phlegm: water: cold and humid: phlegmatic.

According to the theory of the four elements, heat was associated with perfection and strength, and cold with things undeveloped. For this reason many (including the probable originator Empedocles, *c.* 490–430 BC) believed that the source of innate heat (or life) was the blood. Aristotle (384–322 BC) subsequently proposed the heart, but whichever it was, the innate heat required cooling and this was achieved by the pneuma inhaled during respiration.

Phlegm was, as we have seen, the humour responsible for most diseases. Moreover, being stored in the brain it was ideally situated for causing harm as it could pour down and drown the organs below it. (A cataract was, for example, thought to be due to the watery phlegm flooding down like a river's cataract across the eye.) Nature dealt with phlegm either by losing it through the nostrils or by drying up the excess with fever or, locally, by inflammation and abscess formation. Thus we can see how fever came to be regarded as an important aspect of prognostication, particularly when associated with the ancient Chaldean system of numbers adopted and adapted by Hippocrates.

It was, however, possible to help Nature, as the Greeks realized when they saw how the phlegm (the buffy coat) was increased in disease. Drawing off whole blood (in the haematological sense) would also remove the excess phlegm. And so, with what appeared to be impeccable logic, the era of blood-letting came into being. It was an integral part of the doctrine of the humours and was widely regarded as the best means of removing morbid material from the body. (Other methods of restoring the balance between the humours included purging, giving enemas, administering hot

and cold baths, creating issues to promote the flow of pus – phlegm – and much else, usually unpleasant, besides.) At first, the physician chose for his phlebotomy a vein in an area where he reasoned the phlegm had accumulated; in this way he would leave healthy blood behind. But this gave way to bleeding through the most convenient vein, usually one in the antecubital fossa (in the front of the elbow).

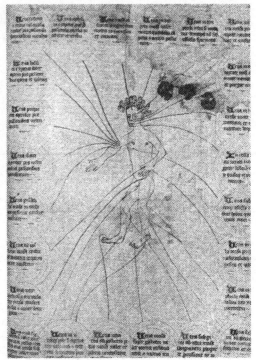

A blood-letting chart. Late 14th century. This indicated the best place to bleed for the disease in question. (*Bodleian Library, Oxford.*)

Then when Arabic medicine was in the ascendant (during the Dark Ages) the principle on which blood-letting was based was turned upside-down. The Arabs believed it was preferable to redistribute the phlegm rather than remove it. Consequently they let only small amounts of blood from carefully selected veins. This was known as revulsive bleeding as opposed to the derivative bleeding of the Hippocratic school. During the early Middle Ages bitter argument raged over the respective merits of the two systems, but eventually the derivative won and blood flowed freely in the interests both of preserving health and treating all manner of disease until modern scientific thought and knowledge ousted the doctrine of the humours in the mid-19th century.

A blood-letting scene. By Romeyn de Hooch (or Hooghe) (1645-1708). In the picture on the wall, one of the Stations of Christ's Passion is demonstrated to the dying man comparing it, by inference, to the medical scene below.

Despite the paradoxes imposed by the doctrine of the humours, the ancients (including Galen, 130–*c.*200, whose influence ruled medicine for the best part of fifteen hundred years) believed that blood (in the haematological sense) was a homogeneous red fluid manufactured in the liver. Galen, in fact, adjusted the humoral theory to suit his own requirements so that maladjustments of the two biles and the phlegm produced diseases in their own right, whereas diseases associated with

disorders of the blood (the humour, but approaching the haematological usage) were due to upsets of the pneuma. With the exercise of a little faith, this could be seen as groping in pitch blackness towards the respiratory function of blood.

Early references to the formation and function of blood that seem to have a modern flavour are leapt upon for this very reason, though the original observers cannot possibly have understood the significance of what they saw. They simply observed, recorded and sometimes made an attempt at explanation in contemporary terms. For instance, Hippocrates related pallor and weakness to corruption of the blood, but it would be most unwise to put a modern interpretation on this.

Pliny the Elder (23–79) has also left a number of tempting observations on the blood. In his *Naturalis Historia* (Bk XI, Ch. 86) he wrote of the bone marrow: "in the young it is of a reddish colour, but it is white in the aged. It is only found in those bones which are hollow." Could he have had even a flickering insight into where blood was formed? And in Chapter 90: "Those animals in which the blood is more abundant and of an unctuous nature, are irascible; it is darker in males than in females, and in the young than in the aged… There is great vitality, too, in the blood, when it is discharged from the body, it carries the life with it…. The blood is the only substance in the body that is sensible of temporary increase, for a larger quantity will come from the victims if they happen to have drunk just before they are sacrificed."

He is, however, firmly on his home ground in Book XXVIII, Chapter 10: "The blood of the human body is most efficacious, according to Orpheus and Archelaüs as an application for quinzy; they say, too, that if it is applied to the mouth of a person who has fallen down in a fit of epilepsy he will come to himself immediately." A few pages previously Pliny had again referred to this use of blood for epilepsy; patients were, he said, in the habit of drinking blood, particularly of gladiators – draughts that were teeming with life. (A footnote in the 1893 English translation mentions that Louis XV of France (1710–74) was accused by his people of taking baths of infants' blood to repair his premature decrepitude.)

When men began to think for themselves again and to question Galenic dogma, investigation of the blood was influenced by alchemical practice and overlaid by abstruse philosophical argument. The main direction of study was, however, towards chemical function. Michael Servetus (1509–53) noticed that something happened to blood in the lungs where it was cleaned of its sooty vapours and became reddish. Then Richard Lower (1631–91), after a series of typically well-observed experiments, wrote: "we must next see to what the blood is indebted for this deep red coloration. This must be attributed entirely to the lungs, as I have found that the blood, which enters the lungs completely venous and dark in colour, returns from them quite arterial and bright…. Further that this red colour is entirely due to the penetration of particles of air into the blood is quite clear from the fact that, while the blood becomes red throughout its mass in the lungs (because the air diffuses in them through all the particles of blood, and hence becomes more thoroughly mixed with blood), when venous blood is received into a vessel, the surface and uppermost part of it takes on this scarlet colour through exposure to the air." The element in the air responsible for the scarlet colour was subsequently shown by Antoine-Laurent Lavoisier (1743–94) to be oxygen.

The extraction of these few facts ignores the general picture of the time which was confused and complicated; chemists, cock-a-hoop over their discoveries, were indiscriminately attempting to apply them to physiology – notable among the red herrings was the phlogiston theory of Georg Ernst Stahl (1660–1734). And, strange though it may seem, the slow blossoming of microscopic study only added to the contention. Iatrochemists (those who studied the application of chemistry to medical theory) could not reconcile the peculiar bodies – sometimes the fruits of optical aberration – seen by others in the blood with their own theories.

Jan Swammerdam (1637–80) was the first to see the red blood corpuscles. In 1658, while examining the blood of a frog under the microscope "I saw a serum in the blood, in which were a vast number of orbicular particles, of a flat oval but regular figure. These particles seemed also to contain another fluid: but when I viewed them sideways, they resembled crystalline clubs, and several other figures; that is, according as they were turned about in various directions in the serum of the blood. I

observed besides, that the colour of objects always appeared the more faint, the more they were magnified with a microscope."

The next to show that blood was more than a chemical or mystical fluid was Marcello Malpighi (1628–94) who, besides viewing the red cells in 1666, found that when he washed a blood clot he was left with strands of fibres that formed a compact network. He had discovered fibrin.

Thus far no one had seen human blood cells. Swammerdam's work was on the frog – and in any case was not published until nearly eighty years later (by Boerhaave) – and Malpighi's observations were merely the result of a rather sketchy study of the mesentery of a hedgehog. But then along came Antonj van Leeuwenhoek (1632–1723) – spelt Leewenhoeck in the *Philosophical Transactions of the Royal Society*. In 1674 he reported to the Royal Society: "I have divers times endeavoured to see and to know, what parts the *Blood* consists of; and at length I have observ'd taking some Blood out of my own hand, that it consists of small round globuls driven thorough [*sic*] a Crystalline humidity or water: Yet, whether all Blood be such, I doubt. And exhibiting my Blood to myself in very small parcels, the globuls yielded very little colour."

Leeuwenhoek carefully recorded what he had seen – round globules as opposed to the oval ones he had observed in frogs and fish. Furthermore, he evidently guessed that the colour of blood came from these cells. His doubt on the matter was shortly to be resolved by Herman Boerhaave (1668–1728) who in 1708 wrote: "And while in life the blood appears uniformly red; under the microscope one may see rarefied red spheres in a clear limpid serum." Unfortunately he had diluted the blood with water and in consequence was describing the swollen haemolysed ghosts. This unnatural view may have been responsible for his theory of 'error loci'. He proposed that there were four orders of capillaries, the largest of which carried the red cells, the second largest the serum, the third the lymph and the smallest a tenuous fluid. If the red cells found their way into the second order (error loci) the result was disease.

But the most outstanding work came in the second half of the 18th century from the pen of William Hewson (1739–74). He began the third part of his *Experimental Inquiries*, published after his early death from a dissection wound, by pointing out that if the lenses of compound

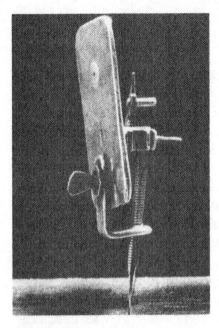

One of Leeuwenhoek's microscopes. These are unrecognizable as such today: the viewing took place on a horizontal plane as opposed to the familiar vertical. A small lens was firmly clamped between two vertically mounted brass plates while the specimen was mounted on a pointed holder opposite. Focusing was achieved by the use of screw adjustments which could move the specimen in two directions.

microscopes were not adjusted to each other, distortion was more than probable. He then proceeded to show that the red cells were not globules as Leeuwenhoek and others believed, but flat bodies. (The difficulties facing microscopists at that time were immense: Leeuwenhoek had appreciated the deficiencies of compound microscopes and had used a single carefully ground lens.) In addition, Hewson realized that the blood must be diluted if the cells were to be seen clearly. Since his experiments showed that water made them swell and disintegrate and any of the common neutral salts made them shrivel, he used serum for his morphological studies. In particular he was concerned about the dark spot he saw in the centre of the cell: because the corpuscles were flat he reasoned that this dark spot must be a solid particle contained in a flat vesicle that was either empty or filled with a 'subtle' fluid (he had his problems, too). The dark spot, he said, only appeared to be a darker red than the rest of the cell and disappeared when the cell was made spherical with water – both accurate observations.

Hewson also discovered the lymphocyte in diluted lymph from cut lymphatic nodes. These cells, or particles, he found to agree remarkably in their properties with the dark spots in the red cells, not only as to size and shape, but in their behaviour in fluids. He further noted that they were taken by the lymphatic vessels into the circulation where they were mixed with the blood and retained for a time before being separated again. But

whether he believed that the lymphocyte and the dark spot were one and the same is open to doubt.

As well as studying the cells, Hewson was intrigued by the coagulation of the blood. He rightly believed that this was caused by the formation in the plasma of an insoluble substance which he called 'coagulable lymph' and which we know as fibrinogen. But no one else understood what he had achieved and even Andrew Buchanan (1798–1882) who extracted fibrinogen by squeezing a clot of blood through a linen cloth, seems to have been perplexed by what was happening. He knew, though, that it was something worthy of note since the liquid he obtained would coagulate hydrocele fluid. The fact that fibrinogen was the sole precursor of fibrin was finally demonstrated by Olof Hammarsten (1841–1932) in 1876.

Alas, it was fashionable to pour scorn on microscopic findings and Hewson's work on the blood cells was ignored. The power that shaped opinion largely lay in France and typifying the prevailing attitude were the views of François Magendie (1783–1855). In 1817 he wrote that he had been able to see, with loupe or microscope, the transparent particles in innumerable multitude tumbling over each other in the blood of cold-blooded animals, yet never in the blood of warm-blooded ones since the membranes were opaque. Nevertheless, he agreed that their existence had to be admitted.

But his magnanimity went just so far and no further. He believed that what people were seeing was the product variously of imagination, error and optical illusion. Hewson's cells were, he thought, most likely bubbles of air. The strange part about this is that Magendie was an enthusiastic experimental microscopist, yet he persisted in diluting blood with water and in attributing the many-shaped globules he saw to the positioning of his optical system.

❦

However, by the time he came to deliver his lectures on the blood in 1837–38, Magendie was resigned to the existence of the red cells and had turned his sceptical eye on the leucocytes, the existence of which had

recently become apparent – though who first described them is uncertain. "Independently of the red globules," he wrote, "there are others of another kind in the blood, as I mentioned to you, differing from those in point of size, conformation, and colour; they are known as the white globules. They are first recognised by their greater size, and, in addition, they may be known by having neither central spot nor prominence, but a small part of lighter colour than the rest which gives them a peculiar appearance;

"Whatever the nature of these latter [the white cells] may be, I have never observed them in the blood in circulation. It has been supposed that they are nothing more than minute fragments of fibrine, which adhere to the object-glass in consequence of their coagulating. M. Letellier affirms, that if red globules be left in a vessel, white ones may be seen to gravitate to the bottom; this militates in favour of their being formed of fibrine."

The seal was, nevertheless, finally set on the existence of the granulocyte by William Addison (1802–81), a Malvern general practitioner, in 1841. In the Preface to his book written two years later he said that his instrument makers had recently fitted his microscope with a new object glass that gave him a magnifying power of 700 diameters linear. This directed his "attention more particularly to the cause of the innumerable and various appearances presented by pus globules; and I now believe that the irregularity in shape and outline, and the appearance of conspicuous granules, nuclei, or discs, either in these globules or in mucous globules, is connected with the cessation of the active movements of these minute molecules. The perfectly circular and uniformly molecular mucous globule is a living cell; while these globules presenting the characters which have hitherto been considered characteristic of pus globules are, in my opinion, dead ones." The phagocytic property of the leucocyte, which Addison so nearly discovered, was eventually demonstrated by Theodor Langhans (1839–1915) in 1870.

One year before Addison published his book, Alexander Donné (1801–78) described the platelet. "The little globules are particles no larger than one three-hundredth of a millimetre in diameter, closely resembling the tiny particles in chyle." Addison also saw the platelets and may have appreciated their relationship to the formation of fibrin although this was not clearly defined until 1882 and the work of Giulio Bizzozero (1846–1901).

❦

So, at the beginning of the 1840s a fair amount of both chemical and microscopical knowledge was in existence, but it lacked co-ordination. This essential quality was given to haematology by Gabriel Andral (1797–1876) who described the modifications that occurred in the proportions of several constituents of the blood – including the globules, fibrin, solids of the serum and water – in health and disease (for example, anaemia, plethora, fever, haemorrhage, various organic diseases).

Previously disease of the blood had been unchartable territory, though one condition can be extracted from the state of ignorance and given a certain individual standing. Chlorosis (the green sickness or the disease of virgins) once extremely common is now rare, a change that can probably be attributed to improved conditions of living despite the fact that iron-deficiency hypochromic anaemia (the essence of chlorosis) is still very much with us today.

Chlorosis has considerable antiquity, for probably the 'mildew' numbered among the curses for disobedience to God (Deuteronomy, Ch. 28, v. 22) is the green sickness as is the smiting with 'mildew' that Haggai (Ch. 2, v. 17) talks about. Coming closer to our own time Shakespeare (1564–1616) has Falstaff say: "for thin drink doth so over-cool their blood, and making many fish-meals, that they fall into a kind of male green-sickness" (*II King Henry IV*, IV, 3).

The first recognizable medical account of chlorosis was given in 1554 by Johannes Lange (1485–1565): "Since the qualities of her face, which in the past year was distinguished by rosiness of cheeks and redness of lips, is some how as if exsanguinated, sadly paled, the heart trembles with every movement of her body, and the arteries of her temples pulsate, and she is seized with dyspnoea in dancing or climbing the stairs, her stomach loathes food and particularly meat, and the legs especially at the ankles, become oedematous at night."

Unfortunately, his advice about treatment cannot live up to his excellent clinical description: "I shall communicate the trusty advice from the rich store of the medicine of Hippocrates, who says in his book on diseases of Virgins: the cure of this disease is venesection if nothing

hinders. I therefore say, I instruct virgins afflicted with this disease, that as soon as possible they live with men and copulate, if they conceive they recover,..."

The continued emphasis on chlorosis is indicated by Joseph Lieutaud (1703–80) who introduced some degree of measurement into the thinking on anaemia – though he considered the disease to be a loss of quantity as opposed to quality. Having said that "the complexion and all the skin has a cadaveric colour" he went on: "Thus I have seen it in several cachectics principally in girls who have been for a long time subject to paleness, with suppression of the menses."

But even in the late 1830s, bleeding was still being recommended. Magendie, giving a clinical description of chlorosis in his lectures, went on to say: "In order to remedy these organic disorders, the practitioner bleeds the patient, and gives preparations of iron, which, according to the current belief, possess the property of recomposing the blood." This, to Magendie, was not the contradiction it seems to us. As he believed the disease was due to an alteration in the blood, it was perfectly reasonable to remove it and then give something to 'recompose' it.

⚬∿⚬

With the acceptance of the red cell as something more than a bubble of air and the dawning appreciation that there was a firm link between the cell and anaemia, accurate measurement became essential. Although Magendie, in his 1837–38 lectures, had talked about measuring red cells with an optical micrometer and had proposed a means for counting them, nothing worthwhile developed until Karl Vierordt (1818–84) came up with what must have been remarkably accurate results from an ingenious but crude technique. He simply diluted blood by a known amount and then drew a known quantity in uniform lines on a glass slide; when the lines were dry, he counted the red cells. During 1851 and 1852 he made periodic counts from his own blood: his average figure was 5 174 400 cells per mm^3. Three years later Antonj Cramer (1822–55) introduced the capillary cell on which subsequent visual counting techniques were based. Now though, laboratories are equipped with electronic particle counters,

autoanalysers (for blood chemistry) and photoelectric equipment (for haemoglobin estimation); however, microscopical examination of the appearance and relative proportions of the various cells still remains an essential part of the haematologist's work.

The next major discovery came in 1868 when Ernst Neumann (1834–1918) showed that the red blood cells of mammals were produced from colourless nucleated cells in the bone marrow. Although not everyone agreed unhesitatingly, Neumann's work put paid to much speculation and also silenced the many voices that, down the ages, had cried their beliefs about the origin of blood.

The last of our landmarks was the introduction by Paul Ehrlich (1854–1915) in 1891 of dyes to the study of the chemistry and morphology of the blood cells.

But the vital element is still missing from the story. Oxygen was known to be transported by the blood, yet the how retained its mystery into the second half of the 19th century. To Vincentii Menghini goes the credit for showing, in 1746, that the insoluble part of blood ash contained particles which were attracted to a magnet. This was interesting because iron had been used since antiquity in therapeutics as a strengthening agent – the theory of similarities.

In 1797, William Charles Wells (1757–1817) noted that the colour of blood came not from the iron but from a complex organic substance. This point was confirmed by Jöns Jakob Berzelius (1779–1848) in his chemistry textbook – previously, in 1812, he had also confirmed Menghini's observation that the blood contained iron. What he could not work out was the form in which the iron was present, though he realized that it was the colouring matter (soon to be called haemoglobin) that took up oxygen and that iron was somehow or other implicated: "the mode in which the iron is combined with the colouring matter will probably long remain unknown." The starting point for modern research into the metabolism of iron was provided by another of the chemists who were now on far more certain ground than a hundred years previously – Ernst

Felix Immanuel Hoppe-Seyler (1825–95). During the 1860s and 1870s he crystallized haemoglobin and made an extensive study of its chemical composition, properties and compounds.

And so today, with all its technological advances, has done nothing to shake the ages-old belief that blood is life. Truly, as Mephistopheles (in Goethe's [1749–1832] *Faust*, I,4) said when insisting that Faust sign away his soul with blood in exchange for renewed youth: "Blood is a very special juice."

9

"DEATH, LIKE BIRTH, IS A SECRET OF NATURE"
The Medical History of Marcus Aurelius

"Death, like birth, is a secret of nature." This quotation comes from a truly amazing philosophical work, the *Meditations* of Marcus Aurelius (121–180). It is a 'diary' kept during the last ten years of his life in which he recorded, not events, but his thoughts and emotions thus giving us a wonderful glimpse into the inner life of a remarkable philosopher and emperor. He probably started writing as a response to the Marcomannic wars, the horrors of which affected him deeply; and in the way that the survivors of the Western Front in the Great War were unable to speak of their experiences, so the wars receive hardly a mention in the *Meditations*.

These wars on the Danube during Marcus's reign have a greater significance than might at first appear. During the reigns of his immediate predecessors, Trajan (52–117), Hadrian (76–138) and Antoninus (86–161), the tribes had only indulged in recreational raping and pillaging – nothing really serious. But by the 160s they were in need of territory. So, when three of the thirteen legions in the north were sent to the wars in the east, at the end of which the army returned depleted by plague, the tribes saw their opportunity and began to make trouble in

A bronze, originally gilded, statue of Marcus Aurelius erected in c.166. The emperor appears vertically elongated compared with the horse, probably because the statue was designed to be viewed from below, suggesting a position on top of a triumphal arch. In the tenth century it was located north of San Giovanni in Laterano. In 1538 it was moved to Piazza del Campidoglio. It was recently restored and moved indoors to the Palzzo Nuovo. Note the absence of stirrups; these were introduced from China only in the 7th or 8th century. (*Mansell Collection.*)

earnest. Initially they were contained, but the wars were a turning point in the history of the Roman Empire and marked the beginning of the decline to its fall in the fifth century.

Marcus Aurelius was the last of the so-called 'Five Good Emperors' of Rome who reigned from AD 96 to 180. The others were Nerva (35–98), Trajan, Hadrian and Antoninus Pius, none of whom was the son of his predecessor. Marcus was born in 121, the son of Annius Verus and Domitia Lucilla, both of whom came from wealthy families with assured places in public life and both of whom had a previous Good Emperor somewhere close in their family trees. Annius Verus died when Marcus was about four or five and he was then brought up by his grandfather, another Annius Verus. In 136 he was betrothed to Ceionia Fabia, sister of Lucius Commodus. Two years later he and Lucius Commodus were both adopted by Antoninus Pius who, in the summer of that year became emperor on the death of Hadrian. Marcus's betrothal to Fabia was called off and he was betrothed instead to Faustina, daughter of Antoninus. He married her in 145 and by 170 she had borne him at least fourteen

children; she died in 175 while accompanying Marcus on a campaign to the eastern provinces.

Antoninus Pius died in 161 and Marcus was faced with the job that Antoninus had groomed him for; however, he refused to be made emperor unless equal powers were conferred on Lucius Commodus, his adoptive brother. Lucius died in January 169 at the start of the Emperors' return from the northern wars to winter in Rome. He was 39 and died apparently from a stroke. Needless to say rumours that Marcus had had a hand in his death soon surfaced and later writings were full of conspiracy theories also implicating Faustina.

In 177 Marcus made his only surviving son, the fifteen-year-old Commodus, his co-emperor. And on March 17, 180, Commodus became sole emperor when Marcus died at the start of a new campaign in the north.

Even though the 'Illustrious' Galen (129–*c.*200) was his doctor, we know little about Marcus's health and much of what we do know comes not from Galen, but from his biographers. Marcus was never very strong physically, although at the age of 15 he was fond of boxing, wrestling, running and fowling; he was apparently good at the ball-game and was an excellent hunter. But at that age he met Apollonius of Chalcedon, the foremost expounder of the Stoic school of philosophy, and he fell under the man's spell. He grew serious and reserved; he abandoned the sporting life and began studying philosophy as if his survival depended on it. In consequence he became a Stoic of no mean dedication and determination, living the rest of his life by its principles – which included in-difference to pleasure or pain; uncomplaining fortitude in suffering; austere impassivity; and limitation of wants. Among the lessons he learnt from Apollonius was to preserve his equanimity, even in long illnesses. Interesting – was this simply a generalization or was it specifically directed at Marcus?

The first hint of illness came in 145 when he was 22. On his becoming consul for the second time at this exceptionally early age, his tutor, Cornelius Fronto, wrote him a brief note urging him to have plenty of sleep "so that you may come to the Senate with a good colour and read your speech with a strong voice." This may be the same illness that

The Aurelian Column, Rome. The reliefs on this column, which not unexpectedly stands in Piazza Colonna, depict events that occurred while the emperor was on campaign with his army in the Marcomannic wars. The column was erected in 180; the original statue of Marcus on the top was replaced in 1588, on the orders of Pope Sixtus V, with a bronze one of St Paul.

Marcus himself referred to in a letter written at about the same date: "My present condition, as you can easily judge, is revealed by the shakiness of my handwriting. As far as my strength is concerned, I am beginning to get it back, and there is no trace of the pain in my chest. But that ulcer… I am having treatment and taking care not to do anything that interferes with it. For I feel that a long illness can only be made tolerable by conscientious care and following doctors' orders. Anyway, it would be a bad business if physical illness should last longer than one's mental determination to regain one's health."

There is no clue here or at any time later about the nature of the 'ulcer'. The word *ulcus* translates simply as 'sore' and even to speculate that it might have been thought to be a peptic ulcer is to credit 1st century medicine with 20th century knowledge. Furthermore, there is no evidence that the 'pain in the chest' had the same cause as the 'poor condition of his

stomach and chest' first recorded some twenty-five years later when he was about 45.

A coin showing Marcus age 17.

Whether one would be justified in introducing a psychosomatic element is a moot point, but in view of Marcus's almost over-the-top Stoicism, it is a possibility. Apollonius had taught him to be immutable, even at the loss of a child. This was a hard lesson, because by 169 he had already lost six children, five of them boys. Two sons remained: Commodus, a thoroughly unpleasant child, aged eight, and Annius, aged seven and a charming little boy treated like a doll by his elder sisters. As Marcus remarked, he didn't want them to follow the others. But by the end of the year Annius was dead. He had developed a swelling below the ear, probably mastoiditis, which was operated on – not by Galen – and he failed to recover. Marcus mourned him for just five days, and even then continued with public business. He was now left with only the odious Commodus.

By this time I feel Marcus's autonomic nervous system had taken enough and decided to rebel. There is a long list of possible physiological dysfunctions that could fit the bill particularly, in view of a later episode, peptic ulcer-like symptoms, indigestion, diarrhoea, pylorospasm and so on. Furthermore, other events had already begun to pile up. But before dealing with them, it is important to realize that although Antoninus Pius had groomed Marcus to be his successor, he had never sent him either to the Roman provinces or to the armies to gain experience. Consequently, when war broke out in the east in 161, Marcus sent Lucius to take supreme command which was a joke – Lucius spent the war in Syria living it up with his beautiful Syrian mistress while Statius Priscus fought the battles in Armenia and Avidius Cassius those beyond the Tigris.

When the victorious army returned to Rome in 167, it brought with it considerably more than glory – the 'plague'. But what was it? We have at our disposal smallpox, louse-borne typhus, bubonic or pneumonic plague and possibly typhoid, or even a combination of some or all of these.

It is generally believed to have been smallpox, a view supported by the possibility that it was the Roman army that was instrumental in its spread throughout the Empire and was itself seriously depleted in the process. This belief seems to be based on the fact that the Romans laid great stress on the hygienic well-being of their armies which would lessen the possibility that they could be responsible for spreading a disease of dirt and overcrowding. (At the start of the 20th century, a military hospital was excavated at Carnuntum, Marcus's headquarters on the Danube; it was dated to the 1st century AD. In its layout and equipment, it cast all other such buildings in antiquity into the shade.)

Nevertheless, louse-borne typhus could be a strong contender responsible, as it has been, for devastating epidemics recurring over centuries in temperate climates in times of war and famine; it carries a mortality of about 10 per cent and 75 per cent of cases occur in people under thirty. Smallpox (variola major) has a mortality of from 25 – 50 per cent. Bubonic plague kills about 60 per cent of those affected and pneumonic plague kills them all. (These are figures that apply to modern times and are not necessarily relevant to the 160s; we can only make a guess at these.)

The tribes along the northern frontier took advantage of a depleted Roman army forcing Marcus – the novice campaigner – and Lucius Commodus to go north in the spring of 168 to deal with them. But by the time they reached Aquilea, the site of modern Venice, the tribes had either been pacified or defeated and the two emperors decided to winter there. However, Galen was unhappy about the state of Marcus's health and recommended that, on account of the cold, the damp and the plague the two emperors should return to Rome. They set off in January 169 and after they had been travelling for only two days Lucius had a 'stroke' and died.

Marcus continued to Rome with the body where he was faced with the funeral arrangements, clearing up Lucius's affairs, ensuring that his wife (Marcus's daughter, Lucilla) married a man who would be no threat to Marcus himself, raising new legions and the money to pay not only for them but also for the effects of the plague. And in the middle of all this Annius died.

In the autumn of 169 Marcus returned to the northern frontier

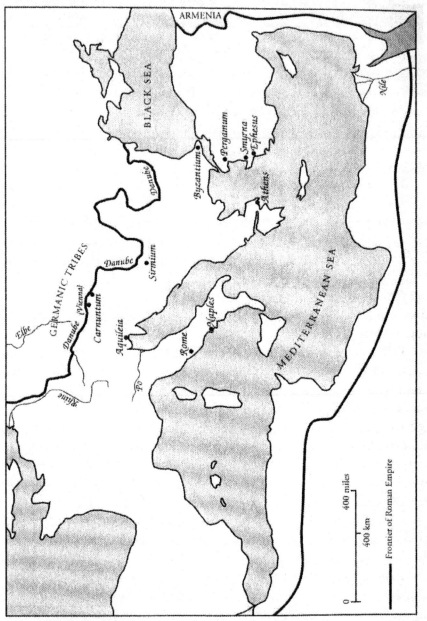

Roman Empire at the time of Marcus Aurelius.

where for the next two years the army fared badly – as did Marcus. During the winter of 170–71 his physical weakness was more in evidence than the previous winter and he would often order a review of the legions and scarcely have left his quarters before retiring again. He found the damp coldness particularly hard to endure. Fortunately, in 172 the tide turned and the barbarians were defeated. Nevertheless, Marcus remained based at Carnuntum until 174 when he moved his headquarters to Sirmium where he was joined by Faustina and his youngest child, Sabina, who was only three years old. For the time being Roman domination was secure across the Danube.

During these years on the frontier Marcus is recorded as eating only at night, taking nothing during the day except for the theriac he had asked Galen to prepare for him. This theriac was like no other. Galen had doubled the number of its ingredients to a hundred and told Marcus to take it in honey and wine. It was, he maintained, a remarkable remedy for all internal disorders, especially those of the stomach. It certainly eased the pains in Marcus's chest and stomach, but at the expense of making him drowsy due no doubt to the amount of opium it contained – Galen was nobody's fool.

When Marcus stopped taking the theriac, the pains returned and he was unable to sleep. So it was back to the theriac. This gives an idea of how intense these pains must have been, but Marcus, the true Stoic, made no complaint. I think it also indicates that the condition, whatever it was, was organic rather than psychosomatic, but it does not rule out the possibility of a psychosomatic origin when the pains were first recorded.

Marcus gives us a clue to his attitude to pain in his *Meditations*: "About pain: the pain which is intolerable carries us off; but that which lasts a long time is tolerable." He backed this up further on by quoting the saying of the philosopher Epicurus (341–270 BC): "Pain is neither unbearable nor unending, so long as you remember it has its limits and so long as you add nothing to it in your imagination."

Both Cassius Dio, a biographer, and Galen note that sleep was a problem for him; he found it difficult to get himself out of bed at dawn, which is not surprising if he had had a bad night and taken a dose of theriac. And even when he did sleep, he was often troubled by disturbing dreams.

The year 175 brought more trouble in the eastern provinces where Avidius Cassius, believing his emperor to be dead reckoned that he would make a good replacement; but before any harm was done he was assassinated by a loyal centurion. Nevertheless, even when Cassius's head was laid before him, Marcus continued with his decision that the eastern provinces should be inspected to ensure their allegiance. He therefore summoned Commodus from Rome to join him at Sirmium and with the court in attendance, they set off. It was on this expedition that Faustina died at the age of about 45.

A medallion showing Marcus age 56 and Commodus age 16.

Another year later, in 176, it was a sick Marcus who returned to Rome with his son. The physicians who had travelled with him diagnosed a violent fever. Marcus agreed. Galen, in *On Prognosis*, described events: "He had taken a dose of bitter aloes the day before at the first hour, and then the theriac, as was his practice every day, at about the sixth hour. Then he had a bath at sunset and a little food, and there ensued colic pains and diarrhoea, which made him feverish."

His doctors saw him at dawn, advised rest and gave him some thick gruel at the ninth hour. They reckoned it was the start of a serious illness. Galen, who had not been on the expedition, having originally been left in Rome to look after Commodus, was called in. He said nothing and did not take Marcus's pulse, as would have been expected. When asked why, he explained that the other doctors, having been on campaign, were better able to make the diagnosis. But Marcus asked him to take his pulse, which he did and pronounced that there was no fever, only an upset stomach.

Marcus was delighted. "That's it! That's exactly it!" he exclaimed. "I feel as though I'm weighed down by cold food."

The usual remedy, said Galen, was peppered wine, but for an

Reliefs at the top of the Aurelian Column. These show the migration of barbarians escorted by Roman soldiers.

emperor he recommended adding a pad of scarlet wool with ointment of nard applied to the anus. "My own usual remedy," Marcus responded, "Pitholaus shall apply it." (Pitholaus was tutor to Commodus.) When this was done, he had his feet massaged followed by a glass of Sabine wine sprinkled with pepper. (This mention of the apparently regular use of nard might suggest that the Emperor was troubled with piles.) From that day until his death four years later, Marcus always referred to Galen as "first among physicians and unique among philosophers."

In August 178 Marcus and Commodus returned once again to the northern frontier and in the following year were victorious over the Germanic tribes. However, while preparing to open the 180 campaigning season by occupying the tribal lands north of the Danube, Marcus fell seriously ill. Seeming to desire death, he stopped eating and drinking. When the army learned how ill he was, they were moved to grief "for they loved him as none other". On the seventh day his condition worsened still further and he allowed only his son to see him, but as soon as Commodus appeared he sent him away in case he would catch whatever it was. He then covered his head as if he wanted to sleep and never woke up. His death took place either at his Sirmium headquarters or twenty miles

Relief from the Column showing a German chief looking up at Marcus and pleading with him. The figure behind Marcus could be Commodus.

further north at Bononia, the Danubian port of Sirmium.

What killed him? Marcus's apparent understanding that his disease was catching might point to its being the plague (whatever that might have been). But Cassius Dio stated that his death was deliberately brought about by his doctors, as "I have been plainly told", so that they would gain favour with Commodus. However, Dio also states his own view that the death was not a result of the disease from which he was still suffering – the stomach and chest complaints – which still leaves us without a clear pointer.

I am not going to speculate about possible diagnoses, only to repeat my feelings that his chest and stomach complaints at their start could have been psychosomatic and that in the end they became organic. Finally, I offer my belief that, thanks to Galen, he was addicted to opium.

A postscript: Commodus became sole emperor and was considered a greater disaster for Rome than the plague. He was assassinated in 192.

10

DURER:
The man and his art

The artistic output of Albrecht Dürer (1471–1528) is full of perplexities. More ink has been spilt arguing over analyses of the meanings hidden in his *Melencolia I* than over any other picture, except the enigmatic *Mona Lisa* of his contemporary, Leonardo da Vinci (1452–1519). Yet so immediate is the uncomplicated appeal of some of his work that reproductions of the *Young Hare* (1502) and the *Hands of an Apostle* (1508) hang in homes all over the world today. In the broad view, his art can be divided into three categories: the realistic watercolours of landscapes he painted on his early travels to the artistic centres of southern Germany and Switzerland; the portraits, altar-pieces and other commissioned work; and the engravings and woodcuts he executed in an attempt to resolve his spiritual conflicts.

Albrecht Dürer, the third son among the eighteen children of Albrecht Dürer, a jeweller of Nuremburg, was born on May 21, 1471, into a Germany on the brink of turmoil. The Renaissance had begun more than a century earlier in Florence where a new idea of beauty challenged the Christian concept. The Alps were a barrier to its northward spread, but ripples of the movement were felt with a kind of disconcerted

eagerness. Artists in the North turned towards an unsoftened realism; their nudes – and there weren't many of them – were uncomfortable in their stark nakedness. Modesty and the climate were against an unfettered joy of human beauty. The artistic Renaissance required an interpreter for the North, and the man it found was Albrecht Dürer. On his return from his first visit to Italy, he brought an appreciation of light, movement and sensuality that were essentially Italian, yet his approach remained Teutonic. He succeeded in uniting the disparate temperaments of the two, as in the exquisite copperplate engraving of *Adam and Eve* (1504).

An artist, no matter how talented, needed an introduction into society if he was to achieve commercial success. In Dürer's case this came from Frederick the Wise, Elector of Saxony (1463–1525), whose likeness he painted in 1496. Thereafter his future was assured, and he never lacked commissions for portraits or religious works. In the former, particularly, he deviated from the Italian fashion by concentrating on the character of the sitter rather than the outward 'beauty'.

But more than the artistic turmoil, it was the social and religious convulsions in Germany that affected him deeply. 'Epidemics of fear', waves of mass hysteria, swept the country. A second Flood was confidently predicted. Comets and meteors were interpreted as signs of God's wrath. Every event that seemed unnatural was a call to mankind to repent and atone for its sins. And God did not stop at warning; he punished. Plague, both bubonic and pneumonic, flowed and ebbed across the land, terrifying in its manifestations, destroying whole cities. The dancing mania increased the horror as those caught in its grip seemed to defy their fate, until at last they, too, sank exhausted to their deaths. (This mania began as outbreaks of ergot poisoning, St Anthony's fire, due to the use of contaminated flour, but inevitably it led to waves of hysterical imitation.) And there was famine.

Starving, panic-stricken peasants left their homes, compelled by some incomprehensible drive to wander, to escape to a better land. They did not find it; they simply formed themselves into marauding bands to plunder and ravage wherever the spirit moved them, until eventually their excesses were put down with a cruelty that surpassed their own.

Over all was the fear of Death. It permeated every aspect of life, not

Melencolia I. Copperplate engraving, 1514.

as an intellectual curiosity about the hereafter, but as a real, morbid state of mind. The discoveries and scientific progress of the 14th century made matters worse. The hidden was illuminated, but by contrast the only mystery that really concerned the people – the mystery of existence – was plunged still deeper into darkness. Dürer was a pious man and a fervid disciple of Martin Luther (1483– 1546). Yet his sensuous nature,

Self-portrait in the nude. Pen and brush, *c.*1503.
Dürer was unwell when he drew this picture and he
looks older than his 33 years.

combined with the freedom learnt in Italy and now claimed for his art, troubled his soul. He shared the superstitions of ordinary folk, which became more intense for him as his religious bent was stimulated by the visions of St John the Divine in the Book of Revelations, a text thundered abroad by every vagabond prophet who could read. He endeavoured to find the way to salvation in his work but the results were not visions of the future, merely reflections of the tortured age. Significantly, his religious engravings and woodcuts have a unity of composition; the individuals are at home in the landscapes. But in those in which he depicted pagan myths he was less happy; the landscapes are echoes of the peaceful watercolours he painted in his youth – they are almost identifiable – yet the human figures do not belong. The scenery has become menacing and the characters are confusions of violence or terror, with Death never far away.

Many of Dürer's pictures were allegorical, the significance of which was plain to those familiar with the symbols. But the key is lost to us today. *Melencolia I* is replete with inner secrets – the comet, the hour-glass, the bell, the scales, the compass, the female figure herself. Even the inscription on the scroll carried on the wings of a bat and set below a rainbow is a mystery. At pictures such as this, we can but look and wonder.

If Dürer's art poses many problems that we may never solve, his illnesses are little less obscure. Of particular interest are the *Self portrait in the Nude* of about 1503 that shows an enlarged testicle on the left side (the portrait would be most unusual if it were not a mirror image), and *The*

The sick Dürer. Pen and watercolour, 1512-14 or 1509-20.

Sick Dürer, a watercolour sketch of himself in a loincloth, dating from 1512–1514 (or perhaps 1509–1520), with his left index finger pointing to the upper right quadrant of his abdomen, the region of his gall-bladder (if the portrait is not a mirror image he is pointing to the region of his spleen). "Where the yellow spot is and my finger points, I am sick within." In the absence of further clinical information, a speculative trip through the causes of testicular enlargement (though we shall return to one possibility below) and of pain in the right (or left) hypochondrium would be a pretty profitless exercise – even if we knew whether the pictures were mirror-images or not. However, during his visit to The Netherlands in 1520–21, Dürer developed a recurring fever after a fruitless six-day voyage in a gale to see a whale stranded on a beach in Zeeland. He spent large sums on drugs, and the doctors he consulted were at a loss to know the cause – as indeed are we, although this particular illness has been attributed to malaria. This has led to the suggestion that the portrait is not a mirror image and that the finger is pointing to the spleen; it would also mean that the 1509–21 range of dates would be valid. If nothing else, the Dürer saga demonstrates the appalling obstacles to reaching a diagnosis from the past.

He was also prone to melancholy particularly when unwell, but it was the melancholy of mental exhaustion common among artists after a period of intense creative effort, rather than a morbid depression. Dürer was probably aware of the comment by the physician, Marsilio Ficino

(1433–99): "All men who have excelled in art have been melancholy."

With the return of Columbus's (1451–1506) men from discovering the New World, a new scourge was let loose upon suffering Europe. Once its venereal origin was appreciated, syphilis was regarded as a personal punishment for man's sins as opposed to the communal one of the plague. Dürer now had this to add to his spiritual troubles, and one of the diagnoses advanced to account for his testicular enlargement is syphilis. But this, I believe, is unlikely, because in 1506 he wrote to his friend, Willibald Pirkheimer (1470–1525): "Give my compliments to our Prior and ask him to pray for me that I may be saved, and especially from the French [syphilis], because I know nothing of which I am so much afraid, since nearly every man has it; it eats up many people so that they die thus." So, it would seem, he had been saved until that date, and the example of two other friends, the renowned syphilitics Conrad Celtis (1459–1530) and Ulrich von Hutten (1488–1523), may well have saved him subsequently, though the spectre of the disease continued to haunt his mind.

In the latter part of his life Dürer had searched in vain for a scientific explanation of human beauty. He had tried to resolve the body into geometrical patterns, hoping that the pentagram and other occult symbols would provide the key. But it was not to be, and on April 6, 1528, the wasted body of Albrecht Dürer released his soul to continue this quest for the philosophers' stone of art – the eternal truth of beauty.

11

THE DEATH OF LORD BYRON

News of Lord Byron's death at Missolonghi in Greece reached London on May 14, 1824, and it is no exaggeration to say that the loss of this romantic hero shook the very heart of the nation. The news "came upon London like an earthquake", the *London Magazine* reported. Thomas Carlyle (1795–1881) is quoted as saying: "My God, if they had said that the sun or the moon had gone out of the heavens, it could not have struck me with the idea of a more awful and dreary blank in the creation". Mary Shelley (1797–1851) commented: "God grant that I may die young!" Yet, despite the attendance of medical men during Byron's final illness and the performance of an, admittedly perfunctory, post-mortem, the cause of death is still in doubt. Attention instead has been directed at his feet and personality.

In an article in *The Daily Telegraph Magazine* (April 19, 1974) Peter Quennell wrote: "The disease that killed him, modern diagnosticians suggest, was not marsh fever, but a 'chronic inflammatory process of the brain', or perhaps acute uraemic poisoning." This, however, merely repeats the medical opinions obtained by Leslie Marchand and published in his *Byron: A Biography* (1957). So, *pace* Marchand and Quennell, I want to

propose marsh fever in the form of blackwater fever together with cerebral (nervous) malaria. But to be fair, it could have been their medical understanding that let them down: marsh fever *is* malaria; the post-mortem appearances of the brain in cerebral malaria could suggest a 'chronic inflammatory process'; and acute tubular necrosis of the kidney may occur in malaria and is a cause of uraemia.

Although well aware of the dangers of selection, I must first pick out some salient features of these types of malaria. Blackwater fever, although uncommon, is found wherever there are hyperendemic foci of malaria – and in these places malignant tertian infection (*Plasmodium falciparum*) is always predominant. Greece was one of these areas. The disease attacks visitors to the area, especially those treated with quinine, and is rare among the indigenous inhabitants; nevertheless, to become 'indigenous' residence in the area for, usually, between six months and five years is necessary. Reinfection is important, the previous attacks having been in-adequately treated. Heat, cold or fatigue may precipitate an attack and alcoholism predisposes. The main naked-eye appearance in cerebral malaria is hyperaemia which is usually prominent throughout the neuraxis. Other changes occur but they are either microscopic or were not recognized at the time of Byron's death. A wide variety of psychotic episodes, which usually develop between the ages of 25 and 35, may be laid at the door of malarial infection; predisposing factors are repeated heavy infection with *P. falciparum* and lowering of resistance by alcohol, exhaustion and so on. Finally, the patient may appear 'a changed man'.

And so to Byron (1788–1824). Having spent the early summer of 1823 in Genoa, he left on July 15 for Cephalonia via Leghorn, where he landed on August 3. On the 11th he and his party took a trip to Ithaca. On the second day he looked terrible and had to lean on a stick but said nothing about feeling ill. Then on the evening of the 15th he flew into an ungovernable rage at the abbot of a monastery they were visiting: "My head is burning; will no one relieve me from the presence of this pestilential madman?" But the next morning he could hardly give credit to his own frantic conduct.

On January 5, 1824, still full of his hopes to unite the Greeks and win their freedom, he landed at Missolonghi which Colonel Leicester

Stanhope (1784–1862 – 5th Earl of Harrington), an agent of the London Greek Committee, referred to as an unhealthy swamp. A few days later Byron wrote to his friend, Charles Hancock (1795–1868): "I take it that a man is on the whole as safe in one place as another; and, after all, he had better end with a bullet than bark in his body", from which it seems reasonable to infer that he was no stranger to quinine. (And certainly he was no stranger to alcohol.)

After he had been at Missolonghi for nearly six weeks the end began in dramatic fashion. William Parry, the firemaster (artillery), wrote of the evening of February 15: "Lord Byron had scarcely drunk the cider, when he complained of a very strange sensation, and I noticed a great change in his countenance. He rose from his seat, but could not walk, staggered a step or two, and fell into my arms… In another minute his teeth were closed, his speech and senses gone, and he was in strong convulsions…When he fell into my arms, his countenance was very much distorted, his mouth being drawn on one side."

This description was confirmed by Dr Julius Millingen (1800–78) who, with Dr Francesco Bruno, had been summoned. Byron himself wrote two days later that the attack was "of a convulsive description, but whether Epileptic, Paralytic or Apoplectic, is not yet decided by the two medical men… It was very painful, and, had it lasted a minute longer, must have extinguished my mortality – if I can judge by sensations."

The medical men were insistent on bleeding their patient who was equally insistent that he would not be bled; nevertheless, he finally agreed to allow Bruno to apply eight leeches to his temples. There was great difficulty in stopping the bleeding and at one stage Byron fainted.

During the latter days of February Byron gradually regained his strength, but the spark was missing. "That wonderful elasticity of disposition, that continued flow of wit, and that facility of jest, by which his conversation had been so highly distinguished, returned only at distant intervals; for he fell into a state of melancholy…" wrote Millingen. "Flashes before his eyes, palpitations and anxieties, hourly afflicted him; and at times such a sense of faintness would overpower him, that, fearing to be attacked by similar convulsions, he would send in great haste for medical assistance." Nevertheless he refused to be beaten and was soon

riding and taking exercise again, though on March 1 and 2 he was unwell.

Throughout March and the first week in April the weather was atrocious and Byron was subject to momentary bouts of irritability and anger, mostly over trifles and seemingly aggravated by excitements and forced inactivity. On April 9 he insisted on taking a ride but was caught in a downpour; soaking wet and sweating he returned, as was his custom, in an open boat. "Two hours after his return home", wrote his friend Count Pietro Gamba (1801–27), "he was seized with a shuddering: he complained of fever and rheumatic pains." And Millingen remembered: "He complained in the evening of shooting pains in his hips and loins".

Lord Byron.

The next day, despite still complaining of pains in his bones and a headache, he went riding again. Late that night he told Bruno that "he had cold shivers alternating with hot spells and wandering pains over his body." On the 11th Parry grew alarmed when he realized how ill Byron was and how his talk was rambling. Fever, pains and headache continued, though their intensity tended to fluctuate, and when he tried to get up to go riding he was compelled to return to bed. During the night of the 15th, "he was seized by a violent coughing which finally caused him to vomit."

On the 16th his doctors again overcame his resistance to bleeding and removed a full pound, though, said Millingen, "the relief, obtained, did not correspond to the hopes we had anticipated." So, two hours later, they relieved their patient of another pound. By this time Parry was extremely anxious, for Byron "was alarmingly ill, and almost constantly delirious... I earnestly implored the doctors not to physic and bleed him,

and to keep his extremities warm, for in them there was already the coldness of coming death."

From this time on he grew steadily worse, complaining of numbness in his fingers and of want of sleep. On the 17th "he drank great quantities of nitrates", wrote Bruno, "which did not however produce urine in equal proportion, and what he passed appeared raw and of the colour of coffee". He was bled again on the 18th of a few more ounces and purged once more, but he lapsed into coma and at 6 pm on the 19th he was dead. He was 36 years old.

An account of the post-mortem and of the local ceremonies appeared in the *Telegrafo Greco* and subsequently in newspapers on the Continent and in England and America. However, the version I wish to use was published in Larrey's *Clinique Chirurgicale* (1829, Vol. 1, pp 330–2). Dominique Jean Larrey (1766–1842 – Surgeon-in-Chief to Napoleon's Imperial Guard) quoted from a letter given him by Baron Puymaurin, a member of the Chamber of Deputies.

"We shall transcribe here", Larrey wrote, "an excerpt from a letter of one of his companions describing the necropsy of Lord Byron who, at an early age, died in Greece of a fever which appeared to have settled in the brain. 1. The bones of the head were remarkably dense; the cranium was without sutures and resembled that of an old man of 80 or 90 years of age; it might be said to have been but one bone without diploë. 2. The dura mater was intimately adherent to the inner surface of the cranium; and the vessels of the membrane were injected and distended. 3. The communicating vessels between this membrane and the pia mater were filled with gas and whitish serum. 4. The cerebral substance was traversed by many vessels containing black blood; the lateral ventricles were filled with clear serum: the other ventricles and the spinal canal also contained a good deal of similar fluid. 5. The medullary substance extended beyond its ordinary limits into the midst of the cortical substance, the thickness of which was correspondingly much reduced.

"6. The convolutions of the brain appeared more numerous than is common, and the fissures which separated them very deep. (I have also had occasion to notice the same phenomenon in the brain of other illustrious personages.) 7. The total weight of the brain, excluding the

spinal cord, when stripped of its membranes was about six pounds [one *poids du marc* equals eight Imperial ounces]. The rest of the autopsy of the body of this great man revealed nothing peculiar, except perhaps a slight hypertrophy of the heart, and an accumulation of dry faecal material, which implies an obstinate constipation, to which this lord, indeed, is said to have been subject all his life."

The hypertrophy of the heart was a simple work hypertrophy resulting from Byron's passion for long-distance swimming (as indeed was the enlargement of the lungs, not mentioned by Larrey); and in the absence of anything pointing to an exotic or eponymous condition we may safely assume that the premature obliteration of the sutures and loss of diploic structure was without clinical significance. The weight of the brain, which works out at some 1·36 kg or about 3 lb, was also quite within normal limits. However, the reason I wished to use this particular version of the post-mortem report is that Larrey included it under the heading *De la nostalgie* and concluded that Byron fell victim to extreme melancholy (which might possibly be equated with present-day depression). Nostalgia was a very real disease in those days and one with recognized pathological changes in the brain.

Nevertheless, I have no doubt that Byron's friend, John Cam Hobhouse (1786–1859), was far closer to the truth when he wrote: "Had he [Byron] lived I am not sure that he could not one day or the other have had cause to regret that he had not fallen by the fevers of Missolonghi, just as Pompey grieved that he had not died in Campania."

12

LARREY:
What manner of man?

Dominique Jean Larrey (1766–1842) was undeniably one of the greatest of military surgeons. Yet his character and achievements have never really been appreciated on this side of the Channel. Most people, if they have heard of Larrey at all, would say he was Napoleon's surgeon and, if pressed further, might recall that he invented something called a flying ambulance and was surgeon-in-chief of the Grande Armée. But these are only half truths. Larrey was never Napoleon's personal surgeon – this job was held by Alexandre Yvan (1765–1839) from 1796 until he deserted his master at the first abdication; Yvan was in any case far more to Napoleon's surgical taste as he held conservative views about amputation and the use of the scalpel generally. Larrey, therefore, had to limit his ambition to becoming a surgeon to the Imperial household. This was to prove no easy matter.

When appointments were made to the First Consul's household, no absent surgeons were chosen, and Larrey was still in Egypt. He was, however, appointed First Surgeon to the Consular Guard by an order dated November 1, 1800. So when, in 1804, the Consular Guard became the Imperial Guard – an army of the elite within an army – he became its

Surgeon-in-Chief. Unfortunately, though, in that role he was seen to be an uncomfortable threat by those who sought power and influence at Court, and his ambition was thwarted over and over again by the devious actions of, amongst others, Jean Nicolas Corvisart (1755–1821), physician to his majesty, and Antoine Dubois (1756–1837) and Alexis Boyer (1757–1833), surgeons to the Household. Reasons were not always hard to find. For instance, Larrey had invalided Dubois home from Egypt with dysentery, but he knew, and Dubois knew, that it was lack of guts. Put someone under an obligation like that and you've got yourself an enemy for life.

Dominique Jean Larrey. A portrait by his friend, Anne Louis Girodet (1767-1824).

Nevertheless, in 1813, Larrey's claim could be denied no longer and at the eleventh hour he was appointed to a year-old vacancy in the Imperial Household.

So far as Larrey's achievements in battle are concerned, he should be remembered not just for inventing a flying ambulance but for establishing and putting into practice the whole principle of casualty evacuation as we understand it today. His flying ambulance – the vehicle – was simply the first link in the superb system he built up, virtually from scratch, of caring for the wounded from battlefield through clearing stations to base hospitals.

As early as October 1797, while on a tour of inspection in Italy after the fighting had ended, Bonaparte saw an ambulance division on its daily manoeuvres. He was most impressed with its efficiency and military competence and remarked to Larrey: "Your work is one of the greatest conceptions of our age." The pity of it for the French soldier was his reluctance to proceed beyond the compliment.

Larrey's two-wheeled ambulance.

Larrey's problems with Napoleon Bonaparte (1769–1821) probably began in Egypt when he, as Surgeon-in-Chief to the Army of the Orient, chose to remain with the soldiers rather than submit to Bonaparte's expectation and accompany him back to France. Then, when he did return two years later in 1801, he knew Bonaparte would want to meet him in Lyons, but he put his wife before his future emperor and went home to Paris. I believe Napoleon never truly forgave him and when the new appointments were handed out, Pierre François Percy (1754–1825) was named surgeon-in-chief to the army which became the Grande Armée.

Larrey didn't do much to endear himself to the military either. In the negotiations with the British over the departure from Egypt, the French generals said the sick should be left behind until they were fully fit again. Larrey stormed to his feet: "What you really want is to avoid a long quarantine at Toulon and arrive with a fine-looking army in great shape. You raised the question of scurvy: well, your fears are groundless, the disease is not contagious. The sick will embark apart from the rest of the army, and I shall indicate those who cannot be moved. Furthermore, I insist that the best ships shall be made available for the sick and wounded and that these shall sail first." The French sat in stunned silence but Larrey got his way.

By remaining as surgeon-in-chief to the Consular Guard it could, of course, be argued that Larrey got the best of the bargain. But so far as the army as a whole was concerned it meant that it was the Guard who derived most benefit from Larrey's genius. However, this is not to imply, as some have done, that Larrey's excellent system was restricted to the Guard, for, whenever circumstances permitted he would go out of his way to help the casualties of the line. In fact, Percy was frequently late on campaign – by no means always his fault – and Larrey would be ordered to take complete surgical charge.

This happened, for instance, on the 1805 campaign leading up to Austerlitz. But at Jena the following year when the Imperial Guard was not committed, Marshal Bessières (1766–1813), commander of its cavalry and newly arrived in company with Larrey's ambulance divisions at Gera, refused him permission to go to the assistance of Percy and his surgeons on the field of battle. Nevertheless, Larrey did operate on those of the walking wounded who managed to make their way back to Gera some eighteen miles from the battlefield. As he wrote to his wife, Charlotte (1770–1842): "The Emperor and all the wounded did not cease calling my name on that brilliant but ghastly day." Without Larrey's presence any attempt to deal methodically with the casualties and to evacuate them with any semblance of order fell apart at the seams.

Larrey did, however, eventually succeed Percy as surgeon-in-chief of the Grande Armée in February, 1812 – in retrospect, not really the best of times. He held the job until the first abdication. But on Napoleon's return from Elba Percy, old and infirm, was re-appointed.

So much then for an outline of Larrey's career. When we come to an assessment of his character we are on less secure ground. Contemporary diaries, memoirs and so on tell us little or nothing. We have to rely mainly on the judgments of Napoleon; for instance in his will he wrote: "The most virtuous man that I have known" (here Napoleon was using the word virtuous in the Roman Republican sense of valour or courage dependant on a sense of personal honour – really untranslatable today as the concept no longer seems to exist.)

And in his conversations on St Helena with Dr Barry O'Meara (1786–1836) he had more to say: "Larrey was the most honest man, the

best friend to the soldier that I ever knew... He tormented the generals, and disturbed them out of their beds at night whenever he wanted accommodations or assistance for the wounded or sick. They were all afraid of him, as they knew he would instantly come and make a complaint to me. He paid court to none of them, and was the implacable enemy of the army contractors."

And in his *Mémorial de Sainte Hélène*, Emmanuel Las Cases (1766–1842) recorded: "I hold him in the highest esteem. If the army were to raise a monument to memory of one man it should be to that of Larrey. He has left in my mind the idea of a truly honest man."

Possibly, though, the most telling remark was to Dr Archibald Arnott (1772–1855), again on St Helena: "He did more for the morale of my army than any man I know." It has been said that "fear can kill with a scratch. Morale can save life in seemingly impossible situations."

Then there was Louis Thiers (1797–1877) who, in his monumental history of the Consulate and Empire, recorded how, during the retreat from Moscow, Larrey had entrusted some wounded Frenchmen to the care of three Russian officers whose lives he had saved. Thiers wrote: "God alone knows whether they paid this debt contracted with the best of men."

And finally, we have the brief comment of an American doctor, J. Mason Warren (1811–67), who wrote to his father in 1832: "I made a very pleasant and instructive visit, a few days since, to the Hôtel des Invalides, where I attended Larrey in his wards. He is a short, corpulent man, with a very agreeable face. His hair, which is gray, falls in curls over the straight, ornamented collar of the military coat that he wears during his visits. He was very polite to Dr Pierson."

However, as Larrey himself was very well aware, he had his failings. For instance, a British naval surgeon, John Waller, translated Larrey's *Mémoires* in 1815 and wrote in his Introduction: "On the whole, however, notwithstanding a tolerable proportion of disgusting egotism and vaunting, the book, as a system of military surgery... is an undoubted acquisition to the medical world." Not too bad really considering the date. And a German, Johann Heinrich Kopp (1777–1858), writing about his trip in 1824 to French hospitals, recorded how it had become the fashion under the Bourbons to belittle Larrey's surgical ability and to emphasize

his tendency to boast and to exaggerate his past exploits.

Larrey did, however, deeply regret those aspects of his character that put people's backs up. For instance, when his ship was lying in quarantine in the Toulon roads on his return from Egypt he received news from Charlotte that some so-called friends (of whom Dubois was one) had been spreading malicious gossip about him. He wrote back: "It would give me the greatest pain to incur anyone's hatred. I know that my defects and my extreme self-assurance invite criticism from those who wish me ill; but if they understood my feelings and my goodwill they would be aware of my generosity and my esteem."

Larrey in later middle age. A lithograph by F. S. Delpech. (*Wellcome Library, London.*)

There is, however, no doubt that Larrey did hold a very high opinion of himself and expected others to do likewise. Nevertheless, if a man is to be judged by the company he keeps, Larrey ranks high indeed since he numbered among his closest friends three of Napoleon's finest soldiers. Desaix (1768–1800) who had covered himself with glory on the Rhine, had conquered Upper Egypt and had turned Napoleon's defeat at Marengo into victory at the cost of his own life. Marshal Lannes (1769–1809), Duke of Montebello, highly regarded by Napoleon both as soldier and friend, who died at Essling after a ricocheting cannon-ball had

made a mess of both his legs. And Marshal Duroc (1772–1813), Duke of Friuli, killed, during the campaign in Saxony, by another ricochet that removed the front of his abdominal wall. Both these friends died in agony while Larrey could only watch, grief-stricken and unable to help. In a way these friendships were surprising, if we remember the social void that existed (even in the glorious days of the Revolution) between the fighting man and the surgeon. Socially, the status of an army medical officer was low and the conditions of service did nothing to attract the best type of man. Pay was poor and, particularly on active service, irregular. A medical officer had neither military rank nor authority. Combatant officers on the other hand lined their pockets handsomely with the spoils of war and petitioned their sovereign for rewards.

In such a situation an idealist could only be his own worst enemy, and Larrey was an idealist. Life in the army medical services of the Consulate and the First Empire was not easy anyway, but for a humane surgeon who would not conform and who believed in the principles of the Revolution it could be crucifying. Larrey found petitioning for rewards he maintained were his due a distasteful practice; and in treating casualties he took the wounded in order of their surgical need (social triage, maybe, but most certainly not battle triage as we understand it today) and he took them regardless of rank or even nationality – a habit that did not go down well with those who were more equal than the rest. "To perform a task as difficult as that which is imposed on a military surgeon," he wrote in his 1813 campaign journal, "I am convinced that one must often sacrifice oneself, perhaps entirely, to others; must scorn fortune and maintain an absolute integrity; and must inure oneself to flattery."

The extent to which he succeeded in his chosen task can be measured by the devotion he inspired among Napoleon's soldiers. For instance, the whole of the second day at the river Beresina during the retreat from Moscow he spent on the east bank looking for his wagons and ambulances and forcing them into line for crossing. When his own time came to cross, he found the way totally blocked. But he was recognized and at the mere mention of his name the ranks opened and men rushed to help him. "I owe my life to the soldiers," he wrote. "In the end I was seized by strong hands and literally pushed across the bridge."

Larrey's 1813 campaign journal. The opening page, January 1, at Königsberg.
(*Wellcome Library, London.*)

This emotion though was far from being shared by others. Napoleon, as I said earlier, remarked that the Administration both hated and feared him – feelings that derived mainly from the incompetence of its staff – and remember, too, Larrey's stand over the evacuation of his casualties from Egypt. But among his professional colleagues it was jealousy that was at the root of his troubles. His brilliance as a surgeon, both diagnostically and operatively, was quite uncanny; by comparison, his colleagues were ignorant and lacked any comprehension of what he was about. Larrey, in his turn, couldn't understand why they failed to follow his example. Again in his 1813 journal, he wrote: "I often think that those who cling to conservatism must recognize the need for operation, even though it may call for ingenuity, yet they fail to perform it through fear or some equally futile reason. They are guilty men."

This 1813 journal also contains some really soul-searching pages which I feel bear comparison with Beethoven's (1770–1827) Heiligenstadt testament. This was a letter the composer wrote to his brothers, Carl (1774–1815) and Johann (1776–1848), in 1803, bemoaning the effect his deafness had had on his relationships. The letter began: "O ye men who think or say that I am malevolent, stubborn or misanthropic, how greatly do ye wrong me, you do not know the secret causes of how I appear to others; from childhood my heart and mind were disposed to gentle feelings of goodwill..."

The passing of time never mellowed Larrey, although he was always desperately concerned about how he appeared to others. In another entry in his 1813 journal he wrote: "I confess I have never had any desire other than that of helping the wounded, no intention other than that of doing right... I have always been, and doubtless always will be, the victim of my sincerity and openness. Often the Emperor has reproached me for being able to see merit in others yet not in myself... I hate foolishness and politics. The truth, even when others cannot see it, marches always before me; I follow it blindly and am in danger of falling into the abyss if that is where it leads me.

"The misfortunes of others affect me strongly. Disasters afflict my soul and plunge me into the deepest grief; I often think I can do something to help, and even attempt to remedy the situation. But such is my nature that I am thrown off balance and reason is no longer in control."

However, it was because of his 'defects' that he was able not just to survive the horrors of Napoleonic warfare, but to keep fighting injustice, corruption and incompetence to the day he died. Others just swam with the tide or were submerged completely. Yet never once did Larrey allow his compassion and gentleness towards the sick and wounded to be eroded to the slightest degree. As a military surgeon he stood alone.

I would now like to see whether taking a view of Larrey in of the light of the Peter principle (Peter L J, Hull R. *The Peter Principle*. New York, 1969) might help explain some aspects of his character. The principle states that "in a hierarchy, every employee tends to rise to his level of incompetence." Did Larrey exemplify this principle when he became

Surgeon-in-Chief of the Grand Armée (about 400 000 men) or was he thwarted by the obstructive tactics of the Administration combined with a medical staff that was inadequate both in numbers and in innate medical ability? Or was it, perhaps, something quite otherwise instead?

I have already mentioned one event that might be considered to show the Peter principle in action: namely Napoleon's appointment of Percy as surgeon-in-chief on his return from Elba. Percy was then 61 (Larrey was 49); Percy had shown signs of heart trouble in Spain and had not seen active service since 1811. The fact that Percy was a disaster does not affect the argument – he was chosen in preference to Larrey who retired in a fit of the sulks and Napoleon had to send Antoine Drouot (1774–1847), second-in-command of the Imperial Guard, to persuade him to come back to his old job of surgeon-in-chief of the Guard.

At Ligny, two days before Waterloo, the regiments of the line, who bore the brunt of the battle against Blücher (1742–1819), had no organized system of casualty evacuation and when the French moved on the next day, amongst those left behind was Percy complaining of his heart. For the last time Larrey stepped into the breach but there was little he could do.

Moreover, despite the fact that Larrey had conducted the surgical affairs of the Army of the Orient with impeccable skill and efficiency, Napoleon probably believed him unsuited to the top position in view of his seeming greater concern with the details of operation and dressing than with the broader sweep of administering the surgical services. Once, in the Kremlin, Napoleon had taken Larrey to task for "wasting time on surgical details" when, as surgeon-in-chief he should have been better employed. How much of this was due to an inability to delegate and how much to the impossibility of his doing so, is problematical.

But what must seem like a classic instance of the principle at work was Larrey's turning up for the battle of Borodino with only himself and two assistants. His feelings when told by Napoleon to make arrangements for a forthcoming major battle scarcely do justice to the occasion: "I was greatly disturbed by the news" was how he expressed his reaction in his *Mémoires*. Five ambulance divisions and all the surgeons of the reserve had had to be left at Smolensk because of the total lack of co-operation on the

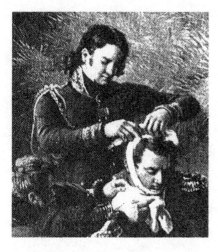

Larrey at the battle of Borodino. Detail from the painting *Battle of La Moskova*, September 7, 1812, by Louis François Lejeune (1775-1848). (*Musée de Versailles.*)

part of the Administration; the one ambulance division he did take forward became fully occupied dealing with the casualties after Valutina. Mercifully, a twenty-four-hour hold-up before the army reached Borodino to begin the battle allowed some transport and supplies to catch up and he found time to appropriate forty-five regimental surgeons. (In their normal jobs these men stayed with their regiments and had nothing to do with the evacuation of casualties. Larrey acquired them to staff the corps and divisional ambulances – dressing and clearing stations. The infantry and cavalry regiments were still left with just about adequate surgical cover. The Grande Armée was some 103 000 men strong of whom about 21 000 were wounded and 6 600 killed.)

Admittedly everything had been against him – shortage of staff and equipment from the start of the campaign, a bloody-minded Administration and lines of communication that Napoleon seemed determined to stretch till they broke. However, it could be argued that, whatever the practical difficulties to be faced, no surgeon-in-chief should have got himself into such a position. So was it incompetence or was it inevitability? A pointer in Larrey's favour was his exemplary performance throughout the 1813 campaign in Saxony which culminated in the immaculate evacuation of casualties by road and river after the battle of Montereau (a mere forty miles from Paris) on January 18, 1814 – and that with an ambulance service far below strength. At this battle the Grande Armée had been reduced to about 30 000 men with some 2000 killed, wounded and missing.

Napoleon's remark in the Kremlin about Larrey wasting time on surgical details – a comment supported by Larrey's own account of his

actions in the battles of 1813–14 – could give us an answer. He was a superb chief surgeon to the Imperial Guard where he could hold the entire system, both surgical *and* administrative, within the palm of his large hand – and let no one run away with the idea that the Guard was small; it comprised some 50 000 of the near half million men who crossed the Niemen into Russia. So was it a question of numbers? In a way, yes. Unfortunately the real answer is that we will never know; Larrey might well have been able to cope with the Grande Armée had he had sufficient competent surgeons so that he could devote himself to administration.

Larrey was indeed fortunate with the Guard where he was free to exercise both his surgical and administrative skills side by side. But to be surgeon-in-chief of an army the size of the Grande Armée, a man had to be an administrator first and a surgeon second. And this was something Larrey could never be: the sick and wounded came first whatever the cost.

So here we have the answer as we are now able to explain Larrey's character in philosophical terms. He was the embodiment of the Kantian philosophy of the categorical (or moral) imperative, according to which – in the medical setting – the patient comes first, whatever the circumstances, and no one should be neglected. This is in direct conflict with utilitarianism as later propounded by John Stuart Mill (1806–73) which, in its simplest form, may be expressed as the greatest good for the greatest number – and this necessarily means that there have to be sacrifices. (There is no evidence that Larrey was a follower of Immanuel Kant (1724–1804) or was even aware of his existence. He simply put into practice a way of life that was expressed in philosophical terms by Kant.)

However, conflict between medicine and its administrators is a perennial problem. Larrey could find no solution, and today we are searching still and with a desperation just as great. In this context the lesson we have to learn from Larrey is that never ever must doctors allow the control of their destiny to slip from the hands of those whose primary concern is the care of the sick.

13

SOME MUSINGS ON SHAKESPEARE'S MEDICAL SOURCES

So much has been written about Shakespeare (1564–1616), the man and his works, that he will doubtless provide a source of academic exercise for as long as the English language is understood. One of the more intriguing problems – apart, that is, from whether he was really the Earl of Essex (1566–1601), the Earl of Oxford (1550–1604), Francis Bacon (1561–1626) or all of them rolled into one – is where did he get his knowledge?

An obvious medical source would seem to be his doctor son-in-law, John Hall (1575–1635), the son of a doctor practising in Bedfordshire. When he was fourteen he went up to Queen's College, Cambridge, and after the customary seven years took his M.A. degree in 1597. He then went abroad to study medicine – the usual practice since neither Oxford nor Cambridge had much to offer by way of practical training. It is uncertain where he went, but at all events he returned, presumably with an M.D. which he did not incorporate at Cambridge, his own university. Instead, he settled for the alternative of obtaining a licence to practise medicine from the Bishop of Worcester. He may have done this because the practice of incorporation was falling into disrepute as it was believed

Hall's Croft, Stratford-upon-Avon.

that the ethical standards of medicine abroad were lower than in England. Or it may simply have been that as a practical physician and devout churchman he preferred the bishop's licence to the degree of a university that virtually discouraged practical medicine.

We do not know for sure when Hall arrived in Stratford-upon-Avon; all we can be certain of is that in 1601 he bought the house now known as Hall's Croft in Old Town, and that on June 5, 1607, he married Susanna (1583–1635), Shakespeare's elder daughter, who was then twenty-four and well-known for her work among the poor and sick of the town. Hall was held in high esteem as a doctor; he had probably discarded the more dubious aspects (astrology, astronomy and alchemy) of contemporary medicine, but we should be careful not to make him out to be more than an average country physician. Nor is it necessary for, as I shall show, I believe his medical learning and ability had little or no influence on Shakespeare's writings.

The Halls' wedding took place about the time that *Coriolanus* was written, and in this play Menanius tells a tale about the body's members rebelling against the belly (Act I, sc. 1). The theory goes that Shakespeare heard this Aesop's fable in physiological guise from Hall. Fair enough. But there is better to come. Working backwards to find where Hall got the story, we come to Montpellier in the mid-16th century where Rabelais (1495–1553) was lecturing on medicine – and Rabelais had himself adapted the fable. This is the sort of evidence advanced for Hall's having been a student at Montpellier some fifty years after Rabelais's death. Too tenuous to be accepted? Yet it does indicate what we are up against.

Hall's Croft. The dispensary.

However, if William Shakespeare was indeed the author of the plays, why is there no record of the fate of the manuscripts? They are not mentioned in his will, although he disposed carefully of his best bed and other household stuff to his daughter Susanna and his son-in-law. Apart from the fact that manuscripts in Elizabethan times were not considered of value in our sense, it seems likely to me that the originals had passed into the hands of actors, managers or publishers and were never returned to the author.

It has, however, been suggested that they were kept at New Place, Shakespeare's home which he left to the Halls and into which they moved shortly after Shakespeare's death in 1616. We are asked to believe that when Hall found the manuscripts, he destroyed them. The argument runs that Hall, being a strict Puritan, was overcome with guilt at inheriting

New Place, Stratford-upon-Avon, home of Shakespeare and, later, the Halls.

such sinful documents. Expurgation could only be achieved by the destruction of all books and manuscripts, thereby extinguishing his father-in-law's memory. Such would not fit in with the known facts of Hall's character or with his relationship with Shakespeare, and there is absolutely no evidence that he did destroy the manuscripts.

After an exhaustive analysis of the medical references and the dates of the plays, R. R. Simpson, a surgeon, in *Shakespeare and Medicine* (1959), concluded "that while there is no evidence that Hall influenced the medical references to be found in the plays of Shakespeare, either in their quantity or their quality, there is some evidence to suggest that, in the portrayal of doctors as doctors in the plays, Shakespeare might have been influenced by the character and qualities of his own son-in-law."

Although I agree whole-heartedly with this verdict, I disagree with Simpson and a number of other commentators in the wide-eyed, amazed manner in which they analyse the medical references in terms of modern medicine. I believe that Shakespeare at some stage in his career had read and had had constant access to many of the medical books of the time – and these would include translations of ancient books (those of Hippocrates, for instance) as well as contemporary works. Also, I believe his plays do not reveal a need for anything more as far as medical facts are concerned. Given these sources, Shakespeare's genius lay in his gift for words and imagery, in his ability to sift the wheat from the chaff, and in his profound understanding of human nature.

New Place. An interior view.

A big mystery in Shakespeare's life is what he did with himself during the so-called 'missing years', 1584–92. They began when he was twenty, an age when he would have been at his most receptive. What facts and learning was he assimilating at this time? To afford a satisfactory explanation any theory as to his whereabouts and occupation must give him the opportunity for gaining at least rudimentary ideas on medicine, music, law, military matters and much else besides. Writers have

introduced him into lawyers' offices, noblemen's households, military expeditions, and other employments that suited their arguments. However, none of these can fulfil the requirements on its own, and the time was too short for Shakespeare to have run through the lot and gained sufficient first-hand experience of all the trades and professions encountered in his plays. What he needed was contact with books and people.

A clue, unfortunately not developed, was given by Dr C. Martin Mitchell in *The Shakespeare Circle* (1947): "Richard Field [1561–?] was a senior boy at Stratford Grammar School when Shakespeare was a junior. The two were life-long friends; Richard went to London as a youth, was apprenticed to the publisher Vautrollier, of Blackfriars, by his well-to-do father, the tanner Henry Field [*d*.1592], a close friend and neighbour of John Shakespeare's [1529–*c*.1601]... Richard Field married Vautrollier's widow and succeeded to the business which was one of the foremost printing houses in London." (In fact Field married Jakin, Vautrollier's daughter, not his widow.) Mitchell goes on to say that another ex-grammar schoolboy and contemporary, George Badger, was also in London apprenticed to the publisher Peter Shortt. Both these houses published works of Shakespeare's between 1593 and 1598.

[Here I must declare an interest. Many doctors when discussing the diagnosis of famous patients of the past manage to make what is known fit a disease within their own specialty. I worked for eight years as medical editor for a firm of publishers.]

I am not saying that Shakespeare worked for Thomas Vautrollier or for Field after Vautrollier gave up his business or died in 1588. In the years we are considering they published only one medical book between them (*see* Ames's *History of English Printers (1471–1600)*), and they had no part in the production of Holinshed's (*c*.1520–*c*.1580) *Chronicles* – sometimes referred to as Shakespeare's bible. (The first edition of the *Chronicles* was published in 1577 by J. Harison and printed by someone not named, but identified on internal evidence as H. Bynneman. The second edition, 1587, was published by J. Harison, G. Bishop, R. Newberie, H. Denham and T. Woodcocks; the printer is unknown). But what I am saying is that, with the help of Field, Shakespeare could have had introductions to other publishing houses and access to many of the books necessary for building

up his store of factual knowledge on all subjects. And, I imagine, he would have felt no hesitation in plagiarizing them, since books in those days had a much more limited circulation than now, and the audiences at his plays were largely illiterate. In a London publishing house, too, Shakespeare would have met authors and, if he had maintained his friendship with Field, also the many notables who are known to have frequented Vautrollier's. Finally, living in London he would have had plenty of opportunity for sharpening his natural gifts of observation of humanity.

I am not equipped, either by training or by temperament, to solve this problem of Shakespeare's missing years. I merely suggest that if the right person were prepared to investigate the history of London's publishing and printing houses at the turn of the 16th century, he might uncover some interesting facts about William Shakespeare. For an encourager, he might identify the mysterious Mr W. H. to whom the Sonnets were dedicated by Thomas Thorpe (*c.*1569–*c.*1635): "To the Onlie Begetter of These Insuing Sonnets Mr W. H. All Happinesse and that Eternitie Promised by Our Ever-Living Poet Wisheth The Well-Wishing Adventurer in Setting Forth." As Thorpe was the stationer for whom the Sonnets were printed, I feel that his typesetter is a stronger candidate for dedicatee than William Herbert (1580–1630 – 3rd Earl of Pembroke and nephew of Sir Philip Sydney (1554–86)) the current popular choice, even though Herbert was a poet and patron of the arts.

14

SIX DOCTORS AND A GOLD-HEADED CANE

In the 17th and 18th centuries the physician's cane was virtually his badge of office and their heads provided an excellent excuse for ostentatious display. Not all the heads were of gold, some were of silver and some of materials such as wood or ivory that could be carved and decorated. Many were hollow to contain a sponge soaked in an aromatic or antiseptic substance, the popular belief being that sniffing the sponge while in consultation with the patient would ward off the noxious elements of the disease. It was also an admirable way of overcoming the ubiquitous stench of both patient and environment. However, a more satisfying use for a hollow head was to hold a glass phial containing alcoholic refreshment. Not to be outdone, the quacks of the day, many of whom made an excellent living with their remedies, also carried canes in imitation of their qualified colleagues.

At this time England was a study in the extremes of human living. At one end, the great mass of the people, poor, unwashed, stinking, disease-ridden wretches eking out a pitiful existence from the gutters. At the other, the Court and the upper classes, for the most part rich, idle, conforming to a strict code of etiquette with an artificiality of conduct to

A carved wood head representing the figure of Atlas supporting the world and, lower down, a snake (from the Balkans).

help alleviate their boredom. This artificiality showed itself in their manners and clothing and reached its apogee in the Regency period when the veritable 'tulips' of fashion, the Corinthians, would spend hours concocting elaborate arrangements of their neckcloths. The distinctions of class and trade were finely drawn and adhered to rigidly.

During the 17th century physicians had been consolidating their position and the fashionable practitioners had become accepted by Society. The prevailing conditions were such that an educated man could, and often did, excel in more than one sphere of learning. The system of patronage and the inheriting of wealthy practices gave the outstanding physicians opportunities for becoming extremely cultured men, and many achieved literary fame or could hold their own in the most exalted circles.

In the matter of sartorial splendour physicians had tended to lag behind as shown by the occasion, in 1628, when Peter Chamberlen (1601–83 – Peter the third of obstetric forceps fame) appeared before the Royal College of Physicians dressed in the gay frivolous manner of the Court. He was severely reprimanded by the President and refused admission to fellowship until he could return clad in a more sober, dignified way as befitted a physician. But times changed, aided by a reaction to the puritanism of Oliver Cromwell's (1599–1658) Protectorate, and with the restoration of the monarchy, doctors blossomed forth in a magnificence of dress.

A full-skirted coat of velvet, satin or brocade resplendent with broad cuffs and many gilt basket buttons was worn over a lavishly embroidered

An engraved ivory head with a carved snake and buckle
(from Istanbul).

waistcoat. Buckskin trousers fitted into highly
polished top boots or were buttoned just below the
knee over fine stockings and buckled shoes. A
powdered wig topped by a three-cornered hat
completed his attire. As a touch of supreme
arrogance his gauntleted gloves would be borne by
a lackey walking a respectful distance behind his
master; in winter he would wear a muff to preserve
the delicacy of touch so essential in a day
when diagnosis depended on the exercise of the
unaided senses.

The taverns, coffee houses and clubs were the
great meeting places of the day. At the clubs the
physician talked with the learned men; in the coffee
houses and taverns he sharpened his wits with the
literati, betweenwhiles writing prescriptions for the
apothecaries on the strength of their description of
the patient's symptoms. For this service at second
hand he charged a fee of half a guinea. An artifice, not
unknown at the time, was for a physician, anxious to
create the impression of a large busy practice, to
arrange to be summoned from church, whereupon he
would gallop madly through the streets flourishing
his cane and scattering all before him.

The most famous of all the canes was
equipped with a gold crutch handle on which were eventually engraved
the five coats of arms of its owners. This cane, which is still in existence
and kept in a safe at the Royal College of Physicians in London, is of
malacca and beautifully balanced. It achieved an immortality through
writing its autobiography by the hand of William McMichael
(1784–1839), a distinguished Fellow of the Royal College. In this, the

The gold-headed cane. The visible coat of arms is that of Anthony Askew. A cord was originally passed through the hole at the top of the shaft.

cane describes its adventures in the hands of its successive masters; a device that proves an excellent way of telling the history of the Royal College and of a number of its famous fellows, both past and contemporary with the particular owner.

Two misconceptions may be encountered; one is that the cane went with the office of President of the Royal College of Physicians, and the other that there were five owners. In fact only one (William Pitcairn) was a president, and the cane was owned by six men (there were two Pitcairns, uncle and nephew).

John Radcliffe (1650–1714), the original owner, had an extensive and extremely well-to-do practice, numbering royalty among his patients. He attended William III (1650–1702) in 1689 and cured him of asthma, the dregs of the smallpox that had fallen on his lungs. Five years later he was blamed for the death of Queen Mary (1662–94), from smallpox, but stoutly maintained that he had been called in too late. Radcliffe's manner was perhaps unfortunate for royal circles as he was renowned for speaking his mind. He made no secret of the fact that he was uncultured, but his medical knowledge was outstanding and his prognostic ability almost uncanny. At all events his patients overcame their fear of his tongue to retain his services and after his death his fortune was sufficient to found the library, infirmary, and observatory at Oxford which bear his name,

and to endow two Radcliffe travelling fellowships. (There was also £500 yearly for ever, towards mending the diet at St Bartholomew's Hospital – the hospital still (2005) receives £300 twice a year.)

Radcliffe fell from royal favour when, shortly before his death, he refused to attend Queen Anne (1665–1714) in her final illness. However, his pupil and friend, Richard Mead, to whom he had already entrusted many of his patients, took over and later, while discussing the queen's case, Radcliffe handed him the gold-headed cane with the advice, "Use all mankind ill". Nevertheless he was at heart kind and generous.

Richard Mead (1673–1754), utterly unlike Radcliffe in manner and approach, was in correspondence with many of the scholars of Europe. He was an enthusiast for vaccination against smallpox and held sound commonsense views on matters of public health. While in Mead's care, the cane met Sir Hans Sloane (1660–1753), the first medical baronet whose private museum subsequently formed the foundation of the British Museum, and paid a visit to the Tower of London during Mead's successful attempt to obtain the release of Dr John Friend (1675–1728) who had been incarcerated for his Jacobite sympathies.

The next owner of the cane was the dandified Anthony Askew (1722–74). How the cane came into his hands is uncertain, but as he bought much of Mead's library it seems likely that he also bought the cane. In his youth Askew had travelled extensively in the East, which added to his fascination since, in those days, this was an unusual accomplishment. He was a great scholar and brought bibliomania into fashion. So proud was he of his library that he would not let others touch the rarest of his books, but exhibited them under glass.

About two years after Askew had bequeathed the cane to William Pitcairn (1711–91 – remembered for his wise use of opium in fevers) it entered the Royal College of Physicians for the first time in the hands of a president. Seven years after resigning from the presidency Pitcairn gave the cane to his nephew David Pitcairn (1749–1809), a kind, gentle and dignified man who treated his patients with great consideration and often refused to charge a fee when this would cause hardship. While on his deathbed, his old friend Matthew Baillie (1761–1823) called and was presented with the cane. Baillie was to be the last individual owner.

On his mother's side he was a nephew of the famous Hunters, John (1728–93) and William (1718–83), and when he came to London he was supervised by William. In his book on morbid anatomy, dedicated to David Pitcairn, Baillie used the lung of Samuel Johnson (1709–84), the lexicographer, to illustrate emphysema. However, Baillie was inclined to be blunt and, in his busiest period, rather irritable with patients who poured out their troubles at length. In taking a history his questioning was brief but much to the point and afterwards he would give a concise account of the case to the doctor who had called him in consultation. He would lecture clearly on the disease to the patient and his relatives who were at this period of history beginning to show an interest in medical matters, a trend that has gathered force ever since. In his treatment he refused to try anything ingenious, subtle or far-fetched, relying on simple measures.

By the time the gold-headed cane came to Baillie, canes were no longer considered necessary appendages of the profession and so were seldom seen. When Baillie died in 1823, his widow presented the cane to the Royal College of Physicians where it has since remained. A fitting epitaph may be culled from the cane's autobiography:

"Formerly the entree of palaces had been open to me; I had been freely admitted to the houses of the great and rich; but now I was doomed to darkness… having become to a certain degree an object of curiosity, my seclusion has occasionally been broken in upon by a temporary exhibition to a visitor."

15

HISTORY INFORMS
THE FUTURE –
ONE WAY OR ANOTHER

Billroth was stoned in the streets of Vienna. He had, on January 29, 1881, carried out the first successful gastric resection for carcinoma, but had followed this with two failures. The public with its insatiable curiosity about matters surgical thereupon reacted towards the 'father' of gastric surgery with this unseemly behaviour.

A lesser man than Theodor Billroth (1829–94) might easily, there and then, have given up the struggle, but ten years later he had removed forty-one cancerous pyloruses with sixteen operative deaths – a dismal performance perhaps, when measured against today's results, yet we must remember that Billroth was carving a completely new path with none of the modern aids, such as blood transfusion, fluid replacement, antibiotics, radiology and so forth, at his disposal; anaesthesia was still in its infancy, and his patients were desperately ill. Without his persistence and that of his pupils and assistants gastrointestinal surgery would have been much longer in reaching the state it – and the patient – enjoys today.

Medicine, for better or worse, is no longer answerable to itself and God alone; it has a social responsibility and, in return, society must accept its responsibility to behave in an informed manner towards medicine. Society has thus, in a sense, gained a new freedom, but as Edmund Burke (1729–1797), the 18th-century statesman, remarked about the opening years of the French revolution, "the effect of liberty to individuals is that they may do what they please: we ought to see what it will please them to do, before we risk congratulations."

Times may have changed since Billroth's day, but human emotions have remained much the same. His public may be excused their reaction since surgery had only a few years previously been utterly transformed and the populace had no comparable situations for their guidance. Even so it is difficult now to understand why they responded so violently; we can only guess that they were deeply afraid of the unknown. Today we have history to guide us yet it would seem that there are still many whose emotions unwisely overrule their judgment, or whose actions and words are born of ignorance. The wave of what can only be described as hysteria that followed Christiaan Barnard's (1922–2001) two heart transplantations in 1967–8 serves as a shining example.

The story covers virtually the whole of mankind's history – his attitudes to life, his beliefs and the reasons for them. Significant here is Aristotle's (384–322 BC) statement that the heart is the seat of the soul, of the emotions, the very source of life. Traditional beliefs die hard and the Aristotelian outlook is still very close to the surface even in an educated and sophisticated society. The heart is also the shrine of romantic love. Admittedly the Greco-Romans had a try at making the liver the home of the soul, but without success. Had this caught on or had someone decided instead on the kidneys, there would undoubtedly have been the same outburst when these organs were first transplanted.

The history of heart transplantation reflects the history of surgery, particularly the reactions of the profession and the public, and the circumstances surrounding 'firsts': the early mortality and morbidity rates, and the length of time before operations became acceptable and why.

More specifically it reflects the story of organ transplantation. If we ignore legend (which nevertheless indicates that the subject has been

hovering around since ancient times) this has been pursued scientifically since the start of the 20th century; Alexis Carrel (1873–1944) and Charles Guthrie (1880–1963) were far from alone in the early days, and quite a few kidneys were transplanted from animals into human patients, although not into the anatomically-correct place. Survival times ranged from hours to days. Many organs now transplanted clinically were transplanted experimentally in animals, though usually into sites, such as the neck, where their behaviour could easily be studied. Notable exceptions were the abdominal organs.

Nevertheless, the general attitude was one of despair until the modern era began. Two significant events marked its start: Sir Peter Medawar's (1915–87) demonstration in 1944 that rejection of skin grafts was due to an immunological reaction (later it was shown that organs were rejected by the same mechanism), and Willem Kolff's (*b*.1911) invention of the artificial kidney which enabled patients with renal failure to be maintained and brought into a state fit for surgery. But this, in turn, created problems. Considerations other than purely medical ones became only too apparent. The technique was costly, almost prohibitively so, and patients had to be selected. In some hospitals, committees were set up to decide which patients should receive treatment, since it was felt the problem was one for society rather than medicine. Eventually, home dialysis became available, though some surgeons regarded this as merely a short-term lifeline until a suitable kidney became available for transplantation.

From about 1950 onwards the transplantation ball gathered momentum to be given added impetus with the discovery of immunosuppressive drugs in the early 1960s. A vast amount of experimental work was done and applied clinically with varying degrees of success.

But by 1964 Richard Lower (*b*.1929) and Norman Shumway (1923–2006) of Stanford University, California, could give the clear warning: "with a definite increase in survival of renal homografts it seems logical to conclude that cardiac homografts are just around the corner. Perhaps the cardiac surgeon should pause while society becomes accustomed to resurrection of the mythological chimera." He did not.

That same year James Hardy (1918–2003) of the University of

Mississippi, who had been working intensively on the subject since 1956, transplanted a chimpanzee's heart into a human patient – he had fully intended to use a human heart but when all was ready the intended donor lingered on, although his brain was irretrievably damaged. The recipient lived only a few hours. News of the operation leaked out to the press who at first believed the human donor had been used; when the truth was told the excitement died down. This is of both interest and significance in the assessment of human reaction to major medical and surgical events that may be perceived as threatening.

The historical evidence, there for all to read, clearly showed that a human heart homotransplant was an inevitability. The only missing factor was the precise date, but from at least 1964 onwards it was bound to be sooner rather than later. Yet, as events showed, pretty well everyone, medical and lay, was caught on the hop, and reacted in a thoroughly predictable manner. They were afraid and primitive emotions took over. This can be seen in one way by the concern over the moment of death. Deep inside, the man in the street – and a good many medical men besides – feared that his own heart might be taken from him before he was really dead.

So, should the historical evidence have made the profession and interested segments of society sit up and take heed of their responsibilities before the inevitable came to pass? During the best part of twenty years while the surgical teams got on with their part of the job, competently, with integrity and with respect for the sanctity of human life, scarcely a peep was heard from those who were to become their vociferous critics on the moral and ethical issues. But neither did the surgical teams pay heed to the warning given by Shumway and Lower.

Adding to the problem, the amply demonstrated determination of the media coupled with the avidity of their public, has also to be appreciated. The more newsworthy a medical story the more difficult is it for a balanced assessment to be made and what emerges is, as often as not, slanted to worry the man or woman in the street. But members of society want to know what is going on in medicine, and indeed have every right to be informed since they must have an increasing say in how the fruits of modern medicine are to be dispersed. The great difficulty is to inform

them so that each person can make an accurate assessment of the situation and decide on the broader issues, leaving the purely medical details to the doctors who must keep that responsibility. Yet even amongst the well-informed there are those who have opinions that may be driven by forces – such as religion, politics or ingrained prejudices – outside medical science. So, human nature being what it is, history informs us that striking medical advances will continue to be greeted in the same old way by media and public alike. (The recent outcry at the prospect of full facial homographs and the rows over expensive anticancer drugs are cases in point.)

16

CRIMEAN WAR I:
Why the army's medical services were in such an appalling mess at the start

The British public awoke to the fact that all was not well in the Crimea when its breakfasts were disturbed by William Howard Russell's (1821–1907) despatches in *The Times*. His first report concerned the battle of the River Alma (September 20, 1854) and described the plight of the wounded; it was published on October 9. Yet the one that really set the cat among the pigeons appeared on October 13 and was accompanied by an editorial written by the campaigning editor, John Delane (1817–79), taking the Army Medical Department to task for the deficiencies at the British Military Hospital at Scutari.

So just how bad was the situation? Forty years had passed since Waterloo and, except for the Empire-building campaigns in remote parts of Asia and Africa, they had been forty years of peace. The British public did not know what to expect – it certainly was not prepared for the harsh truths of war and the even more ghastly ravages of disease. Moreover, the invention of the telegraph had created a sense of immediacy never before experienced with a foreign campaign – public opinion could alter the course of events.

The human suffering exposed by Russell was simply the end result of what had gone before during those forty years. And what *had* gone before beggars belief.

The problems besetting Dr Andrew Smith (1797–1872), Director General of the Army Medical Department, were many. The Department had been eroded by forty years of Treasury miserliness, and economy had become both a way of life and a state of mind. Smith, in his office in London, had a staff of two medical officers and four clerks and in consequence had to deal with a whole mass of petty detail that should never have reached his desk. The red tape that bound him was unbelievably tangled. For instance, the only direct financial control he had was over the purchase of medicines, dressings and surgical appliances. On matters of policy he had to approach the Military Secretary to the Commander-in-Chief at the Horse Guards and the Secretary *for* War (responsible for overall civilian supervision of the army); for approval of expenditure on equipment and supplies he had to go to the Secretary *at* War (Sidney Herbert (1810–61) – he was responsible for army finance and administration). But the procedure for obtaining medical comforts took the prize. In the words of Alexander W. Kinglake (1809–91 – the author of *Eothen*):

"If the Director General of the Army Medical Department wished to furnish our hospitals in the East some kinds of supplies, as for instance, wine, sago, arrowroot, he had to send his purpose revolving in an orrery of official bodies: For first, he well knew, he must move the Horse Guards, and the Horse Guards must move the Ordnance, and the Ordnance must set going the Admiralty, and the Admiralty must give orders to the Victualling Office, and the Victualling Office must concert measures with the Transport Office, and the Transport Office (having only three transports) must appeal to the private ship-owners, in the hope that sooner or later they would furnish the sea-carriage needed."

Smith's position was at first well nigh intolerable. The Crimea, thanks to the telegraph, was on his doorstep so far as trouble was concerned, but when it came to an accurate understanding of events and an assessment of the appropriate action to take it was still as remote as Timbuctoo. The new dimension that had been added to warfare could only be mastered by

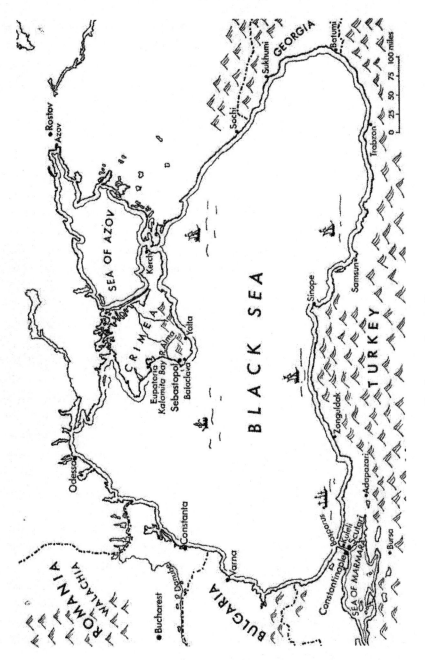

The Crimean theatre of war.

experience. And, to make matters worse, Smith was often kept in the dark about important military decisions.

The Russians had been at war with the Turks since October 1853 and had occupied Turkish territory along the banks of the Danube. Britain did not declare war until March 27, 1854, after six weeks of hurried and inadequate preparation. Smith, however, had been warned on February 22 that troops already gathering in Malta might be sent east to help the Turks. He reacted by despatching three senior medical officers to the Balkans to report on the climate and prevalent diseases; their impressions, which came back during April, were decidedly unfavourable. The climate went to extremes during summer and winter; diseases, such as malaria, dysentery, typhoid and typhus, were endemic; and sanitation was non-existent. The reports also contained valuable recommendations for preserving the health of the troops which Smith passed on to the Military Secretary only to see them rejected.

❧

From the moment of the warning Smith began fighting his way through the administrative jungle in an attempt to ensure that the Department should not be found wanting. Bed coverage (the number of hospital beds likely to be required, expressed as a percentage of the total force) was reckoned to be adequate at about 10 per cent except at times of fighting or epidemic disease when 20–25 per cent was thought to be more realistic. The provision of these beds was traditionally the responsibility of the principal medical officer on the spot – in this case, Dr John Hall (1795–1866), the Inspector General in the Crimean area – but Smith thought he would play safe and sent in a requisition for five thousand beds. However, as the requisition had to be initiated by a non-existent purveyors department, a retired purveyor was added to Smith's staff. The requisition then had to get the approval of the Commander-in-Chief before it could be met by the Board of Ordnance. About half the beds had arrived by June, but the full number did not reach Turkey until Christmas Eve – a delay due to poor delivery by the contractors and severe pressure on shipping space.

Next, Smith set in motion the request for hospital equipment only to find there was none in store (no one had foreseen the need for a general hospital) and again it all had to be ordered from civilian contractors. In fact the only supplies ready for shipment in time were the medicines, dressings and surgical equipment ordered by Smith himself from the Apothecaries Hall – and due to the shortage of ships, they sat on the quayside from February 17 till April 3. As all medical stores were loaded under the orders of the Ordnance Officer at the Tower of London into shipping allocated by the Naval Transport Officer, it is scarcely surprising that priority was given to military materials. Nevertheless, a ship did sail on April 11 containing the complete equipment for a hospital of five-hundred-and-fifty beds as well as spare blankets and sheets together with marquees and bedding for the regimental hospitals. Admittedly it was well below the coverage needed for an army of twenty-five to twenty-eight thousand men but it was the best that could be done.

Smith was also busy seeing to the regimental needs for the treatment and evacuation of casualties in the field. He ordered forty ambulance carts, both two- and four-wheeled (relying, as had been the practice in the Peninsular War, on the local requisitioning of any further carts that might be needed), four large wagons containing stores, three hundred stretchers, regimental panniers, cases of instruments, bandages, splints, everything in fact that was required. But when, early in April, the army arrived in Turkey, its medical supplies had still not left England. The regimental surgeons at Scutari were fortunate in being able to take over the Turkish supplies and equipment in the General Hospital, but those in Gallipoli had nothing. And nothing that Smith had ordered for them reached the regiments until June. However, during May three ships did arrive in Turkey with hospital stores and equipment.

Yet, back in London, Smith believed that all was well and that the army now had medical materials sufficient to last for six months; he relied on Hall to keep him informed of developments locally and to indent for further supplies as necessary.

Unfortunately, even when stores eventually left England some items such as blankets, brandy and port were liable to go missing, and comforts generally were used up in less than three months largely owing to short

ordering by Smith's purveyor. Moreover, as the labelling was left to the Ordnance Officer the stores were frequently addressed to inappropriate personnel who made little or no attempt to dispose of them correctly. When this fact dawned on Smith he addressed everything to senior medical officers personally, but by the time the consignment arrived the nominee had quite likely moved elsewhere. To combat the transport delays Smith should have marked the requisitions for stores 'Urgent' because as Captain A. Milne, R.N., of the Admiralty said in his evidence to the Roebuck Committee, had he seen anything so marked he would have sent them out as hastily as possible by steamer.

Milne's evidence also exposed a shameful blunder over hospital ships. On May 11, Smith had asked the Military Secretary for a liberal supply of well-ventilated ships with ample accommodation to be used as floating hospitals, and for the evacuation of casualties to Scutari and the transport of invalids home to England. Yet Milne declared that the Admiralty had never received such a requisition; though when asked whether he considered it a part of his duty to suggest such a thing, he replied, "No. I thought of it, I must acknowledge, and I must acknowledge that I thought it odd that a requisition was not made." Somewhere along the line, someone had evidently lost or ignored the request. The consequences for the sick and wounded were beyond description and the waste of medicines and supplies arising from the need to equip available transports as temporary hospital ships was deplorable.

✺

At the end of May the army, under Lord Raglan (1788–1855), set out for the Black Sea port of Varna in Bulgaria. The troops were in good heart and eager to drive the Russians out of the occupied territories. As it happened, they never saw the Russians who left of their own accord; instead they met all the diseases forecast by Smith's medical officers and took not the slightest precautions against them – despite the fact that the principles of sound sanitary conduct for an army in the field were well known and had been so for a hundred years.

Varna was a sordid insanitary place and the dilapidated building chosen

as the general hospital was in keeping with its surroundings. The hospital equipment, sent on from Scutari, arrived on June 3 but the bed cover was only 10 per cent which was marginal even if conditions proved favourable. The army moved inland and camped overlooking marshy ground (thus inviting malaria). Its medical equipment had arrived by this time, though most units chose to leave their large medicine chests behind in Varna. Inevitably, fevers and bowel diseases soon became epidemic and, most disastrous of all, cholera appeared. The regimental surgeons quickly ran out of medicines, and because of shortage of transport the authorities refused to send them their medicine chests. The hospital at Varna was overwhelmed.

By the end of July, despite serious doubts about the health of the army, it was decided to invade the Crimea. Hall was not told about this officially but on the strength of rumour he asked the quartermaster-general for conveyance for four hundred tons of stores plus the wagons, men and horses of the ambulance train; the vessels should then be kept as hospital ships. Hall had to fight every inch of the way, first to get transport from the Commissariat to carry stores to the quay, then to persuade the Agent of Transport to provide boats to carry them out to the waiting *John Masterman* which already was loaded with the complete equipment for a six-hundred-bed hospital as well as reserves of medicines, dressings and a small amount of medical comforts. However, only three of the ambulances were taken on board and nowhere in the remainder of the fleet could Hall find space for the others. He protested strongly but to no avail. Also sailing from Varna were *Cambria* and *Andes*, both equipped as hospital ships yet both too small to be really effective for the evacuation of casualties. Two thousand men were left at Varna either sick or dead.

When Hall sailed on September 4, stores were still arriving from England – no one had told Smith that Varna was being abandoned. To make matters worse, the stocks at Scutari had fallen dangerously low as Ward, the purveyor, was keeping no records and had not asked Hall for replenishments. Nevertheless, Hall himself took no steps to re-route unwanted supplies from Varna until just before he left when he ordered a recent shipment to be loaded on *Bombay* and sent to Scutari. He also wrote a brusque note to Ward telling him to indent on Varna for whatever equipment he might need. But even this apparently excellent

idea fell foul of the system, as perhaps Hall should have realized it would.

Ward did as he was told and on September 6 and again ten days later wrote to the purveyor at Varna urging him to despatch without delay as many beds and as much equipment as he could spare. The letters lay undelivered in the office of Rear-Admiral Boxer (1784–1855), Principal Naval Officer at Constantinople, because he did not consider the request to be urgent. In November he did, however, send a ship to Varna and the equipment eventually reached Scutari at the end of the month. Admiral Boxer was also responsible for creating a shortage of medicines and dressings at Scutari by sending a shipment, that arrived in Turkey in September, on to Varna simply because it was labelled Varna and regardless of the fact that he knew the army had already left.

❧

When the British army invaded the Crimea in the middle of September it had no transport so, true to Peninsular tradition, three-hundred-and-fifty local carts were rounded up, twenty-four of which were given to Hall. He kept six and distributed the other eighteen throughout the army to carry the reserves of medicines brought by *John Masterman*. But there were no proper ambulances, not even the three sent from Varna: one had disappeared and the other two were without their horses. Then, unbelievably, Lord Raglan ordered that no regimental hospital equipment was to be carried in the advance on Sebastopol; the regimental surgeons were limited to a pair of panniers, a small box of medical comforts and a bell tent. In other words, while facilities for first-aid were carried, there was not a single hospital bed for the entire army. And the men were ordered to leave their knapsacks behind at Kalamita Bay where they landed.

Disease continued to ravage the army and the sick had to be evacuated. Such transport ships as happened to be available were pressed into service, much to the disgust of their captains; they were invariably grossly overcrowded and inadequately staffed and equipped. Moreover, since a transport was rarely used for sick or wounded more than once the equipment and medical supplies that were carried were dumped at the end of the voyage. Particularly distressing for men suffering from cholera and

dysentery was the shortage of bed-pans and urinals. It is difficult to know whose hell was the worse: that of the men cramped between decks or of those who spent the four- or five-day journey lying unattended on the open deck. In one shipload of four-hundred-and-thirty sick men (mostly suffering from cholera) one-hundred-and-fourteen died during the voyage.

After the battle of the Alma on September 20, the British had eighteen hundred wounded, some of whom were not brought in for forty-eight hours. The surgical operations were carried out under horrifyingly primitive conditions with doors torn from their hinges to serve instead of the operating tables left behind at Kalamita Bay. The one saving grace was chloroform which, contrary to some stories, was used quite freely. Hall was then faced with the problem of getting the casualties to the beaches as he had no ambulances and no medical officers for escort duty. Fortunately the Navy and the French came to the rescue with transport, but Hall had to take some of the regimental surgeons to staff the transport ships though he could do nothing about the lack of orderlies on board. This problem of transport to Scutari persisted into December. On the 17th of that month Hall was eventually allocated two fully equipped steamers that ran a regular service between Balaclava and Scutari, but as they only held one-hundred-and-fifty men each he acquired on December 24 another four ships, all well equipped, supplied and staffed.

When, at the beginning of October, the allies were encamped around Sebastopol, the British sent to Kalamita Bay for their regimental hospitals and stores only to find that the bulk had been spirited away. Mercifully, Hall was able to establish a hospital at Balaclava to cope with the sick and to hold the casualties awaiting transport to Scutari. This hospital consisted of the local school and two marquees; it had on average three hundred to three-hundred-and-fifty patients and was kept fully equipped and supplied from the stores on board *John Masterman*.

For the battles of Balaclava (October 25) and Inkerman (November 5) Hall had obtained twelve ambulance wagons; his only regret was that he had not managed to acquire the full forty originally sent out. Unhappily, though, these two battles made Hall feel that his hospital was no longer safe for long-term casualties and he evacuated two thousand men to Scutari. He knew this would strain the Scutari resources but he

The gale off the port of Balaclava, 14 November, 1854. (*National Army Museum, London.*)

naively assumed that Dr Duncan Menzies, the medical superintendent of the hospital, would by then have received the stores from Varna.

On November 14 a fresh disaster struck. Previously the weather in the Crimea had been mild with mist and rain, but in the early hours of the fourteenth a violent storm struck the Crimea. The loss of *Prince* with all hands was catastrophic for the army as she carried the winter underwear and other warm clothing for the entire force – it almost seems as though some evil genius was at work, since the clothing should have been despatched much earlier except that no one in London could make up their minds whether the army would have to winter in the Crimea or not. Lord Raglan admittedly sent at once to the quartermaster-general's department in Constantinople for whatever warm clothing they could buy, but despite two shipments that arrived from England during December, the last man did not get his full winter issue until January. And yet greatcoats and skin rugs were stored in some of the other ships that survived the storm – they were not issued because no one knew they were there.

Commissariat difficulties on the road from Balaclava to Sebastopol during the wet weather.
(National Army Museum, London.)

Clothing was not the only valuable cargo to go down in *Prince*. She was also carrying desperately needed medicines (including three hundred pounds of opium) for Scutari, but they had not been unloaded there because they had been packed underneath ammunition destined for Balaclava.

The storm also played havoc with communications (not to mention living conditions) ashore. The dirt road from Balaclava became a mud bath and the resulting difficulties of transport persisted throughout the winter. Virtually everything had to be carried the three or so miles by men up to their thighs in mud. Men could ill be spared from military duties either to restore communications or to carry supplies; in consequence the troops grew weaker and fell sick, thus further reducing their effectiveness. Even when help was provided something inevitably seemed to go wrong; for instance, a large cargo of vegetables arrived in November but the men found them difficult to carry and so most just rotted in the hold. Again, on November 17 Smith ordered forty thousand gallons of lime juice to be distributed throughout the winter to prevent scurvy; twenty thousand gallons arrived in early December but due to an administrative error it was not distributed for another two months.

To conclude this sorry tale of disasters, the pieces of which were picked up at Scutari, we discover that suits of hospital clothing, boards and trestles for beds, and other miscellaneous items such as knives, forks, plates and cups were in store at Balaclava but the regimental surgeons were unaware of their existence – nothing was issued, everything had to be indented for. Hall reckoned, however, that by mid-January the troops in the field had all that they required. But the damage had been done; sickness continued to tear the army apart and only the arrival of better weather and the Sanitary Commission was able to bring this under control.

Hall's failure from the start had been in not keeping his superior in London fully informed. Whether from inability or unwillingness he failed to send back accurate appreciations of the changing situation. As a result Smith knew nothing of the transport and shipping difficulties and of their aggravation by the large numbers of sick; he learnt of shortages only through other sources and did not know what to make of them as Hall was silent on the subject. In desperation he decided to communicate directly with Menzies.

❧

Menzies meantime had been coping adequately with his job of medical superintendent at Scutari despite his problems with the purveyor. When *Bombay* arrived from Varna in September loaded with 5200 sheets, 3500 blankets, 1700 rugs and palliasses, and more than 1000 sets of hospital clothing, he was almost equipped to deal with the 2000 patients for whom he had accommodation – the missing items were a thousand or so of the beds ordered by Smith that had been sent to Varna. His medical staff consisted of himself (he was responsible for all the major operations), one staff surgeon, seventeen staff assistant surgeons and three local civilian doctors. They were already at full stretch dealing with the sick when the casualties from the Alma arrived; only by commandeering the services of seventeen regimental surgeons and ten naval surgeons from the transports was he able to meet the challenge. At this stage, too, he was just able to avoid serious overcrowding by the use of the convalescent hulks in the harbour. These ships served a valuable purpose as they freed beds in the hospitals for

new arrivals. Unfortunately though, transports frequently arrived without warning and before space could be cleared for the casualties by the transfer of convalescents to the hulks. The casualties were nevertheless disembarked – a move that simply reinforced the picture of misery and chaos.

On October 18, at the height of the furore created by Russell's despatches, Smith wrote to Menzies telling him that if the reported shortages of lint, linen and medicines were correct, he should purchase them at once with funds made available to the British Ambassador in Constantinople. The Ambassador, Lord Stratford de Redcliffe (1786–1880), on the instruction of the Foreign Office, offered Menzies directly any financial assistance he might need. Menzies refused, saying the hospitals were perfectly well supplied and that, in any case, he was daily expecting additional stores from England and Varna. The next ship from England did not arrive until November 28, the same time as the Varna stores eventually reached Scutari. Menzies's refusal seems inexplicable though he may have been wary of this strange channel of communication and have seen himself having to pay the bill in the end. So, instead of accepting the offer he made a desperate plea to Admiral Boxer on November 5 to send to Varna for stores which, as we have seen, was successful. However, when the ship returned on November 21, for some reason she was not unloaded until the first week in December. By early November, too, Smith realized that his beds had either not yet left England or were on tour around the area and so he ordered another two thousand followed by four thousand more a month later – sufficient to bring the bed coverage up to 30 per cent – but they only arrived between February and May 1855 at a slower rate than the influx of casualties.

Thankfully the whole system started to become more human towards the end of 1854, largely due to the efforts of Sidney Herbert. The purveyor at Scutari (a Mr Wreford who had replaced Ward during October) was subordinated to the orders of the medical staff in everything concerned with the welfare of the sick, which meant that he could no longer be obstructive on financial grounds. Medicines could also be issued without the counter-signature of the medical superintendent. In December Smith's need to "send his purpose revolving in an orrery of official bodies" was brought to an end by order of the Secretary for War

and he was thus able to buy medical comforts direct from the contractor. He was soon after permitted to obtain his other medical supplies through the Commissariat Department which had been removed from Treasury control and placed under the War Office. Then on December 29 the Duke of Newcastle (1811–64 – the Secretary for War) ordered that two hundred tons of medical comforts and medicines should be sent, with priority, every fortnight until the middle of March; thus, after the end of January, Florence Nightingale's own stores were no longer needed (*see* Chapter 17). And finally the transport difficulties and delays were overcome by the creation of a Transport Board which took over the roles played by the Admiralty and the Ordnance Board.

In February 1855 the Hospital Commissioners submitted their report. Their recommendations for improving the administration at Scutari were put into effect without delay and as the war dragged on most of their other advice was acted upon. Then, on March 6, the Sanitary Commission descended upon the hospitals at Scutari; it had powers to act and under its guidance these hospitals – and later the others in the area – were brought up to thoroughly acceptable hygienic standards.

⚬❧⚬

In his despatch published on 13 October Russell had singled out the Army Medical Department for special attention: "It is found that the commonest appliances of a workhouse sick ward are wanting, and that the men must die through the medical staff of the British Army having forgotten that old rags are necessary for the dressing of wounds."

But Russell was painting only the side of the picture he saw. How did Smith view the situation from his desk in London in the light of all the actions he had taken in the earlier part of the year?

On October 20, 1854, just a week after this report was published, Smith received a letter from Hall in which he said he had been to Scutari and had "much satisfaction in being able to state that the whole hospital establishment has now been put on a very creditable footing, and that the sick are all doing as well as could possibly be expected."

Smith's perplexity was further increased when a letter arrived from

the dispenser at Scutari saying that the surgeons in charge of the wards were "willing to assert publicly that no one under their care suffered from want of any stores. I further emphatically say that an assertion that I had not a supply of lint, linen, bandages, dressings and necessary medicines sufficient for any emergency would be unfounded".

Smith himself saw no reason to doubt this letter. Why should he? "No-one", he later wrote to Hall in January, "can look over the long and full lists of medicines, medical comforts, etc. which have been sent to Scutari during the last six months without being convinced that there must be an ample supply at that station for the wants of the whole Army."

So where did the truth lie? A clue that it depended very much on attitude and experience comes in a letter written on January 1, 1855, by a young assistant surgeon, Edward Mason Wrench (1833–1912), from Balaclava: "Last week I had two letters from Scutari – the first was from a man who had not been out here [i.e. Balaclava], he described it as very uncomfortable, and a horrid place; the other was from Hervey Ludlow who has been out here and sent to Scutari invalided – he writes that it is a sort of Paradise compared to Balaclava."

The official record of events in the Crimea is enshrined in the painstakingly compiled records of the various Government commissions. Here again attitudes are in evidence, as when Mr Ward, the 67-year-old purveyor at Scutari, questioned there by the members of the Hospitals Commission in December, 1854, replied that though he had served through the whole of the Peninsular War "the patients never were nearly so comfortable as they are here... Even when we returned to our own country from Walcheren and Corunna the comforts they got were by no means equal to what we have here."

But in England, where a tide of humanitarianism was already on the flood, comparisons with the Napoleonic Wars were just as invalid as they would be today and Russell's message was falling on the ears of a people ready to listen. He may have been guilty of exaggeration and distortion; he may not have appreciated the difficulties created by outworn regulations that crippled initiative; but what he wrote came as the truth day after day to the breakfast tables of the nation.

17

CRIMEAN WAR II:
The nurses

The sick, like the poor, have always been with us and caring for them has been an integral part of existence. Yet the emergence of nursing as a highly trained profession began little more than a hundred-and-fifty years ago. In the middle of the 19th century, 'nursing' was in the hands of a pretty miscellaneous collection of women who between them looked after the physical and spiritual needs of the sick. They had in common their sex and a lack of special training for the work. They differed in their religious persuasions and in the fervour with which they tried to obtain converts – the sick patient was considered particularly susceptible to indoctrination; indeed the soul was often ministered to at the expense of treating the body. And be-devilling the entire structure of nursing, nurses and the nursed was social class.

The most remembered today was the professional nurse, whose shocking reputation for drunkenness, immorality, coarseness and bad language is not to be wondered at, considering that she often came from the lowest strata of Victorian society and had to work extremely long hours in depressing and deplorable conditions. She was personified by Sarah Gamp; yet despite Dickens's (1812–70) assurances in the later

editions of *Martin Chuzzlewit* that he had drawn Mrs Gamp from life, the paid nurse was not always so vile – her character suffered at the hands of reforming zealots. Florence Nightingale (1820–1910), a most astute observer, saw her other side (though admittedly she was referring to those who had passed the selection for service in the military hospitals of the Crimea). "Nurses" she wrote, "are careful, efficient, often decorous, and always kind, sometimes drunken, sometimes unchaste." And when at first this type of nurse disappeared from the hospital wards, the patients, particularly the men, felt they had lost a point of contact with their own familiar world outside.

Nursing in hospital was done by these professional nurses though their duties amounted to little more than a specialized form of domestic service; most of what today would be regarded as nursing responsibilities were carried out by the doctors and medical students. For instance, doctors would change dressings, apply poultices and give enemas – temperature, pulse, blood pressure and respiration charts and other aspects of modern nursing routine were in any case non-existent.

The hospital was the nurse's home. Her bed was usually in the ward with the women patients or in a cubby-hole off the men's ward, but sometimes she might sleep in the attic or basement. She could be on duty for twenty-four or even forty-eight hours at a stretch and would cook her meals in the ward kitchen. She learnt her job by carrying out the doctors' orders, but promotion rarely came her way. The ward sisters (not to be confused with the Sisters of religious orders – though the title did originate from this source) were usually better-class widows of respectable character whom circumstance had forced into earning a living. They were responsible for the running of their wards, for seeing that the nurses behaved themselves and that the doctors' instructions were carried out.

At the opposite pole to the professional nurses were the 'Ladies', the voluntary workers of good family who were usually inspired by Christian charity to help others less fortunate than themselves. In many instances their resolve was strengthened by a desperate need to break out from the monotonous seclusion of life in a Victorian home; virtually every other avenue of employment was closed to them if they wished to remain members of society. Mostly, their activities were restricted to visiting the

sick poor in their homes and supplying them with suitable comforts. Their nursing responsibilities rarely extended beyond soothing a fevered brow or smoothing a rumpled pillow – but in the days when nursing consisted of little more anyway, they had a valuable effect on morale. Florence Nightingale, however, deliberately excluded them from her Crimean party as she wanted only women who could give practical help. The second group of nurses, led by Mary Stanley, who left for the Crimea on December 2, 1854, was, however, of a different fibre and did contain Ladies.

In between the two extremes were the religious orders, Roman Catholic and Anglican, of varying degrees of strictness. They learnt their nursing by experience, so their effectiveness depended on that experience. These Sisters of Mercy or of Charity (they were known by a variety of names) visited and nursed the sick – usually the sick poor – in their homes, but sometimes they brought the patient back to their convent. As Florence Nightingale noted (again about those selected for service in military hospitals), "Sisters of Mercy, as regards ward service, are decorous and kind, and sometimes inefficient and prudish." Members of the Anglican orders were mostly daughters of middle-class families whose motives were much the same as those of the Ladies.

A rather confusing feature of mid-19th century English medicine is the inter-relationship between nursing, hospitals, the home and social class. Nobody, rich or poor, went into hospital if they could possibly avoid it. So long as there was someone to look after them at home, patients were more comfortable, better treated and certainly safer from the dangers of infection than they would be in hospital. The better-off could afford to employ nurses (of widely varying degrees of experience and ability) to help in caring for the sick person's needs. These nurses either lived in or visited as circumstances demanded. The poor helped themselves, though they might be fortunate in scraping a penny or two together for a visit from a nurse with charitable feelings towards someone of her own kind. They might also hope for a call from a Sister of Mercy who was either seeking a convert or simply wishing to give practical comfort as in the case of the Anglican Sellonites during the cholera epidemics of 1849 and 1852 in Plymouth. (They were the only members of Florence Nightingale's party to have had hands-on experience of this sort of nursing.)

Nevertheless the number of poor patients who received any sort of outside help was desperately small. They either died or got better naturally – though maybe with some lingering disability. But if they could not be cared for at home they would find themselves in hospital – or more likely the workhouse since at that time only about eight thousand hospital beds existed in the whole of England and Wales.

Nursing in the army was quite a different affair to nursing in civil life: it was self-contained and run on organized lines designed to meet military, rather than medical, needs. The nursing at the time of the Crimean War was done by male orderlies who were either convalescent patients, pensioners or soldiers temporarily posted by their commanding officers; thus for the most part they were a shifting, untrained population lacking any motivation. Military nursing was a necessary evil to be accomplished with as little disruption to military order as was possible. Practices did, nevertheless, vary in other countries, notably Roman Catholic ones, which helps to explain why the French were able to call on their Sisters of Charity for service in the Crimea.

In British eyes, the army was fully capable of looking after its own. There was no question of outside nursing assistance and, in any case, the quality of such assistance would, in most people's opinion, have made it a positive liability. Under the circumstances, Florence Nightingale's reception at Scutari was surprisingly favourable.

The stumbling block to nursing, both civilian and military, was its centuries-old position as a kind of domestic service – sometimes noble, but for long periods a hateful drudge. Strangely, perhaps, the fortunes of nursing were only loosely linked to those of medicine; the dominating influence was religion, an influence that had in no way abated by the mid-19th century.

For the first fifteen hundred years of the Christian era, nursing had leant heavily on the monasteries. Unfortunately very little is known about nursing in monastic communities except that it was practised more with Christian charity than with a knowledge of medicine. But if proof is needed that nursing was a religious occupation it is given by the effects of the Reformation and the dissolution of the monasteries in the late 1530s in England.

The dissolution of the monasteries marked the end of any passable system of nursing for the best part of three hundred years. Conditions deteriorated as callousness and even brutality entered the scene, and it was the sick poor who suffered most. The philanthropy of the rich no longer had a materially identifiable object, though ladies continued to visit the poor as they had been doing since Greek and Roman times. The few lay hospitals that were left could in no way meet the need, added to which their religious nursing Sisters were expelled, though the old monastic titles of Matron (in charge of the nurses) and Sister (in charge of the wards) were retained. In England there was no such thing as a 'nursing class' and in consequence hospitals had to take what they could get – and that amounted to servants prepared to do unpleasant tasks in unpleasant surroundings. The Protestant Church was not imbued with the same sense of responsibility towards the sick as was the Catholic, and once nursing was dissociated from religion it lost its social standing.

Nursing was thus effectively destroyed and nothing was done to restore it. Women, in general, were subject to a masculine society, their education was neglected, and they were no longer permitted the freedom they had enjoyed in the past – the proper place for a respectable woman was in the home. The mere suggestion of a career was unthinkable. The propriety of nursing, even as Christian charity, had been forgotten. Women took up 'nursing' only when they saw no other way to survive.

The Continent did not suffer as badly at the Reformation as did England. The hospital system was stronger and the nursing orders were determined to carry on – with varying degrees of success. However, there were abuses and to combat these the Sisters of Charity were, in 1633, born through the inspiration of the great social reformer, Vincent de Paul (*c.*1580–1660), and his devoted follower, Louise le Gras (1591–1660). The Sisters came from humble backgrounds all over France; they were subject to no vows or regulations since the institution was not religious in the monastic sense, though Vincent did emphasize that their calling was sacred. He appreciated that a monastic life with its religious observances was in conflict with the demands of nursing, particularly in people's homes. The Sisters of Charity passed through the Dark Age of nursing, from the 17th century to the middle of the 19th, like a shining light.

Never before this period nor since were conditions in civil hospitals so bad – open windows and ventilation were anathema; damp seeped in, walls were mildewed and fungous growth sprouted in corners; cockroaches and bugs flourished; the patients were filthy and crawling with vermin; dirt was everywhere and with it the germs of disease which spread feverishly from malnourished patient to malnourished patient. The 'nurses' were supposed to scrub and do the laundry, to empty spittoons, close-stools (commodes) and bedpans but without an adequate sanitary system effort was pointless. Nursing care just did not exist.

Reaction, when it came, was slow moving. The way was prepared by poor-law reform and by the developing revolution in public health and hygiene which began in the 1830s and continued for the best part of Queen Victoria's (1819-1901) reign. The slums of industrial towns were festering sores where epidemics spread like wildfire; the morbidity and mortality rates throughout the country thoroughly alarmed the authorities and forced them into acting on the reports produced by the philanthropists.

The welfare of the individual sick person, however, took second place to the public health and despite scattered attempts to improve matters it took the Crimean War and the energy of Florence Nightingale to get nursing reform off the ground. Previous ventures were mostly overtly religious – if not to start with, they had become so. The early ones had been Roman Catholic and strongly influenced by the French model; for example, the Sisters of Mercy founded by Catherine McAuley (1788–1873). This order was originally intended to give a home to destitute girls but in 1830 it concentrated on nursing; the Bermondsey branch, opened in 1839, provided five extremely able nuns for Florence Nightingale's party.

The first Protestant nursing order to appear in England was founded in 1840 by Mrs Elizabeth Gurney Fry (1780–1845). It was known as the Protestant Sisters of Mercy or the Nursing Sisters, and for the first time training of a sort was given – though to say that it approached the Nightingale concept would be an overstatement; nevertheless it was a firm step in the right direction. The order was the first to be approached by Florence Nightingale when forming her party for Scutari, but its Lady Superintendent refused to comply with the conditions laid down by the Government.

In 1845 the Park Village Community (whose members were also known as Sisters of Mercy) was founded by the Rev. Edward Pusey's (1800–82) High Church movement. This was followed in 1848 by the Sellonite Sisters of Mercy and by St John's House, Westminster, another High Church sisterhood which sent six of its members with the Nightingale party. Others including the Protestant Institution for Nurses in Devonshire Square – they refused to allow any of their members to work outside their own control – were formed soon after. The thin end of the wedge had thus been inserted into Victorian society: nursing was on the verge of becoming respectable, even though it was still regarded more as an act of charity and religious devotion than as the physical care of a sick body. Moreover, despite these nursing orders being sponsored by the Church of England there was a constant suspicion that they were sailing under false colours – a suspicion that in many cases, both individual and collective, proved to be true. The Catholic tradition in nursing was strong.

So, when public opinion demanded that nurses be sent to the Crimea the nation found that it did possess a varied assortment to choose from, but mostly they were women living an other-worldly existence doing work that ill-prepared them for the real task of nursing they would meet at Scutari. Their response, nevertheless, was immediate:

"Many was the band that was that week organized for the work;" wrote Frances Magdalene Taylor, a Lady Volunteer, who went out in Mary Stanley's party, "many were the individuals who in their secluded homes determined to offer their services for this purpose, and applied for information and permission to the official authorities." But it was a fluttering movement lacking direction and leadership. Had these Sisters and Lady Volunteers ventured as such to the Crimea, they would have received short shrift from the military and been packed off home on the next boat. What was missing was an administrative genius capable of welding a motley collection of women into an effective unit with a single purpose – a leader with strength enough to subdue their religious fervour and differences, to control the behaviour of the professional nurses, and with influence in high places to ride through governmental red tape. The genius was there, standing in the wings, well rehearsed and simply awaiting her cue.

By any standard the 34-year-old Florence Nightingale was a remarkable woman. She had an assured command of both people and events and she moved in the upper reaches of Victorian society, travelling extensively on the Continent and numbering among her friends Elizabeth Barrett Browning (1806–61), George Eliot (1819–80), Lord Shaftesbury (1801–85), Lord Palmerston (1784–1865) and Sidney Herbert (whom she first met in Rome in 1847). Yet for ten years she had been struggling to free herself from the entangling web of that society. For ten years she had known that her purpose in life was to reform nursing and to ensure that those who nursed were properly trained for the responsibility. For ten years, despite strong family disapproval and social disbelief, she had prepared herself for the moment when the world would listen to her – the moment that came with the calamity of the Crimea. She visited hospitals and nursing orders on the Continent, studying their administration, watching operations, all the while compulsively taking notes and drawing comparisons. She obtained a multitude of public health and hospital reports and filled notebook after notebook with comment and observation; she was sent private reports on hospitals from friends in Paris and Berlin; eventually, thanks largely to her social connections, she was recognized for what she had made herself: the leading expert on hospitals and sanitary conditions in Europe. Then in the spring of 1854 she began to visit hospitals in England with the express purpose of gathering ammunition for her campaign to reform the terrible working conditions of nurses. In this she had the unqualified support of Sidney Herbert who was himself seeking reliable information about the bad pay and worse lodging of nurses in an attempt to focus public opinion on the evils. Both were fighting an uphill battle as public opinion accepted the status quo and in any event could not see how change could come about.

But then came Russell's despatches. After the first, describing the plight of the wounded after the battle of the Alma on September 20, which was published in *The Times* on October 9, Florence Nightingale acted. She gathered a small party of about half-a-dozen professional nurses and, with herself in charge, was prepared to sail on the 17th. On the 12th she had seen Lord Palmerston who had given her expedition his approval. On the 13th she had visited Dr Andrew Smith who, in his usual rough

manner, had informed her that all was well in Scutari and, in answer to her question about what she should take with her, had assured her that nothing was needed (all of which he believed to be true). He did, however, give her a letter of introduction to Dr Duncan Menzies, the medical superintendent at the Scutari General Hospital.

But, on the 15th Sidney Herbert, the Secretary at War, wrote to her officially asking her to take a party out to Scutari. This put an entirely different complexion on the matter, particularly as Herbert suggested increasing the number of nurses to at least forty. The old plan was scrapped, but as Florence Nightingale wanted to leave within a week, the new party had to be assembled without delay. A headquarters was therefore established at the Herberts' London home at 49 Belgrave Square. Here, a committee consisting of Miss Mary Stanley (sister of Arthur Stanley, Dean of Westminster), Mrs Charles Bracebridge (*d.*1874), Lady Charlotte Canning (1817–61) and Lady Laura Cranworth began to interview applicants – a task that slowly dampened their original enthusiasm. Out of some sixty or seventy hopefuls only eleven were considered to have had sufficient experience of nursing in hospital and even they were not of the best calibre – only one gave a reason other than money for wanting to be included in the party. The number of these professional nurses was made up to fourteen by the addition of three from the aborted expedition.

The uniforms issued to these nurses were hastily made and mostly fitted where they touched. They were also hideously unattractive, consisting of a grey tweed dress, a grey worsted jacket, a short woollen cloak, and a white cap. Round the shoulders a holland scarf was worn with the words 'Scutari Hospital' embroidered on it in red. This uniform did, however, succeed in its primary objective which was to identify the wearer as a nurse and so save her from the unwelcome attentions of the troops. The nuns and Sisters in the party were spared the charade and were allowed to wear their own habit or uniform dress.

While the committee was sifting the professionals, Florence Nightingale was going the rounds of the institutions and communities in London. From these she collected ten Roman Catholic nuns (five from the convent in Bermondsey and five from the orphanage in Norwood)

and six Sisters from St John's House – although the Master took two days to agree to Miss Nightingale's terms. Towards the middle of the week Miss Priscilla Lydia Sellon (1821–76) came forward with the offer of some of her own Sisters and the services of eight were accepted even though this meant sending to Devon for four of them. The party was completed by Selina Bracebridge, who was in charge of the domestic side, and by Charles (*d.*1872), her husband, who saw to the financial and travelling arrangements. Florence Nightingale herself was in charge and on the 19th she received formal Cabinet confirmation of her appointment as Superintendent of the Female Nursing Establishment of the English General Hospitals in Turkey. This grandiose title makes it plain that she was going to Scutari not as a practising nurse but, as she wished, as an administrator. The Commander in the Field, Lord Raglan, was informed of her impending arrival as was Dr John Hall, the Inspector General in the Crimean area, and the Purveyor-in-Chief. Smith wrote personally to Menzies with instructions that every help should be afforded to Miss Nightingale and her nurses. It was the Director General's wish that the medical officers "should use every endeavour to render the nurses useful in their position". Although Sidney Herbert believed that there were sufficient doctors and supplies at Scutari, he was uneasy about the reports he was receiving and he warned Florence Nightingale that he was immediately sending out a commission to look into the state of the hospitals and the condition of the sick and wounded. This was the Hospitals Commission – made up of Benson Maxwell, a barrister, and Drs A. Cumming and P. Sinclair Laing. The purpose of the Commission was solely to establish the facts, not to take any action.

After the Nightingale party had left for Scutari, Mary Stanley continued to recruit – but with an ulterior motive. In the privacy of her heart she had become a Roman Catholic (she made this public knowledge when she was received into the Catholic church in the spring of 1855) and, probably out of jealousy, she wished to establish Catholic dominance in the Turkish hospitals. By sheer determination and force of personality, Florence Nightingale had succeeded in getting together a group of women who agreed to abide by her orders in all matters relating to the hospital, to attend primarily to the bodily needs of their patients, and never to

introduce religious subjects except with patients of their own faith. Mary Stanley's venture came close to wrecking all this.

The Stanley party, which arrived in Scutari on December 15, consisted of fifteen Roman Catholic nuns, nine Lady Volunteers, and twenty-two nurses. The nuns recognized the authority only of their Mother Superior and were chiefly concerned with gaining souls. The Ladies, for the most part, resented having to perform menial tasks and believed that they should be waited on by the nurses. And the professional nurses were representative of the worst of their kind – drunken, coarse, promiscuous and useless.

The religious dissension stirred up by these new arrivals in what had hitherto been an atmosphere of almost miraculous harmony was quite shameful. For Florence Nightingale, though, already facing a challenge to her authority as a result of the actions of one her Sisters and coping with a medical disaster that had still to reach its height, this new disruptive influence could well have been the breaking point. But her courage and determination brought her triumphantly through.

Although women continued to come out to the Crimean theatre, the original party were the only nurses to work through the whole winter and to see order brought out of the most appalling chaos. They were something very special – and Florence Nightingale realized this. "Our own old party," she wrote to her sister, "which began its work in hardship, toil, struggle and obscurity has done better than any other... The small beginning, the simple hardship, the silent and gradual struggle upwards; these are the climate in which an enterprise really thrives and grows."

18

CRIMEAN WAR III:
Hospital organization and administration

Despite their own undoubted deficiencies, the hospitals at Scutari would almost certainly have been able to cope (according to early 19th-century standards) had the rot not already set in at the front. Their staff inherited the consequences of disaster elsewhere, but instead of meeting the crisis as a challenge, they stubbornly played the game according to the regulations. Nevertheless they were not alone in this, as the response of virtually everyone in authority in the whole theatre of war was obtuse beyond belief. It was not conflict with the Russian enemy that so nearly destroyed the British army; it was disease: cholera, dysentery, typhus, scurvy, gangrene and the aggravation of cold, exposure and malnutrition. Infectious diseases, the curse of armies for centuries were still mysterious unknown quantities, and without a knowledge of their cause, control was a haphazard business. Although sanitation and hygiene were acquiring an aura of respectability, the reasons were charitable and empirical; thus they were easily ignored in conditions where rigid enforcement held the sole hope of salvation. The discovery of bacteria lay only a decade in the future, but it might just as well have been a million years.

Disease was nothing new to the army, so why were the pressures on the hospitals not anticipated by the medical administration?

The answers lie in the management by the Commander-in-Chief, Lord Raglan, of his troops and of their medical support which precipitated the situation, and in the out-of-date medical organization that had to deal with the consequences. Moreover, the fact that the Army Medical Department was, as it had always been, a civilian department did not improve matters, as it and its staff were devoid of military authority. (Not until 1898 did the Department become the Royal Army Medical Corps with officers and men having substantive military rank.) Its administration, too, was hopeless: when the Department had come into being with the creation of the Standing Army in 1660, it was separated into two branches, staff and regimental, each working within its own special compartment, and each with its own sphere of responsibilities with the result that the seeds of administrative chaos were present from the very start. Nevertheless, at its origin the system did what was required of it passably well, but by the middle of Queen Victoria's reign it was suffering from severe hardening of the arteries. An example of this is Staff Surgeon First Class Duncan Menzies's predicament.

When, in April 1854, the British army was gathering at Scutari there was no thought of establishing a military general hospital (a staff responsibility). The regimental surgeons simply moved into the large Turkish military hospital (by agreement) where each ran his own regimental hospital with Menzies acting as the co-ordinating staff officer. At the end of April, Menzies realized that the formation of a general hospital would be inevitable so he wrote to Dr Andrew Smith, Director General of the Army Medical Department, asking for the regulations governing general hospitals. Smith, in London, replied that there were none. As he wrote later:

"The untoward position in which I found myself, led me immediately to require the records of the Department to be searched, in the hope that they might, by supplying information in reference to the events which were observed, and the wants that arose during the campaign in Spain and Portugal, afford what under existing circumstances was so greatly needed. The search however proved unproductive, as only two or three valueless documents were found."

To have no regulations or orders to follow – not even ones applicable to the Peninsular War – was a catastrophe in itself. Small wonder then that, when the regimental hospitals moved out of the building in early June and Menzies became the medical superintendent of what had suddenly become a general hospital, he followed so far as he could the only rules available to him – those for regimental hospitals. However, the administration and the functions of the two styles of hospital varied considerably. In consequence, people were playing one game according to the rules of another, and if someone chose to be bloody-minded (as usually happened) he could obstruct the whole field of play. The situation at Scutari and the trials and tribulations to be endured can thus be better understood if we know a little about the various rules and how they came into existence.

⚬❦⚬

But first, a fundamental aspect of the military mind should be appreciated. War was a game full of complex rituals, played according to certain well-defined rules, and any change was vigorously resisted. This attitude was acceptable when war was a small, almost tribal, affair, but it was responsible for many catastrophic incidents (of which the Crimea is one of the best known) when war outgrew its childhood. Part and parcel of the attitude was the view that the military machine was all-powerful and that anything that interrupted play was a nuisance – and among the greatest nuisances were the sick and wounded, together with those who tried to help them. The Surgeon-in-Chief of the French Grande Armée, Pierre François Percy (1754–1825), for instance, was driven to remark in 1799: "What administration! To see the indifference, the lethargy of all those at the head of affairs. When one speaks to them about the hospitals, one would believe that the sick and wounded cease to be men when they can no longer be soldiers." It was a state of mind that knew no frontiers. Indeed, with few exceptions, such as the Roman army and the British army under Marlborough (1650–1722), the value to an army's morale of a good medical service passed unappreciated throughout history until the 20th century – the concept of morale was in any case ill-formed.

The Army Medical Department, under its Director General, had absolute control over its staff officers, but was responsible for the regimental surgeons only insofar as their professional standards and conduct were concerned. For the rest, these surgeons were entirely under the military discipline of their commanding officers; they, in fact, held commissions in their regiments and wore the regimental uniform.

The staff medical officers were inspector generals, deputy inspector generals and staff surgeons; their duties were a mixture of the administrative (particularly in the senior two ranks) and the medical. The staff surgeons usually served in garrison or general hospitals, but when in the field they were employed at brigade, or sometimes divisional, level. Like the Department itself, staff officers were all civilians, though in 1841 the staff surgeon first class had been given the equivalent rank of major and the staff surgeon second class that of captain – but this was an empty gesture on the part of the Commander-in-Chief as the ranks still carried no military authority. A staff surgeon might be superintendent of a hospital but he had to have a field officer (who might be of lower rank) in overall command to maintain discipline. Assisting the staff surgeons in hospitals were staff assistant surgeons.

However, the heart of the army's medical organization was the regimental surgeon who, at the time of the Crimea, had two regimental assistant surgeons under him. Medically the regiment looked after its own; it carried with it the paraphernalia for setting up a regimental hospital, including a marquee for occasions when no suitable building could be found, beds, bedding, ward utensils such as urinals and bed pans, dressings and a large chest containing six months' supply of medicines. Transport for all this was a regimental responsibility. For the sake of convenience and mutual support a number of regimental hospitals would sometimes come together as a brigade hospital, as happened at Scutari before the army moved on to Varna.

Regulations governing regimental hospitals began to appear around 1770. Most dealt with matters of conduct, rations and pay while a soldier was ill, but one was to be the cause of considerable misery at Scutari: every man had to bring with him into the hospital his knapsack containing a clean shirt, a hairbrush and comb, eating utensils and other necessaries.

The disregard for the realities of warfare was sublime. Admittedly there was provision for clothing and anything else the sick man might require to be properly brought in, but this had no relevance whatsoever in the Crimean situation. On arrival at Scutari virtually no one had a knapsack (they had been abandoned on Lord Raglan's orders when the army landed at Kalamita bay) but as the regulations decreed that they did have their knapsacks, in the eyes of authority they all did have them, and there were no rules whereby the deficiencies could be made good.

The staffing of the regimental hospitals was again a regimental concern; medical orderlies and non-medical personnel such as cooks, ward-masters, storemen, office staff and so forth were detailed by the commanding officer; the band provided the stretcher-bearers. Soldiers' wives who followed the regiment were at first encouraged to undertake nursing duties and to do the cooking and washing, but gradually they were edged out until by 1832 they were no longer employed in any capacity. Although none of the soldier orderlies had special training, the system worked reasonably well (by 18th-century standards); indeed many orderlies had long experience and performed their tasks admirably. Convalescent patients also helped. Nevertheless, Florence Nightingale tactfully drew attention to one of the serious defects in the system: the lack of training of *all* those who nursed the sick and wounded.

One other rule, which was workable so long as the system continued to function as the administration intended but was a the cause of friction at Scutari, concerned food and the paying for it. When a soldier was a patient in his regimental hospital, his basic ration was drawn by his Company; other items he might need were bought by the hospital sergeant out of stoppages levied on the patient's pay.

Thus, during peacetime the regimental hospital system could fulfil its obligations which amounted to being self-contained and not bothering anyone else. But during a war, the situation changed, a fact that was appreciated, however reluctantly, by the authorities who formed general hospitals that would accompany the army overseas to give support after battle and to hold the long-term sick when the regiment was on the move – they were established in existing hospitals or, in the early period, in large buildings.

❧

In 1690 when staff hospitals first appeared they were of two sorts: the fixed hospital which developed into the general hospital, and the marching hospital which developed into the flying hospital. The marching hospital was, as its name implies, reasonably mobile and had its own tentage and transport wagons. Its function was to act as a casualty clearing station between the regimental hospital and the fixed hospital; it was an invaluable part of the system since it meant that there were clear administrative and transport links between front and rear. Flying hospitals were, however, perversely done away with during the Peninsular War (their transport wagons littered the roads); instead, the staff surgeon who was acting as senior medical officer to the brigade had to apply to the Commissary General for transport to evacuate the sick and wounded. The consequence, so far as the Crimean War was concerned, was a great administrative divide between the regiments at the front and the general hospital at Scutari.

The general hospital, which today is an indispensable part of casualty evacuation and treatment, has had an extremely chequered career; in fact, so many have been the low points that it is impossible to choose the lowest, but certainly the state at the beginning of the Crimean campaign is a strong contender. In contrast to the regimental hospitals, general hospitals were unpopular with all concerned: with the casualties because they were removed from friends and a familiar environment; with commanding officers because the men were lost to them for an excessive length of time; and with many senior doctors for a variety of reasons, both administrative and medical. But overshadowing all these reasons was the terrible fear of infection; even in those days it was known that when men were crowded together infectious diseases spread like wildfire and a particularly vicious form of wound infection known as hospital gangrene was an ever-present menace. This was nothing either new or peculiar to British military hospitals; during Napoleon's campaign of 1813, the hospitals from Dresden to the Rhine and beyond were quite justifiably called the sepulchres of the Grande Armée.

In wartime, general hospitals were accepted as a necessary evil but in

peacetime their number was reduced to absurd levels. Indeed for a long while no arrangements were made in Britain for dealing with the sick returning from overseas. The Transport Commissioners were responsible for them so long as they were being transported, but what happened to them after they were landed was no one's concern. Their plight was pitiful and a shame to the country. Relief of a sort came only in 1781 when the first general military hospital was opened in England. Nevertheless between 1802 and 1806 the general hospitals at Gosport, Plymouth and Deal had been closed by the surgical member of the Army Medical Board on grounds of economy – when it was found that it cost 17d a day to keep a man in a general hospital, but only 10d in a regimental hospital, the fate of the general hospital was sealed.

So, in 1809 some six thousand sick and wounded arrived in Portsmouth from Corunna to find not a single hospital ready for them. Only the prompt improvisation of Dr James McGrigor (1771–1858), the local inspector of hospitals, saved the situation from complete disaster, but even so probably a thousand men died unnecessarily before the three general hospitals were reopened. Then in the years of peace after Waterloo the Government turned the economic screw and the Army Medical Department was squeezed to the bone. General hospitals were cut back again so that apart from two of minor importance, there was only Fort Pitt at Chatham to cater for the troops invalided home from garrisons overseas. McGrigor, who became Director General in 1815 and held the post until 1851 (he was knighted in 1831), was not unduly upset by this, despite his previous experience, since he was a staunch believer in the regimental system. The net result was that by the time war was declared in the Crimea, no general hospital had been established for forty years and indeed any thought that one might be needed – certainly in Europe – had been regarded as faintly ridiculous.

❧

Female nurses had been employed in military general hospitals until the early 19th century and had featured prominently in all major campaigns. However, the provision of other subordinate staff such as

medical orderlies, cooks, clerks and remaining non-medical personnel fell to the lot of the units in the field – and this was a disaster. Not surprisingly, human nature being what it is, the commanding officers seized on the opportunity to offload their more difficult and undesirable characters with the result that ill-discipline, drunkenness and thieving were the rule.

The administration of the few general hospitals that did exist was in little better state and did nothing to enhance their reputation. The military commandants could be posted elsewhere at a moment's notice, so there was lack of continuity at the top. Added to this they disliked the job and were invariably ignorant of hospital organization and administration, so there also inefficiency and lack of enthusiasm. The absence of a firm administrative hand was sorely felt at Scutari. Nevertheless, so far as the hospital inmates were concerned, the greatest deficiencies were in food, clothing, medicines and dressings, the responsibilities of the purveyors and apothecaries.

The purveyors' original task had been to distribute food to the sick and wounded, but they soon gained responsibility for contracting for supplies and for cooking the food. Later, in 1795, they were given the jobs of finding accommodation for the hospital and of providing beds, bedding, ward furniture and lighting. Theirs, too, was the responsibility of finding subordinate staff either by requesting headquarters to detail men from the regiments or by recruiting them from civilian sources. Purveyors were at first drawn from staff and regimental surgeons, but with the start of the Peninsular War this practice ceased as qualified men were in short supply and urgently needed for medical duties; the purveyors' clerks became the purveyors. During this war they became responsible for the arms, accoutrements, clothing and other necessaries of the patients; the rations, medical comforts and other stores they obtained through the Commissariat Department – or if this proved impracticable, by local requisitioning. The cost of items the patients needed in hospital was paid to the Medical Department by the regiment from stoppages in the soldiers' pay.

Later, after the war, most of the stores had to be obtained by the Ordnance Department before being transferred to the purveyor. But the

next event was to have the most profound repercussions at Scutari: the Accountant's Branch of the Medical Department was closed for reasons of economy and its responsibilities taken over by the Secretary at War. As a result the purveyors thought that they were now answerable to the War Office and not to the Director General. So, when Dr Menzies was trying to establish a general hospital at Scutari he could get no co-operation from the purveyor (whose responsibilities in this respect were enormous, both as regards finance and supplies); Mr Ward said that he either made decisions on his own or referred matters to the War Office.

But hospital duties were not the end of the purveyor's responsibilities. In 1827, McGrigor, the then Director General, had laid down that during the evacuation of casualties the purveyor was responsible for the hospital equipment carried on transport ships, and also for the cleanliness, ventilation and general equipping of the vessels. When the casualties were landed, he had a duty to see that medical comforts, supplies of food and cooking utensils were carried on the wagons and that stretcher-bearers were available to carry the wounded into hospital. Yet three years later, such was the rundown of the Army Medical Department that the office of purveyor had become obsolete. Consequently in 1854 veterans of the Peninsular War had to be brought out of retirement to perform a most formidable and demanding job, the existence of which, officially at any rate, was in limbo. Hence the elderly Mr Ward at Scutari and hence an explanation for the inflexibility in the hospital management.

The apothecaries, as the name indicates, had charge of the medicines, dressings and instruments in a general hospital; and, like the hospital itself, they faded away after Waterloo until in 1830 they were no longer needed. The Army Medical Department became responsible for assessing the quantity of drugs and dressings required and from 1842 had obtained half the supply from the Society of Apothecaries in London and half from two commercial firms – an arrangement that worked perfectly satisfactorily. However, in October 1854 the appointment of apothecary was resurrected and qualified medical officers were given the equivalent rank of lieutenant. The apothecary appointed to Scutari was Dr Reade, and when he died on November 25 of the same year, it was found that he had kept no accounts or records.

Finally, adding to all these fertile sources of inefficiency was the telegraph. Previously, once an expedition with its equipment and surgical staff for a general hospital had left England, its principal medical officer took full administrative control — no other course was possible — and replacement medical officers and supplies were despatched on request or as London felt was necessary. But thanks to the telegraph the Crimea was no longer remote; the Director General retained command of a medical service whose reported misfortunes left him utterly bewildered. The seeds of administrative chaos, germinating over many years, certainly came into full flower in the first winter of the Crimean War.

❧

The nature of the hospital buildings at Scutari was responsible for some of the problems facing both doctors and nurses. In a nutshell these were caused by the vast size of the buildings (despite which they became desperately overcrowded), their appalling latrines, and the dilapidation and unsuitability of the barracks for use as a hospital.

The General Hospital, Scutari. *(Mansell Collection.)*

The General Hospital had originally been a Turkish military hospital and, with one formidable drawback, not too bad a one at that: spacious and well ventilated, with an adequate water supply, bathing facilities, and stoves in the wards. There were beds for six hundred and sixty patients in the wards with perfectly adequate overflow accommodation for another four hundred and twenty-six in the corridors. The drawback was the nature of the latrines; these were of the Turkish squatting variety with drains discharging straight into the sea, with no intervening water traps and no flushing system. There was nothing to stop the smell wafting back into the wards and an on-shore breeze was distinctly unwelcome. Since 'polluted air' was believed to be responsible for the transmission of disease, the soldiers threw any rubbish they could find into the drains in the vain hope of blocking the stink. Fatigue parties were ordered to clear the mess but they fought a losing battle. The engineers were called in to help, but they could do nothing to improve matters since the drains were deeply embedded in the fabric of the building. Only in the spring of 1855 after the Sanitary Commission had arrived were new flush lavatories installed and the sewage outflows water-trapped.

Another disturbing feature of the hospital environment was the closeness of the burial grounds. Apart from the demoralizing effect of this, the Turks buried the dead neither deeply nor securely with the result that still more noxious odours drifted into the hospital when the wind was in the south.

The Barrack Hospital was a different story. The Sultan Seline Barracks had been built as barracks and were commandeered as a depot when the British army began to concentrate at Scutari for the forthcoming campaign. They were taken over as a (general) hospital in September 1854 with Staff Surgeon First Class McGrigor (no relation to Sir James McGrigor) as superintendent – but once a barracks, always a barracks unless expensive modifications are undertaken. The building was immense, on two and three floors set around a central parade ground. It would have been a hospital administrator's nightmare in the best of circumstances. Parts of it were in a shocking state of disrepair; the latrines were of the same style as those in the General Hospital but with worse problems as, after heavy rain, they were prone to flood back into the

The Barrack Hospital, Scutari. *(Mansell Collection.)*

wards. Men in the last stages of bowel diseases had neither the will nor the inclination to paddle across the floor through an inch of sewage to reach the latrine, so they did not. The water supply was sufficient in quantity but was not laid on in the wards and could only be drawn at two or three places – on one occasion the water was found to be filtering through the carcase of a horse. And there was no operating theatre, for which reason the hospital was originally intended only for the sick – when wounded in need of surgery began arriving, they were operated on where they lay in the wards and corridors.

The parts of the building that were usable from the start gave adequate space for about one thousand and sixty-five beds in both wards and the inner corridors that overlooked the parade ground. However, the beds in the wards were Turkish divans – low wooden shelves set around the walls. Besides complicating the problems of nursing, these were extremely difficult to clean and harboured rats. When, in November 1854, the sick and wounded descended in a flood on Scutari, Menzies was compelled to open the dilapidated parts of the buildings as well.

Although the barracks had become a hospital, they still retained some of the functions of a depot. Reinforcements on their way to the Crimea were quartered there, and the wives and children left behind lived in some of the rooms in squalid, filthy conditions. These women and soldiers heaped yet more problems on Menzies's plate as they were usually drunk

and noisy and could not be kept from the wards. Mercifully, though, the departing regiments had left behind more than a hundred sick in the General Hospital with orderlies, cooks, store-keepers and others to look after them. Although these men formed the nucleus of Menzies's subordinate staff, the blessing was decidedly mixed since the regiments had inevitably left their worst behind. The military commandant of the hospital was a Major Sillery (the same rank as Staff Surgeon First Class Menzies) who was not renowned for the exercise of initiative when the going grew tough.

cXWo

Estimates of the number of casualties in the Crimea vary widely, nevertheless those for the month of January, 1855, indicate the size of the medical disaster when it was at its height. Out of an army of 30 000 men, 11 328 were admitted to hospital; of these 3168 died. These figures include only 119 wounded. On average 26·8 per cent of the army's strength was sick during each month of that winter; the next year between October 1855 and March 1856 it was 3·6 per cent which was lower than the rate for troops in the United Kingdom. By the spring of 1855 Scutari had been transformed and the death rate had fallen from the 36 per cent level of January to 5·2 percent in May.

Dramatic though these figures are, they do not reveal the full extent of Florence Nightingale's accomplishment: this comes in a comparison with the medical services of the other armies and what they managed to achieve.

The French system centred around the Divisional Ambulance in the field (the equivalent of the British flying hospital so lamentably missing since the Peninsular War). Their regimental medical service was little more than a first-aid post which treated only those casualties exempted from duty for a day or two. The more seriously wounded and ill were evacuated to the Divisional Ambulance where those likely to recover in a matter of weeks were retained, while the rest were sent back to the general hospitals at base (in this case Constantinople). The French Sisters of Charity were not allowed in the Divisional Ambulances because, so it was rumoured, of the corruption of the French Intendance upon whom the Sisters quietly

exercised a most unwelcome surveillance. (The Intendance was the civilian administration in charge of the medical services. Its corruption was legendary and during the Napoleonic wars it had been in constant conflict with the medical officers who were then, as in the Crimea, completely under its thumb.) The Sisters served in the French general hospitals in Constantinople where, apparently, they did all the cooking for the officers and that of the extras for the men. Florence Nightingale observed that they seemed more like 'consolatrices' in the wards, but with admirable housekeeping qualities. They did, however, have some nursing duties as is shown by their visiting her at Scutari to see how she coped with bedsores (a curse in all the hospitals) and to borrow air pillows and water beds.

The Russian system of nursing seemed, to Florence Nightingale, by far the best she had known and to be the only perfectly organized system in the Crimean War. A Sister had charge of everything relating to the bedside care of the patient; she received her orders from the medical officer, attending him on his rounds and conferring with him afterwards. She was even responsible for the 'felchers' or dressers, and for the orderlies so far as their bedside conduct and duties were concerned. Away from the bedside, the felchers were under a senior felcher who in turn was under a medical officer; and in all that pertained to discipline, clothing, meals and so forth, the orderlies were under the control of a non-commissioned officer.

The 'nurses' were of two sorts: there were the Sisters of the Elevation of the Cross who were generally widows of officers, though a few were Sisters of Charity. They had been formed by the Grand Duchess Helena Pavlovna and placed by her under the orders of the famous civilian surgeon Nikolai Ivanovich Pirogoff (1810–81), to whom had been given supreme surgical command in Sebastopol. Under these Sisters were the female nurses who were usually wives or widows of soldiers.

Completely distinct from the sisters and nurses were the 'Frauen des Barmherzigen Wittwen Instituts'. These Widows, roughly equivalent to the English 'Ladies', had been instituted some forty years previously by Mary of Wurttemberg (1759–1828), for many years the venerated Empress-Mother. Florence Nightingale thought it possible that the pressures of war rendered their services rather nondescript as they were neither Sisters nor nurses, and perhaps, as she waggishly remarked,

because they did not come under his orders, Professor Pirogoff had not a good word to say for them.

This, then, was the quality of the other two important medical services. Yet the Crimean War was a significantly greater medical disaster for their armies than it was for the British. The death rates per thousand from disease were: British, 119·3; French, 253·5 (the highest in history); Russians, 161·3. The Russians, who had twice as many killed and wounded as the allies put together, suffered terribly from infected wounds and hospital gangrene raged through their wards. Pirogoff knew that segregating the patients would help stem the epidemic but he could not shift authority and so antagonized the government with his criticisms that he was compelled to resign his professorship at St Petersburg. More than 14 000 Russians died of their wounds, compared with 1800 British and 4300 French.

However, the change that Florence Nightingale brought about is strikingly illuminated by comparing the figures for deaths from disease (excluding cholera) in 1854 and 1856. In 1854 there were 2373 British who died and 1857 French. In 1856 the figures were 17 129 French (an alarming number that was in part accounted for by a severe epidemic of typhus (a louse-borne disease that typically occurs in overcrowded, unhygienic conditions) and only 218 British.

⚬�khжⲟ

Looking back from our privileged position, there was a terrible inevitability about the whole Crimean episode. So many different threads were being drawn to a close. In particular the fluctuating story of nursing care and the evolution of the Army Medical Department were both reaching a climax. A catharsis was desperately sought and that first ghastly winter in the Crimea became the chosen time and place. The outcome for the British was staggering – particularly as the winter of 1854–5 is usually equated in people's minds with conditions throughout the whole war. Out of the opening chaos came an improvement that was scarcely believable, while the French army – whose medical services had been held up as an example – gathered throughout the war the highest sickness rate in history.

19

EVOLUTION OF THE BLOOD-PRESSURE MACHINE

Scientific curiosity and need-to-know were the two driving forces leading to the measurement of the blood pressure. The governing factor was what was available by way of technical instrumentation.

Although people have felt the pulse for thousands of years and although the sight of blood pulsing in a series of spurts from a severed artery cannot have been all that uncommon, the concept of 'blood pressure' just did not exist. Indeed, if you think about it, there is much to be said for Johannes Müller's (1801–58) observation in the middle of the 19th century that the discovery of the blood pressure was more important than the discovery of the blood.

But once William Harvey (1578–1657) had discovered, in 1628, that the blood circulated, it was only a matter of time before someone realized that if blood circulates it must exert a pressure on the vessels it flows through. A hundred years were to pass before that realization dawned.

The Reverend Stephen Hales (1677–1761) was an exceptionally curious man. After taking holy orders in 1711 he was presented with the perpetual curacy of Teddington, Middlesex, where he remained for the rest of his life. But his impact was not on the world of the spirit but on

that of science – and a considerable impact it was, too. Among his extensive scientific researches was the first measurement of the blood pressure. But why did he attempt this? Possibly the idea was sparked when he learnt that the blood circulated. Possibly it was to test the prevailing theory that muscular action in some way depended on the force of blood – a theory that he demolished. Or possibly it was simply scientific curiosity. "In natural philosophy", he wrote, "we cannot depend on any mere speculations of the mind; we can only with the mathematicians, reason with any tolerable certainty from proper data, such as arise from the united testimony of many good and credible experiments."

His experiments with the blood pressure are not precisely dated but he first used dogs while still at Cambridge in about 1708. Then, six years later, he repeated the work on horses. He was by now ensconced at Teddington.

"In December, I laid a common field gate on the ground, with some straw upon it, on which a white mare was cast on her right side, and in that posture bound fast to the gate; she was fourteen hands high, and about fourteen years of age; had a fistula of her withers, was neither very lean not yet lusty; having laid open the crural artery about three inches from her belly, I inserted into it a brass pipe whose bore was one sixth of an inch in diameter . . . I fixed a glass tube of nearly the same diameter which was nine feet in length: then untying the ligature of the artery, the blood rose in the tube 8 feet 3 inches perpendicular above the level of the left ventricle of the heart; . . . when it was at its full height it would rise and fall at and after each pulse 2, 3 or 4 inches."

Hales also cannulated the left jugular vein and noted how the height of the column of blood increased with the animal's struggles – at one point it overflowed the four-foot-two-inch long tube. When he cannulated the left carotid artery he most ingeniously joined the brass cannula to the glass tube with the windpipe of a goose for flexibility. In this experiment he let sixty cubic inches of blood at intervals, observing the fall in pressure with each letting. The horse expired when the height of the blood in the tube had fallen to about two feet.

He went on to estimate that the blood pressure in man was about seven-and-a-half feet. This is equivalent to around 220 mmHg or about 100 mmHg above the accepted normal – it was, nevertheless an attempt

in the right direction. Subsequently, when Hales measured the force of the rising sap in trees he used a mercury manometer. Quite why he didn't use this in his animal experiments is unknown, though it may have been due to problems with coagulation of the blood.

Silence then descended for another hundred years or so during which, so far as we know, no one pursued Hales's experiments. Then, when interest revived, the initiative had passed to the Continent. In 1828, 29-year-old Jean-Léonard-Marie Poiseuille (1799–1869) won the gold medal of the Royal Academy of Medicine in Paris for his doctoral dissertation on the measurement of the arterial blood pressure. His manometer was a U-tube filled with mercury with a lead tip containing potassium carbonate to act as an anticoagulant for cannulation of the artery – because it was invasive, the technique could only be used on experimental animals. His work, however, was important because he showed that blood was not returned to the heart by suction of the right ventricle and diaphragm since the arterial pressure was maintained into vessels as small as 2 mm in diameter (which he had cannulated). He also showed that the blood pressure rises and falls on inspiration and expiration.

Next on the scene was Karl Ludwig (1816–95), Professor of Comparative Anatomy at Marburg, who, in 1847, devised a method of recording the blood pressure, but again it was a direct method requiring cannulation of an artery. The principle underlying his idea was simple and although suited to the laboratory was totally impractical for use in the clinic. His kymograph (*kyma* = wave; *graphein* = to write) consisted in a long ivory float resting on a column of mercury

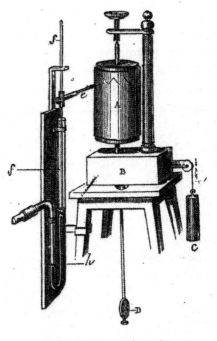

Ludwig's kymograph (1847).

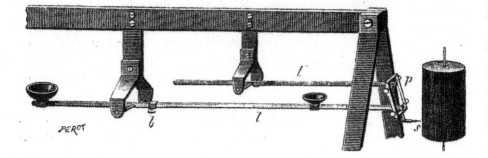

Vierordt's sphygmograph (1855).

in a U-tube; this float was provided with a light-weight arm at the end of which was a stiff brush for tracing the oscillations of the mercury column onto a rotating smoked drum.

In 1855 Karl Vierordt (1818–84), a Tübingen physiologist, turned his attention from counting red blood cells (*see* Chapter 8) to a study of the pulse beat. For this he devised a sphygmograph (*sphygmos* = pulse) – his was a simple apparatus in which a pad (*b* in the illustration) on a horizontally suspended rod was placed over the radial artery at the wrist. This rod had cups at each end into which weights were put until a stylus mounted at the end could trace the beat on a smoked drum. It was then but a small step to attach weights to the end of the rod until the radial pulse was obliterated. Unreliable and prone to variations in the results maybe – but a start had been made.

The next year, J. Faivre, a French physician, realized that with the arrival of anaesthesia ten years earlier he had the opportunity during operations to make direct measurements on human beings. (It is not recorded whether the patients gave informed consent, as would be required today, but it is highly unlikely!) He found the pressure in the femoral artery to be 120 mmHg and in the brachial artery to vary between 115 and 120 mmHg. Eduard Albert (1841–1900), in 1883, cannulated the femoral artery of patients undergoing amputation at the knee. He found the pressure to vary in different individuals between 100 and 160 mmHg.

These were important measurements as they acted as reference points against which future measurements could be evaluated. Even so, the readings had no significance for mid-19th-century doctors. They were still in the stage of scientific curiosity – gathering information.

The application of Vierodt's principle of counterpressure was greatly simplified in the next few years by Etienne Marey (1830–1904), a not-inconsiderable French physiologist. He produced not only a direct-writing sphygmograph but also a version in which the tracing could be made at a distance. The blood pressure was measured by attaching weights to a spring, but it was grossly inaccurate as the resistance of the arterial wall interfered unacceptably with the results.

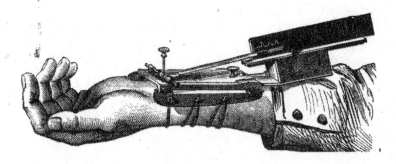

Marey's direct-writing sphygmograph (1863).

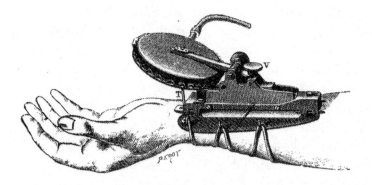

Marey's sphygmograph for writing at a distance (1863).

Marey also applied the principle of counterpressure in a most ingenious fashion – plethysmography (*plethysmos* = enlargement). He enclosed the forearm in a glass chamber filled with water, which was connected to a sphygmograph and a kymograph to record the arterial pulsations in the arm. The chamber was also connected to a moveable reservoir of water (so that the pressure inside could be altered) and to a mercury manometer. The blood pressure was measured, first noting the pressure on the manometer at which the greatest peak-to-peak tracings on the kymograph were recorded, and then gradually increasing the pressure in the chamber by raising the reservoir until the tracings ceased. Ingenious maybe, but too cumbersome for general use.

Previously, in 1855, Marey and his fellow physiologist, Auguste Chauveau (1827–1917), had catheterized both sides of the hearts of horses to study intracardiac pressures and to find out whether both sides of the heart contracted together. Their device for the right heart was almost modern in appearance – as was the procedure itself. At the business end were two separate very small sausage-shaped recording balloons, one to lie in the ventricle and the other to stay in the atrium. The tubes from these balloons ran up inside the catheter to be connected to pens that recorded the pressure changes on a revolving drum. The catheter itself was inserted through the jugular vein. For the left side of the heart they used a rigid metal tube passed down the carotid artery.

The next step was taken by Samuel Siegfried Karl Ritter von Basch (1837–1905). He was born in Prague in 1837 and obtained a Vienna M.D. in 1862; three years later he went to Mexico where he became director of the military hospital at Puebla and physician to the unfortunate Emperor Maximilian (1832–67) – in 1864 he had accepted the title when the French occupied the country, but this was

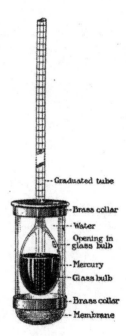

Detail of von Basch's syphgmomanometer (1881). The 'membrane' is the pelotte.

222

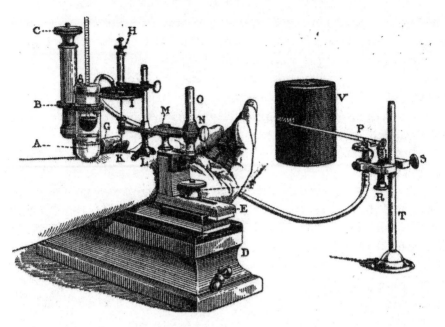

von Basch's sphygmomanometer mounted on a stand. 'A' indicates the pelotte (water-filled india-rubber cap) which rests on the radial artery.

unpopular with the Mexican republicans and after the French troops withdrew, he was captured and shot. von Basch returned to Europe in 1875 and by 1881 had produced an unwieldy device for measuring the blood pressure. He did, however, establish two new and fundamental principles: (1) that counterpressure over the artery could be supplied by a bag containing fluid and (2) that the connection of a mercury manometer to the bag would record the pressure necessary to compress the artery.

Zadek made some slight modifications to von Basch's sphygmomanometer and used it on dogs at the same time as he performed direct measurements on their carotid arteries and found substantial agreement between the two. Both he and von Basch found the normal blood pressure in man to be 130 mmHg with a range of between 110 and 160 mmHg. They noted, however, that some patients with arteriosclerosis gave readings of 180–200 mmHg. Thus the realization that disease could be associated with a high blood pressure was beginning to take shape –

'need-to-know' was taking over from scientific curiosity, though it took another sixty or so years of intensive research before the place of hypertension in the spectrum of disease began to be understood. (A three-volume paperback discussing the literature on blood pressure between 1920 and 1950 contains 16 460 references of which only 238 are on measurement! Studies on human beings were numbered in single figures while animal experiments were ten-a-penny.)

In the 1880s Carl Potain (1825–1901) replaced water with air for compression: a bulb placed over an artery was inflated by squeezing a second bulb. Unfortunately, this simpler method gave erroneous results as it recorded pressure against the more resistant tissues of the arm as well as the pressure directly over the artery. Nevertheless it was a step in the right direction.

The answer came in 1896 when Scipione Riva-Rocci presented a 'new sphygmomanometer' to the Italian Congress of Medicine – the machine that we are familiar with today was beginning to take shape. He enclosed his rubber bag in a cloth sleeve to control the expansion when inflated, and he made it long enough to encircle the arm. Since the bag was originally only 4–5 cm wide it was a source of error as it squeezed the tissues at an angle; it was soon replaced one 12–15 cm wide. The pressure was read either by palpation – a source of subjective error – or by observation of the oscillations transmitted to the mercury in the manometer. The appearance of definite oscillations on slowly deflating the cuff

Riva-Rocci's sphygmomanometer (1896).

indicated the systolic pressure and the change from large to small oscillations, the diastolic pressure. Riva-Rocci said that the mercury manometer was still the most reliable though, to make it easy to read, it was necessary to use only a single limb and not the familiar U-tube. The design of the machine (using a reservoir) meant that at high pressures it gave readings that were too low; also it was fragile and unsuitable for taking pressures above 260 mmHg.

At this period a striking instance of the 'need-to-know' value of blood pressure measurements was provided by the great neurosurgeon, Harvey Cushing (1869–1939). On his return to Johns Hopkins from training in Europe, and while still a house-surgeon, he had plans for adapting the Riva-Rocci sphygmomanometer for use in the operating theatre. He felt there was a need for something better than guesswork through a finger on the pulse if shock was to be studied properly. So he had an assistant take the blood pressure repeatedly during operations and chart the readings. As he said: "On several occasions in critical cases, have we been able to anticipate and to avoid profound states of shock and collapse, and indeed, in some instances, I feel confident that it has been instrumental in saving lives."

Over the following years many modifications and variations were introduced, including folding models which at first were liable to leak. There

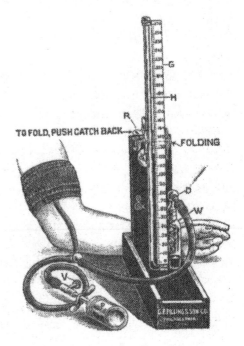

C.J. Martin's modification of the Riva-Rocci sphygmomanometer. This folding model dates from 1905. The view of the mercury column was retained at any point on the scale. When the lid was opened it locked in the vertical position and the mercury tube with its scale was unfolded and pressed upwards until a spring catch held it in position. It is no wonder that leakage was a problem.

were also compressed air manometers, spring manometers and the popular, though now obsolete, aneroid instruments which did away with the need for mercury and could be carried in the pocket.

Unfortunately familiarity breeds contempt, and a survey in 1976 showed that all was not well with either technique or machines. Mercury sphygmomanometers needed to be maintained, serviced and even re-calibrated and when taking the blood pressure the mercury column should fall by no more than 2 cm per heartbeat – not in the all-too-familiar sudden rush. But the greatest concern was expressed over the length of the cuff. This should be sufficient to comfortably encircle the arm. The standard bag at the time was 12 x 33 cm which was too short for some arms. A length of 35–40 cm was suggested as being ideal since overlapping on thin arms was not responsible for significant error. With a bag that completely encircled the arm, width was not critical; but if the bag was too short, width did become important, and with this in mind the World Health Organization suggested a minimum width of 14cm.

The arrival of the electronic age has brought with it automated devices for measuring the blood pressure. These are valuable for twenty-four-hour ambulatory monitoring where the device is worn throughout the entire period; the cuff inflates automatically at preset intervals, say every twenty or thirty minutes, and the readings are recorded electronically for later evaluation. This has led to the introduction of automated devices, available from shops, whereby patients can monitor their blood pressure at home, the readings appearing on a digital LCD screen. The mercury sphygmomanometer is, nevertheless, still a force to be reckoned with in the clinic as it is more accurate than the newer devices, but each has its place.

Index of Personal Names

Subject Index

Larrey: Surgeon to Napoleon's Imperial Guard

Dominique Jean Larrey may rightly be said to have awakened the conscience of mankind to the inhumanity of war. Before him, with few exceptions, casualties had simply been a nuisance to the military command. But Larrey invented a 'flying' ambulance (on the lines of the flying artillery) to rescue the wounded on the field, often himself amputating or dressing under fire. Yet his invention was more than a vehicle, it was the development of a complete system of casualty evacuation back to base hospital – something that survives in principle to our own day. He ignored rank, and indeed nationality, by treating casualties in order of severity. Throughout his career he was in conflict with the Administration to get the necessary essentials for the sick and wounded.

This portrait is based on Larrey's own letters, mostly to his wife while he was on campaign, his journals and notes, including the unpublished collection in the Wellcome Institute. The biography reveals the stark reality of Napoleonic warfare, especially of the Russian campaign, the account of which disposes of the familiar claim that it was the Russian winter that defeated Napoleon in 1812-13 – the entire venture was shockingly mismanaged from the outset. Only the elite of the army, the Imperial Guard, re-crossed the Niemen with any semblance of order.

Excerpts from reviews of the first edition:

Not a book for the squeamish, but one full of interest, splendidly researched, bringing both the character of the Napoleonic wars and of Larrey himself, vividly to life.

The Times

This book is a remarkable literary memorial to a man of immeasurable stature – a hero who scorned the term, a man to whom military medicine owes much, and the world more.

Australasian Post

How Larrey won the Emperor's confidence is described in these pages, and he was never to lose it. It is evident already in the battle of Eylau, "Where the cold was so intense that it froze the urine in my chamberpot," and of which Dr Richardson's account reads like some canto from Dante's Inferno.

The Daily Telegraph

Richardson is more concerned with Larrey's personality and adventures than his surgical studies, but uses some hitherto unpublished material from the Wellcome Institute to enhance an accurate, and very easily read, biography.

The Lancet

The story of surgery. An historical commentary
Revised and expanded edition with bibliography

Since the discovery of anaesthesia a little over a hundred and fifty years ago, advances in surgery have had the drama and excitement of a novel. Here is the full, fascinating story of these advances discussed in an eminently readable book. In lively fashion the author describes such outstanding developments as the discovery of anaesthesia and the gradual evolution of the aseptic ritual. This leads to accounts of the rise of abdominal and brain surgery and of the growth of surgical specialization. Among the specialties covered are ophthalmology, ear, nose and throat, and obstetrics and gynaecology.

The story is full of absorbing accounts of surgical triumphs including the role of Theodor Billroth in the development of abdominal surgery; the unmasking of appendicitis by the Harvard pathologist, Reginald Fitz; the brilliance of Harvey Cushing in establishing neurosurgery; and the work of Halsted in the surgery of hernia and cancer of the breast. The surgery of warfare is reviewed showing not only how it led to progress in civilian practice but also how lessons learned are all too easily forgotten.

This edition contains much new material, particularly on abdominal surgery – the sphere of the 'general' surgeon – and a full bibliography of some eight hundred entries.

Excerpts from reviews of the original edition:

The book is intended for non-medical readers, but the author pays them the unusual compliment of assuming that they would like to know the nature of the problems solved by the great pioneers and the way they attacked them, rather than be told of marvels suddenly achieved by supermen.

Daily Telegraph

The author of this book tells us that it was written 'primarily for the reader with no medical background.' He has actually done better than this. He has produced a readable, up-to-date account of the development of surgery…which can be read with advantage by readers who *do* possess such a background.

British Medical Journal

Its pages contain a very great deal of information not to be found in much larger histories, and which will be new to even well-read doctors.

Lancet

This well written and very readable history of modern surgery is factual and is quite acceptable to the professional and general reader….The professional reader will be impressed with the profound knowledge the author has of the history of surgery, and the general reader will appreciate the interesting way in which the author has made this digest of progress in surgery available as easy and informative reading. It is a magnificent effort beautifully executed.

Annals of Internal Medicine

Heart and scalpel. A history of cardiac surgery
Revised edition with bibliography

Of all the body's organs, the heart is the most dramatic in the field of surgery. Yet without an understanding of the heart's encounters with the surgeon's scalpel, the significance of much recent work – transplantation in particular – can only be two-dimensional. In this eminently readable book, Dr Richardson provides that missing third dimension.

Technical advances are discussed fully, but what the author achieves is more than this: he is deeply concerned with assessing what went on in the minds of men – not only the surgeons, but the physicians, philosophers, and public, whose attitudes all too often made the surgeon's task a battle against desperately unequal odds.

Heart surgery has a long history, extending back centuries before the exciting years of the past half-century when heart-lung machines and cooling first allowed the surgeon to operate inside a motionless heart. These early events are described in this comprehensive book.

Excerpts from reviews of the original edition:

By any standards this is a good book. It sets out to cover the history of cardiac surgery and the technical advances that have gone along with it. It has achieved far more than this. The author has taken a tremendous amount of trouble to establish his facts... He gives us an insight into the complex characters of some of the people who have brought cardiac surgery to its present state.

Medical-News Tribune

The acclaim that is due to the men who explore the heart is muted by professional and ethical considerations. In a work of meticulous and painstaking scholarship, Dr. Richardson goes far to remedy this deficiency by describing in great detail the painful and halting steps of their long and tortuous journey to the heart. Despite the avoidance of sensationalism he shows that truth is stranger than any science fiction and his factual account is more dramatic than the ephemeral programmes of the mass communication media.

The Practitioner

This is a fascinating book and one does not need to be a cardiac surgeon to appreciate it. Dr. Richardson's elegant and lucid prose takes us from Herophilus and Erasistratus to Barnard, Cooley and Shumway in a review of man's efforts to restore the circulation... A favourable feature is the author's attempt to tell us what went on in the minds of the originators, how one finding helped to arrive at the next in the process of exploring the unknown. The story is not one of steady progress and consecutive advance. It demonstrates clearly the sporadic nature of discovery in which bursts of accomplishment are followed by periods of barrenness.

Canadian Medical Association Journal

Flies in Paradise

Writing as Robert Shelley

The gods never intended that we should live for ever – but when it happens, as it did for Paul Baldassare, the imagined blessings are seen for what they are: an agony of existence with, if the gods are kind, fleeting moments of Paradise. But, as Fiametta said when dying of the Black Death, "There *are* flies in Paradise!"

This book is a novel of love and reincarnation set against a backdrop of five thousand years of medical history. In far-off Egypt, as Bal-sarra-uzur, Paul had maintained that disease was sent by the gods and did not have natural causes. For this slur on their character, the gods condemned him to remain on earth until mankind should understand the nature of disease. Throughout his journey he was accompanied by Telesphorus, the immortal son of Aesculapius, who did much to guide him in the right direction and to ease his most desperate moments. But what really saved his sanity was the knowledge that his love, Ishtar, would be reincarnated at points in his existence.

He was in the right place at the right time to witness the significant events along the way. He sat with Hippocrates under the plane tree on the island of Cos; he marched with Alexander to the Indus; he journeyed to the banks of the Danube with Marcus Aurelius; he observed the impact of Christianity and of Islam on the healing art; he watched while Koch stained and fixed invisible bacteria to make them visible under the microscope. On the way, he helped an alchemist create life in the form of a homunculus and served with Napoleon at Austerlitz.

As Paul reflected at the end of his story so far: "If all my years on earth have taught me anything at all, it is that disease is an inescapable part of the human lot."

For Stella

NAPOLEON'S ULCER

and other medico-historical stories